Panda Books
At Middle Age

Shen Rong, a native of Sichuan, was born in 1935 in Hankou. She left junior middle school at the age of fifteen to be a salesgirl in a bookshop for workers. In '52 she transferred to the *Southwest Workers' Daily* in Chongqing, and in '54 she went to study Russian in Beijing. After graduation she worked as a translator in the Radio Station, then for reasons of health went to live with a peasant family in Shanxi. Back in Beijing in '64 she started writing plays. In the '70's she wrote several novels. "At Millde Age", after which this collection was named, won a national best-story award in 1980. It also won its author wider recognition for her skill and courage in raising the problems of middle-aged professionals, praising the heroes and heroines of our times and condemning those who hold up progress. Shen Rong is a member of the Chinese Writers' Association.

Shen Rong

At Middle Age

Panda Books

Panda Books
First edition 1987
Copyright 1987 by CHINESE LITERATURE PRESS
ISBN 0-8351-1609-3
ISBN 7-5071-0005-7/I·6

Published by Chinese Literature Press, Beijing (37), China
Distributed by China International Book Trading Corporation
(GUOJI SHUDIAN) P.O. Box 399, Beijing
Printed in the People's Republic of China

CONTENTS

Preface

A reader is often disappointed when he probes into a writer's life. Writers may have gone through frustrations, struggles, sadness and joy, but who in this world has not had such experiences?

What I can tell my readers is simply a dull story:

A fifteen-year-old girl left her family to go into the world, selling books behind the counter of a bookstore as she held a book in her hands, reading avidly. She was reprimanded by the manager when books on the store racks were stolen, but by reading she acquired knowledge, new interests, ideals and goals. . . . She passed the entrance examination to college and then she worked. Wherever she was, in a government office, in school or in the countryside, she had many dreams which were shattered one after the other. But she never dreamed of becoming a writer. Yet this is what she is now. Was it fated? She would never have started writing if not for her wide social contacts with people of all kinds. In the last twenty years she has written about two million Chinese characters and become a professional novelist.

Time marches on. Now the little salesgirl is a middle-aged woman with a flourishing family: a husband, two sons and their wives, a daughter and two grand-daughters. Her husband is a journalist. Her elder son teaches Chinese to foreign students in Beijing Languages Institute. Her younger son does propaganda work in a Beijing clothing factory. He has acted in a few comedies in his spare time, but unfortunately is still unknown to film-goers. Her daughter is still in her first year in one of the best middle schools in Beijing. A professional woman has to divide her time between her career and her family and more often than not neglects one or the other. She calls herself, "an inadequate wife" and "an inadequate mother"—like Dr Lu in *At Middle Age* although she did not model Dr Lu on herself.

A writer draws nourishment from her national culture and her works grow out of her national soil. My country has an ancient civilization dating back for thousands of years. In her long history she has gone through all kinds of tribulations and is now reborn. She suffered the most in the ten years starting from 1966. The stories in this collection are about people and events in the eighties, but all the main characters lived through those ten years of chaos. They entered the new era with marks left on them by the old. Stories about today cannot avoid yesterday. They show us the life in the period that has just gone by, the worries, sufferings, struggles and hopes of people in that period.

So it is not surprising if readers see tears in this collection.

I lay this painful truth before my readers only because the wounds on the dragon in the East have healed and she is now sailing ahead in the vast ocean.

I hope my next collection will give my readers something to rejoice over.

Shen Rong
Beijing　1986

At Middle Age

WERE the stars twinkling in the sky? Was a boat rocking on the sea? Lu Wenting, an ophthalmologist, lay on her back in hospital. Circles of light, bright or dim, appeared before her eyes. She seemed to be lifted by a cloud, up and down, drifting about without any direction.

Was she dreaming or dying?

She remembered vaguely going to the operating theatre that morning, putting on her operating gown and walking over to the wash-basin. Ah, yes, Jiang Yafen, her good friend, had volunteered to be her assistant. Having got their visas, Jiang and her family were soon leaving for Canada. This was their last operation as colleagues.

Together they washed their hands. They had been medical students in the same college in the fifties and, after graduation, had been assigned to the same hospital. As friends and colleagues for more than twenty years, they found it hard to part. This was no mood for a doctor to be in prior to an operation. Lu remembered she had wanted to say something to ease their sadness. What had she said? She had turned to Jiang and inquired, "Have you booked your plane tickets, Yafen?"

What had been her reply? She had said nothing, but her eyes had gone red. Then after a long time Jiang asked, "You think you can manage three operations in one morning?"

Lu couldn't remember what she had answered. She had probably gone on scrubbing her nails in silence. The new brush hurt her fingertips. She looked at the soap bubbles on her hands and glanced at the clock on the wall, strictly following the rules, brushing her hands, wrists and arms three times, three minutes each. Ten minutes later she soaked her arms in a pail of antiseptic, 75 per cent alcohol. It was white—maybe yellowish. Even now her hands and arms were numb and burning. From the alcohol? No. It was unlikely. They had never hurt before. Why couldn't she lift them?

She remembered that at the start of the operation, when she had injected novocaine behind the patient's eyeball, Yafen had asked softly, "Has your daughter got over her pneumonia?"

What was wrong with Jiang today? Didn't she know that when operating a surgeon should forget everything, including herself and her family, and concentrate on the patient? How could she inquire after Xiaojia at such a time? Perhaps, feeling miserable about leaving, she had forgotten that she was assisting at an operation.

A bit annoyed, Lu retorted, "I'm only thinking about this eye now."

She lowered her head and cut with a pair of curved scissors.

One operation after another. Why three in one morning? She had had to remove Vice-minister Jiao's cataract, transplant a cornea on Uncle Zhang's eye and correct Wang Xiaoman's squint. Starting at eight o'clock, she had sat on the high operating stool for four and a half hours, concentrating under a lamp. She had cut and stitched again and again. When she had finished the last one and put a piece of gauze on the patient's eye, she was stiff and her legs wouldn't move.

Having changed her clothes, Jiang called to her from the door, "Let's go, Wenting."

"You go first." She stayed where she was.

"I'll wait for you. It's my last time here." Jiang's eyes were watery. Was she crying? Why?

"Go on home and do your packing. Your husband must be waiting for you."

"He's already packed our things." Looking up, Jiang called, "What's wrong with your legs?"

"I've been sitting so long, they've gone to sleep! They'll be OK in a minute. I'll come to see you this evening."

"All right. See you then."

After Jiang had left, Lu moved back to the wall of white tiles, supporting herself with her hands against it for a long time before going to the changing-room.

She remembered putting on her grey jacket, leaving the hospital and reaching the lane leading to her home. All of a sudden she was exhausted, more tired than she had ever felt before. The lane became long and hazy, her home seemed far away. She felt she would never get there.

She became faint. She couldn't open her eyes, her lips felt dry and stiff. She was thirsty, very thirsty. Where could she get some water?

Her parched lips trembled.

2

"Look, Dr Sun, she's come to!" Jiang cried softly. She had been sitting beside Lu all the time.

Sun Yimin, head of the Ophthalmology Department, was reading Lu's case-history and was shocked by the diagnosis of myocardial infarction. Very worried, the greying man shook his head and pushed back his black-rimmed spectacles, recalling that Lu was not the first doctor aged about forty in his department who had fallen ill with heart disease. She had been a healthy woman of forty-two. This attack was too sudden and serious.

Sun turned his tall, stooping frame to look down at Lu's pale face. She was breathing weakly, her eyes closed, her dry lips trembling slightly.

"Dr Lu," Sun called softly.

She didn't move, her thin, puffy face expressionless.

"Wenting," Jiang urged.

Still no reaction.

Sun raised his eyes to the forbidding oxygen cylinder, which stood at a corner of the room and then looked at the ECG monitor. He was reassured when he saw a regular QRS wave on the oscillometer. He turned back to Lu, waved his hand and said, "Ask her husband to come in."

A good-looking, balding man in his forties, of medium height, entered quickly. He was Fu Jiajie, Lu's husband. He had spent a sleepless night beside her and had been reluctant to leave when Sun had sent him away to lie down on the bench outside the room.

As Sun made way for him, Fu bent down to look at the familiar face, which was now so pale and strange.

Lu's lips moved again. Nobody except her husband understood her. He said, "She wants some water. She's thirsty."

Jiang gave him a small teapot. Carefully, Fu avoided the rubber tube leading from the oxygen cylinder and put it to Lu's parched lips. Drop by drop, the water trickled into the dying woman's mouth.

"Wenting, Wenting," Fu called.

When a drop of water fell from Fu's shaking hand on to Lu's pallid face, the muscles seemed to twitch a little.

3

Eyes. Eyes. Eyes....

Many flashed past Lu's closed ones. Eyes of men and

women, old and young, big and small, bright and dull, all kinds, blinking at her.

Ah! These were her husband's eyes. In them, she saw joy and sorrow, anxiety and pleasure, suffering and hope. She could see through his eyes, his heart. His eyes were as bright as the golden sun in the sky. His loving heart had given her so much warmth. It was his voice, Jiajie's voice, so endearing, so gentle, and so far away, as if from another world:

> "I wish I were a rapid stream,
> . . . . . .
> If my love
> A tiny fish would be,
> She'd frolic
> In my foaming waves."

Where was she? Oh, she was in a park covered with snow. There was a frozen lake, clear as crystal, on which red, blue, purple and white figures skated. Happy laughter resounded in the air while they moved arm in arm, threading their way through the crowds. She saw none of the smiling faces around her, only his. They slid on the ice, side by side, twirling, laughing. What bliss!

The ancient Five Dragon Pavilions shrouded in snow were solemn, tranquil and deserted. They leaned against the white marble balustrades, while snowflakes covered them. Holding hands tightly, they defied the severe cold.

She was young then.

She had never expected love or special happiness. Her father had deserted her mother when she was a girl, and her mother had had a hard time raising her alone. Her childhood had been bleak. All she remembered was a mother prematurely old who, night after night, sewed under a solitary lamp.

She boarded at her medical college, rising before daybreak

to memorize new English words, going to classes and filling scores of notebooks with neat little characters. In the evenings she studied in the library and then worked late into the night doing autopsies. She never grudged spending her youth studying.

Love had no place in her life. She shared a room with Jiang Yafen, her classmate, who had beautiful eyes, bewitching lips and who was tall, slim and lively. Every week, Jiang received love letters. Every weekend, she dated, while poor Lu did nothing, neglected by everyone.

After graduation, she and Jiang were assigned to the same hospital, which had been founded more than a hundred years earlier. Their internship lasted for four years, during which time they had to be in the hospital all day long, and remain single.

Secretly, Jiang cursed these rules, while Lu accepted the terms willingly. What did it matter being in the hospital twenty-four hours a day? She would have liked to be there forty-eight hours, if possible. No marriage for four years. Hadn't many skilled doctors married late or remained single all their lives? So she threw herself heart and soul into her work.

But life is strange. Fu Jiajie suddenly entered her quiet, routine life.

She never understood how it happened. He had been hospitalized because of an eye disease. She was his doctor. Perhaps, his feelings for her arose from her conscientious treatment. Passionate and deep, his emotions changed both their lives.

Winter in the north is always very cold, but that winter he gave her warmth. Never having imagined love could be so intoxicating, she almost regretted not finding it earlier. She was already twenty-eight, yet she still had the heart of a young girl. With her whole being, she welcomed this late love.

"I wish I were a deserted forest,
......
If my love
A little bird would be,
She'd nest and twitter
In my dense trees."

Incredible that Fu Jiajie, whom Jiang regarded as a bookworm and who was doing research on a new material for a spacecraft in the Metallurgical Research Institute, could read poetry so well!

"Who wrote it?" Lu asked.

"The Hungarian poet Petöfi."

"Does a scientist have time for poetry?"

"A scientist must have imagination. Science has something in common with poetry in this respect."

Pedantic? He gave good answers.

"What about you? Do you like poetry?" he asked.

"Me? I don't know anything about it. I seldom read it." She smiled cynically. "The Ophthalmology Department does operations. Every stitch, every incision is strictly laid down. We can't use the slightest imagination...."

Fu cut in, "Your work is a beautiful poem. You can make many people see again...."

Smiling, he moved over to her, his face close to hers. His masculinity, which she had never experienced before, assailed, bewildered and unnerved her. She felt something must happen, and, sure enough, he put his arms round her, embracing her tightly.

It had occurred so suddenly that she looked fearfully at the smiling eyes close to hers and his parted lips. Her heart thumping, her head raised, she closed her eyes in embarrassment, moving away instinctively as his irresistible love flooded her.

Beihai Park in the snow was just the right place for her.

Snow covered the tall dagoba, Qiongdao Islet with its green pines, the long corridor and quiet lake. It also hid the sweet shyness of the lovers.

To everyone's surprise, after her four-year internship had ended, Lu was the first to get married. Fate had decided Fu Jiajie's intrusion. How could she refuse his wish that they marry? How insistently and strongly he wanted her, preparing to sacrifice everything for her!...

> "I wish I were a crumbling ruin,
> ......
> If my love
> Green ivy would be,
> She'd tenderly entwine
> Around my lonely head."

Life was good, love was beautiful. These recollections gave her strength, and her eyelids opened slightly.

4

After heavy dosages of sedatives and analgesics Dr Lu was still in a coma. The head of the Internal Medicine Department gave her a careful examination, studied her ECG and her case-history, then told the ward doctor to keep up the intravenous drip and injections of opiate and morphine and to watch out for changes in her ECG monitor to guard against more serious complications due to myocardial infarction.

On leaving the ward he remarked to Sun, "She's too weak. I remember how fit Dr Lu was when she first came here."

"Yes." Sun shook his head with a sigh. "It's eighteen years since she came to our hospital, just a girl."

Eighteen years ago Dr Sun had already been a well-known ophthalmologist, respected by all his colleagues for his skill and responsible attitude to work. This able, energetic professor in his prime regarded it as his duty to train the younger doctors. Each time the medical college assigned them a new batch of graduates, he examined them one by one to make his choice. He thought the first step to making their Ophthalmology Department the best in all China was by selecting the most promising interns.

How had he chosen Lu? He remembered quite distinctly. At first this twenty-four-year-old graduate had not made much of an impression on him.

That morning Department Head Sun had already interviewed five of the graduates assigned to them and had been most disappointed. Some of them were suitable, but they were not interested in the Ophthalmology Department and did not want to work there. Others wanted to be ophthalmologists because they thought it a simple, easy job. By the time he picked up the sixth file marked Lu Wenting, he was rather tired and not expecting much. He was reflecting that the medical college's teaching needed improving to give students a correct impression from the start of his department.

The door opened quietly. A slim girl walked softly in. Looking up he saw that she had on a cotton jacket and slacks. Her cuffs were patched, the knees of her blue slacks were faded. Simply dressed, she was even rather shabby. He read the name on her file, then glanced at her casually. She really looked like a little girl, slightly built, with an oval face and neatly bobbed glossy black hair. She calmly sat down on the chair facing him.

Asked the usual technical questions, she answered each in turn, saying no more than was strictly necessary.

"You want to work in the Ophthalmology Department?" Sun asked lethargically, having almost decided to wind up this interview. His elbows on the desk, he rubbed his temples with his fingers.

"Yes. At college I was interested in ophthalmology." She spoke with a slight southern accent.

Delighted by this answer, Sun lowered his hands as if his head no longer ached. He had changed his mind. Watching her carefully he asked more seriously, "What aroused your interest?"

At once this question struck him as inappropriate, too hard to answer. But she replied confidently, "Ophthalmology is lagging behind in our country."

"Good, tell me in what way it's backward," he asked eagerly.

"I don't know how to put it, but I feel we haven't tried out certain operations which are done abroad. Such as using laser beams to seal retina wounds. I think we ought to try these methods too."

"Right!" Mentally, Sun had already given her full marks. "What else? Any other ideas?"

"Yes . . . well . . . making more use of freezing to remove cataracts. Anyway, it seems to me there are many new problems that ought to be studied."

"Good, that makes sense. Can you read foreign materials?"

"With difficulty, using a dictionary. I like foreign languages."

"Excellent."

That was the first time Sun had praised a new student like this to her face. A few days later Lu Wenting and Jiang Yafen were the first to be admitted to his department. Sun chose Jiang for her intelligence, enthusiasm and enterprise, Lu for her simplicity, seriousness and keenness.

The first year they performed external ocular operations and studied ophthalmology. The second year they operated on eyeballs and studied ophthalmometry and ophthalmomyology. By the third year they were able to do such tricky operations as on cataract cases. That year something happened which made Sun see Lu in a new light.

It was a spring morning, a Monday. Sun made his round of the wards followed by white-coated doctors, some senior, some junior. The patients were sitting up in bed expectantly, hoping this famous professor would examine their eyes, as if with one touch of his hand he could heal them.

Each time he came to a bed, Sun picked up the case-history hanging behind it and read it while listening to the attending ophthalmologist or some senior ophthalmologist report on the diagnosis and treatment. Sometimes he raised a patient's eyelid to look at his eye, sometimes patted him on the shoulder and urged him not to worry about his operation, then moved on to the next bed.

After the ward round they held a short consultation, at which tasks were assigned. It was generally Dr Sun and the attending ophthalmologists who spoke, while the residents listened carefully, not venturing to speak for fear of making fools of themselves in front of these authorities. Today was the same. All that had to be said had been said and tasks were assigned. As he stood up to leave, Sun asked, "Have the rest of you anything to add?"

A girl spoke up in a low voice from one corner of the room, "Dr Sun, will you please have another look at the photograph of the patient in Bed 3 Ward 4?"

All heads turned in her direction. Sun saw that the speaker was Lu. She was so short, so inconspicuous, that he had not noticed her following him in the wards. Back in the office where they had talked at some length, he had still not noticed her presence.

"Bed 3?" He turned to the chief resident.

"An industrial accident," he was told.

"When he was admitted to hospital a picture was taken of his eye," Lu said. "The radiologists' report said there was no sign of a metal foreign body. After hospitalization the wound was sewn up and healed, but the patient complained of pain. I had another X-ray taken, and I believe there really is a foreign body. Will you have a look, Dr Sun?"

The film was fetched. Sun examined it. The chief resident and attending ophthalmologists then passed it round.

Jiang looked wide-eyed at her classmate, thinking, "Couldn't you have waited until after the meeting to ask Dr Sun to look at that? If by any chance you're wrong, the whole department will gossip. Even if you're right, you're implying that the doctors in the Out-patients Department are careless, and they are attending ophthalmologists!"

"You're right, there's a foreign body." Sun took back the picture and nodded. Looking round at the others he said, "Dr Lu has not been long in our department. Her careful, responsible attitude is admirable, and so is her hard study."

Lu lowered her head. This unexpected praise in public made her blush. At sight of this Sun smiled. He knew it took great courage and a strong sense of responsibility for a resident ophthalmologist to challenge an attending one's diagnosis.

Hospitals have a more complex hierarchy than other organizations. It was an unwritten rule that junior doctors should defer to their seniors; residents should obey the attending doctors; and there could be no disputing the opinions of professors and associate professors. So Sun attached special importance to Lu's query, since she was so very junior.

From then on his estimate of Lu was, "She's a very promising ophthalmologist."

Now eighteen years had passed. Lu, Jiang and their age group had become the backbone of his department. If promotion had been based on competence, they should long ago have had the rank of department heads. But this had not happened, and they were still not even attending doctors. For eighteen years their status had been that of interns, for the "cultural revolution" had broken the ladder leading to promotion.

The sight of Lu at her last gasp filled him with compassion. He stopped the head of the Internal Medicine Department to ask, "What do you think? Will she pull through?"

The department head looked towards her ward and sighed, then shook his head and said softly, "Old Sun, we can only hope she'll soon be out of danger."

Sun walked back anxiously to the ward. His steps were heavy, he was showing his age. From the doorway he saw Jiang still beside Lu's pillow. He halted, not wanting to disturb the two close friends.

In late autumn the nights are long. Darkness fell before six. The soughing wind rustled the phoenix trees outside the window. One by one their withered yellow leaves were blown away.

Sun, watching the whirling yellow leaves outside and listening to the wind, felt gloomier than before. Of these two skilled ophthalmologists, two key members of his staff, one had collapsed and might never recover, the other was leaving and might never return. They were two of the mainstays of his department in this prestigious hospital. Without them, he felt his department would be like the phoenix trees buffeted by the wind. It would deteriorate from day to day.

5

She seemed to be walking along an endless road, not a winding mountain path which urged people on, nor a narrow one between fields of fragrant rice. This was a desert, a quagmire, a wasteland, devoid of people and silent. Walking was difficult and exhausting.

Lie down and rest. The desert was warm, the quagmire soft. Let the ground warm her rigid body, the sunshine caress her tired limbs. Death was calling softly, "Rest, Dr Lu!"

Lie down and rest. Everlasting rest. No thoughts, feelings, worries, sadness or exhaustion.

But she couldn't do that. At the end of the long road, her patients were waiting for her. She seemed to see one patient tossing and turning in bed with the pain in his eyes, crying quietly at the threat of blindness. She saw many eager eyes waiting for her. She heard her patients calling to her in despair, "Dr Lu!"

This was a sacred call, an irresistible one. She trudged on the long road dragging her numb legs, from her home to the hospital, from the clinic to the ward, from one village to another with a medical team. Day by day, month by month, year by year, she trudged on....

"Dr Lu!"

Who was calling? Director Zhao? Yes. He had called her by phone. She remembered putting down the receiver, handing over her patient to Jiang, who shared her consulting room, and heading for the director's office.

She hurried through a small garden, ignoring the white and yellow chrysanthemums, the fragrance of the osmanthus and the fluttering butterflies. She wanted to quickly finish her business with Zhao and return to her patients. There were seventeen waiting that morning, and she had only seen seven so far. Tomorrow she was on ward duty. She wanted to make arrangements for some of the out-patients.

She remembered not knocking but walking straight in. A man and woman were sitting on the sofa. She halted. Then she saw Director Zhao in his swivel-chair.

"Come in please, Dr Lu," Zhao greeted her.

She walked over and sat down on a leather chair by the window.

The large room was bright, tidy and quiet, unlike the noisy clinic, where sometimes the children howled. She felt odd, unused to the quietness and cleanliness of the room.

The couple looked cultured and composed. Director Zhao was always erect and scholarly looking, with well-groomed hair, a kind face and smiling eyes behind gold-rimmed spectacles. He had on a white shirt, a well-pressed light grey suit and shining black leather shoes.

The man sitting on the sofa was tall and greying at the temples. A pair of sun-glasses shielded his eyes. Lu saw at a glance that he had eye trouble. Leaning back against the sofa, he was playing with his walking-stick.

The woman in her fifties was still attractive, despite her age. Though her hair was dyed and permed, it did not look cheap. Her clothes were well-cut and expensive.

Lu remembered how the woman had sized her up, following her about with her eyes. Her face showed doubt, uneasiness and disappointment.

"Dr Lu, let me introduce you to Vice-minister Jiao Chengsi and his wife Comrade Qin Bo."

A vice-minister? Well, in the past ten years and more, she had treated many ministers, Party secretaries and directors. She had never paid attention to titles. She simply wondered what was wrong with his eyes. Was he losing his sight?

Director Zhao asked, "Dr Lu, are you in the clinic or on duty in the ward?"

"Starting from tomorrow, I"ll be on ward duty."

"Fine," he laughed. "Vice-minister Jiao wants to have his cataract removed."

That meant she was given the task. She asked the man, "Is it one eye?"

"Yes."

"Which one?"

"The left one."

"Can't you see with it at all?"

The patient shook his head.

"Did you see a doctor before?"

As she rose to examine his eye, she remembered he named a hospital. Then his wife, who was sitting beside him, politely stopped her.

"There's no hurry, Dr Lu, Sit down, please. We ought to go to your clinic for an examination." Smiling, Qin Bo turned to Director Zhao. "Since he developed eye trouble, I've become something of an ophthalmologist myself."

Though Lu didn't examine him, she stayed a long time. What had they talked about? Qin had asked her many personal questions.

"How long have you been here, Dr Lu?"

She hadn't kept track of the years. She only remembered the year she had graduated. So she answered, "I came here in 1961."

"Eighteen years ago." Qin counted on her fingers.

Why was she so interested in this? Then Director Zhao chipped in, "Dr Lu has a lot of experience. She's a skilled surgeon."

Qin went on, "You don't seem to be in good health, Dr Lu."

What was she driving at? Lu was so busy caring for others, that she had never given any thought to her own health. The hospital didn't even have her case-history. And none of her leaders had ever inquired after her health. Why was this stranger showing such concern? She hesitated before answering, "I'm very well."

Zhao added again, "She's one of the fittest. Dr Lu's never missed a day's work for years."

Lu made no answer, wondering why this was so important to this lady, and fretting to get back to her patients. Jiang couldn't possibly cope with so many alone.

Her eyes fixed on Lu, the lady smiled and pressed, "Are you sure you can remove a cataract easily, Dr Lu?"

Another difficult question. She had had no accidents so far, but anything could happen if the patient didn't co-operate well or if the anaesthetic was not carefully applied.

She couldn't recollect whether she had made a reply, only Qin's big eyes staring at her with doubt, unsettling her. Having treated all kinds of patients, she had got used to the difficult wives of high cadres. She was searching for a tactful answer when Jiao moved impatiently and turned his head to his wife, who stopped and averted her gaze.

How had this trying conversation finished? Oh, yes, Jiang had come to tell her that Uncle Zhang had come for his appointment.

Qin quickly said politely, "You can go, Dr Lu, if you're busy."

Lu left the big bright room, which was so suffocating. She could hardly breathe.

She was suffocating.

6

Shortly before the day ended, Director Zhao hurried over to the internal medicine ward.

"Dr Lu's always enjoyed good health, Dr Sun. Why should she have this sudden attack?" his hands in his pockets, Zhao asked Sun as they headed for Lu's ward. Eight years Sun's junior, Zhao looked much younger, his voice more powerful.

He shook his head and went on, "This is a warning. Middle-aged doctors are the backbone of our hospital. Their heavy responsibilities and daily chores are ruining their health. If they collapse one by one, we'll be in a fix. How many people are there in her family? How many rooms does she have?"

Looking at Sun, who was depressed and worried, he added, "What? ... Four in a room? So that's how it is! What's her wage! ... 56.50 yuan! That's why people say better to be a barber with a razor than a surgeon with a scalpel. There's some truth in it. Right? Why wasn't her salary raised last year?"

"There were too many. You can't raise everyone's," Sun said cynically.

"I hope you'll talk that problem over with the Party branch. Ask them to investigate the work, income and living conditions of the middle-aged doctors and send me a report."

"What's the use of that? A similar report was sent in in 1978," Sun retorted politely, his eyes on the ground.

"Stop grumbling, Dr Sun. A report's better than nothing. I can show it to the municipal Party committee, the Ministry of Health and whomever it concerns. The Central Party Committee has stressed time and again that talented people and intellectuals should be valued and their salaries increased. We can't ignore it. The day before yesterday, at a meeting of the municipal committee, it was stressed that attention should be paid to middle-aged personnel. I believe their problems will be solved." Zhao stopped when they entered Lu's room.

Fu Jiajie stood up as Zhao entered. He waved his hand in greeting and walked over to Lu, bent down and examined her face. Then he took her case-history from her doctor. From a director he had turned into a doctor.

Zhao, a noted thorax expert, had returned to China after Liberation. Very enthusiastic politically, he was praised for both his political consciousness and his medical skill, joining the Party in the fifties. When later he was made director, he had to take part in so many meetings and do so much administrative work, that he seldom found the opportunity to see patients except for important consultations. During the "cultural revolution", he had been detained illegally and made to sweep the hospital grounds. The last three years, as director again, he had been so tied up with daily problems that he practically had no time or energy for surgery.

Now he had come specially to see Lu. All the ward doctors had gathered behind him.

But he didn't say anything startling. Having read the case-history and looked at the ECG monitor, he told the doctors to note any changes and watch out for complications. Then he asked, "Is her husband here?"

Sun introduced Fu. Zhao wondered why this charming man in his prime was already going bald. Apparently, a man who didn't know how to look after himself couldn't look after his wife either.

"It won't be easy," Zhao told him. "She needs complete rest. She'll need help for everything, even to turn over in bed. Help twenty-four hours a day. Where do you work? You'll have to ask for leave. You can't do it all by yourself either. Is there anyone else in your family?"

Fu shook his head. "Just two small children."

Zhao turned to Sun, "Can you spare someone from your department?"

"For one or two days, maybe."

"That'll do to begin with."

His eyes returning to Lu's thin pale face, Zhao still couldn't understand why this energetic woman had suddenly collapsed.

It occurred to him that she might have been too nervous operating on Vice-minister Jiao. Then he dismissed the thought. She was experienced and it was highly improbable that an attack had been brought on by nervousness. Besides, myocardial infarction often had no obvious cause.

But he couldn't dismiss the notion that there was some

kind of a link between Jiao's operation and Lu's illness. He regretted having recommended her. In fact, Jiao's wife, Qin Bo, had been reluctant to have her right from the beginning.

That day, after Lu's departure, Qin had asked, "Director Zhao, is Dr Lu the vice-head of her department?"

"No."

"Is she an attending doctor?"

"No."

"Is she a Party member?"

"No."

Qin said bluntly, "Excuse my outspokenness since we're all Party members, but I think it's rather inappropriate to let an ordinary doctor operate on Vice-minister Jiao."

Jiao stopped her by banging his walking-stick on the floor. Turning to her he said angrily, "What are you talking about, Qin Bo? Let the hospital make the arrangements. Any surgeon can operate."

Qin retorted heatedly, "That's not the right attitude, Old Jiao. You must be responsible. You can work only if you're healthy. We must be responsible to the revolution and the Party."

Zhao quickly butted in to avoid a quarrel, "Believe me, Comrade Qin, although she's not a Communist, Lu's a good doctor. And she's very good at removing cataracts. Don't worry!"

"It's not that, Director Zhao. And I'm not being too careful either." Qin sighed, "When I was in the cadre school, one old comrade had to have that operation. He was not allowed to come back to Beijing. So he went to a small hospital there. Before the operation was through his eyeball fell out. Jiao was detained by the followers of the gang for seven years! He has just resumed work. He can't do without his eyes."

"Nothing like that will happen, Comrade Qin. We've very few accidents in our hospital."

Qin still tried to argue her point. "Can we ask Dr Sun, the department head, to operate on Jiao?"

Zhao shook his head and laughed. "Dr Sun's almost seventy and has poor eyesight himself! Besides, he hasn't operated for years. He does research, advises the younger doctors and teaches. Dr Lu's a better surgeon than he."

"How about Dr Guo then?"

Zhao stared. "Dr Guo?" She must have made a thorough investigation of the department.

She prompted, "Guo Ruqing."

Zhao gestured helplessly. "He's left the country."

Qin wouldn't give up. "When is he coming back?"

"He's not."

"What do you mean?" This time she stared.

Zhao sighed. "Dr Guo's wife returned from abroad. When her father, a shopkeeper, died, he left his store to them. So they decided to leave."

"To leave medicine for a store? I can't understand it." Jiao sighed too.

"He's not the only one. Several of our capable doctors have left or are preparing to go."

Qin was indignant. "I don't understand their mentality."

Jiao waved his stick and turned to Zhao, "In the early fifties, intellectuals like you overcame many difficulties to return here to help build a new China. But now, the intellectuals we've trained are leaving the country. It's a serious lesson."

"This can't go on," said Qin. "We must do more ideological work. After the gang was smashed, the social status of intellectuals was raised a lot. Their living and working conditions will improve as China modernizes."

"Yes. Our Party committee holds the same view. I talked with Dr Guo twice on behalf of the Party and begged him to stay. But it was no use."

Qin, who was about to continue, was stopped by Jiao who said, "Director Zhao, I didn't come to insist on having an expert or a professor. I came because I've confidence in your hospital, or to be exact, because I have a special feeling for your hospital. A few years ago, the cataract in my right eye was removed here. And it was superbly done."

"Who did it?" Zhao asked.

Jiao answered sadly, "I never found out who she was."

"That's easy. We can look up your case-history."

Zhao picked up the receiver, thinking that Qin would be satisfied if he got that doctor. But Jiao stopped him. "You can't find her. I had it done as an out-patient. There was no case-history. It was a woman with a southern accent."

"That's difficult." Zhao laughed, replacing the receiver, "We have many women doctors who speak with a southern accent. Dr Lu also comes from the south. Let her do it."

The couple agreed. Qin helped Jiao up and they left.

Was this the cause of Lu's illness? Zhao couldn't believe it. She had performed this operation hundreds of times. She wouldn't be so nervous. He had gone over before the operation and found her confident, composed and well. Why this sudden attack, then?

Zhao looked again at Lu with concern. Even on the brink of death, she looked as if she were sleeping peacefully.

7

Lu was always composed, quiet and never flustered. Another woman would have retorted or shown her indignation at Qin's insulting questions or, at very least, felt resentful afterwards. But Lu had left Zhao's office as calm as ever, neither honoured to be chosen to operate on Vice-minister Jiao nor humiliated by Qin's questions. The patient had the right to decide whether or not he wanted an operation. That was all there was to it.

"Well, what big official wants you this time?" Jiang asked softly.

"It's not definite yet."

"Let's hurry." Jiang steered her along. "I couldn't persuade your Uncle Zhang. He's made up his mind not to have the operation."

"That's nonsense! He's travelled a long way to get here and spent much money. He'll be able to see after the transplant. It's our duty to cure him."

"Then you talk him round."

Passing by the waiting-room, they smiled and nodded at the familiar patients who stood up to greet them. Back in her room, while Lu was seeing a young man, she was interrupted by a voice booming, "Dr Lu!"

Both Lu and her patient looked up as a tall sturdy man advanced. In his fifties, he was broad-shouldered, wearing black trousers and a shirt and a white towel round his head. At his cry, the people in the corridor quickly made way for him. A head above everyone else and almost blind, he was unaware that he attracted so much attention as he groped his way in the direction of Lu's voice.

Lu hurried forward to help him. "Sit down, please, Uncle Zhang."

"Thank you, Dr Lu. I want to tell you something."

"Yes, but sit down first." Lu helped him to a chair.

"I've been in Beijing quite a while now. I'm thinking of going home tomorrow and coming back some other time."

"I don't agree. You've come such a long way and spent so much money. . . ."

"That's just it," Uncle Zhang cut in, slapping his thigh. "So I think I'll go home, do some work and earn some more workpoints. Although I can't see, I can still do some work and the brigade's very kind to me. I've made up my mind to leave, Dr Lu. But I couldn't go without saying goodbye to you. You've done so much for me."

Having suffered from corneal ulcers for many years, he had come to the hospital to have a transplant, a suggestion proposed by Lu when she had visited his brigade with a medical team.

"Your son spent a lot of money to send you here. We can't let you go home like this."

"I feel better already!"

Lu laughed. "When you're cured, you can work for another twenty years since you're so strong."

Uncle Zhang laughed. "You bet I will! I can do anything if my eyes are good."

"Then stay and have them treated."

Zhang confided, "Listen, Dr Lu, I'll tell you the truth. I'm worried about money. I can't afford to live in a Beijing hotel."

Stunned, Lu quickly told him, "I know you're next on the list. Once there's a donor, it'll be your turn."

He finally agreed to stay. Lu helped him out. Then a little girl of eleven accosted her.

Her pretty, rosy face was marred by a squint. Dressed in hospital pyjamas, she called timidly, "Dr Lu."

"Why don't you stay in the ward, Wang Xiaoman?" She had been admitted the previous day.

"I'm scared. I want to go home." She began to cry. "I don't want an operation."

Lu put one arm around her. "Tell me why you don't want an operation."

"It'll hurt too much."

"It won't, you silly girl! I'll give you an anaesthetic. It won't hurt at all." Lu patted her head and bent down to look with regret at the damaged work of art. She said, "Look, won't it be nice when I make this eye look like the other one? Now go back to your ward. You mustn't run around in a hospital."

When the little girl had wiped away her tears and left, Lu returned to her patients.

There had been many patients the last few days. She must make up for the time she had lost in Zhao's office. Forgetting Jiao, Qin and herself, she saw one patient after another.

A nurse came to tell her she was wanted on the phone.

Lu excused herself.

It was the kindergarten nurse informing her, "Xiaojia has a temperature. It started last night. I know you're busy, so I took her to the doctor, who gave her an injection. She's still feverish and is asking for you. Can you come?"

"I'll be there in a minute." She replaced the receiver.

But she couldn't go immediately since many patients were waiting. She rang her husband, but was told that he had gone out to a meeting.

Back in her office, Jiang asked, "Who called? Anything important?"

"Nothing."

Lu never troubled others, not even her leaders. "I'll go to the kindergarten when I'm through with the patients," she thought as she returned to her desk. At first she imagined her daughter crying and calling her. Later she saw only the patients' eyes. She hurried to the kindergarten when she had finished.

8

"Why did it take you so long?" the nurse complained.

Lu walked quickly to the isolation room where her little daughter lay, her face flushed with fever, her lips parted, her eyes closed, her breathing difficult.

She bent over the crib. "Mummy's here, darling."

Xiaojia moved and called in a hoarse voice, "Mummy, let's go home."

"All right, my pet."

She first took Xiaojia to her own hospital to see a pediatrician. "It's pneumonia," the sympathetic doctor told her. "You must take good care of her."

She nodded and left after Xiaojia had been given an injection and some medicine.

In the hospital everything stood still at noon, the out-patients having left, the in-patients sleeping and the hospital staff resting. The spacious grounds were deserted except for the chirping sparrows flying among the trees. Nature still competed with men in this noisy centre of the city, where tall buildings rose compactly and the air was polluted. In the hospital all day, Lu had never been aware of the birds before.

She couldn't make up her mind where to take her daughter, hating to leave the sick child alone in the kindergarten's isolation room. But who could look after her at home?

After some hesitation she steeled herself and headed for the kindergarten.

"No. I don't want to go there," Xiaojia wailed on her shoulder.

"Be a good girl, Xiaojia...."

"No, I want to go home!" She began kicking.

"All right. We'll go home."

They had to go along a busy street with recently pasted advertisements of the latest fashions. Lu never so much as glanced at the costly goods in the shop-windows, or the produce the peasants sold in the streets. With two children, it was hard to make ends meet. Now, carrying Xiaojia in her arms and worrying about Yuanyuan at home, she was even less eager to look around.

Arriving home at one o'clock, Lu found a pouting Yuanyuan waiting for her. "Why are you so late, mummy?" he asked.

"Xiaojia's ill," Lu answered curtly, putting Xiaojia on the bed, undressing her and tucking her in.

Standing at the table Yuanyuan fretted, "Please cook lunch, mummy. I'll be late."

In frustration, Lu shouted at him, "You'll drive me crazy if you go on like that!"

Wronged and in a hurry, Yuanyuan was on the point of tears. Ignoring him, Lu went to stoke up the fire, which had almost gone out. The pots and the cupboard were empty. There were no left-overs from yesterday's meals.

She went back into the room, reproaching herself for having been so harsh on the poor boy.

In the past few years, keeping house had become an increasing burden. During the "cultural revolution" her husband's laboratory had been closed down and his research project scrapped. All he had needed to do was to show his face in the office for an hour in the morning and afternoon. He spent the remainder of his day and talents on domestic chores, cooking and learning to sew and knit, lifting the burden entirely from Lu's shoulders. After the gang was smashed, scientific research was resumed and Fu, a capable metallurgist, was busy again. Most of the housework was shouldered once more by Lu.

Every day at noon, she went home to cook. It was an effort to stoke up the fire, prepare the vegetables and be ready to serve the meal in fifty minutes so that Yuanyuan, Fu and herself could return to school or work on time.

When anything unexpected cropped up, the whole family went hungry. She sighed and gave her son some money. "Go and buy yourself a bun, Yuanyuan."

He turned back half-way, "What about you, mummy?"

"I'm not hungry."

"I'll buy you a bun too."

Yuanyuan soon came home with two buns and gave one

to his mother. He left for school immediately, eating his on the way.

Biting into the cold hard bun, Lu looked around at her small room, which was twelve metres square.

She and her husband had been content with a simple life, living in this room since their marriage, without a sofa, wardrobe or a new desk. They had the same furniture they had used when they were single.

Though they owned few material possessions, they had many books. Aunt Chen, a neighbour, had commented, "What will the two bookworms live on?" But they were happy. All they had wanted was a small room, some clothes, and three simple meals a day.

Treasuring their time, they put their evenings to good use. Every night, when their neighbours' naughty children peeped into their small room to spy on the new couple, they invariably found them at work: Lu occupying their only desk studying foreign material with the help of a dictionary and taking notes, while Fu read reference books on a stack of chests.

The evening was not wasted when they could study late quietly and undisturbed. In the summer, their neighbours sat cooling themselves in the courtyard, but the smell of tea, the light breeze, bright stars, interesting news and conversation . . . none of these could lure them from their stuffy little room.

Their quiet life and studious evenings ended much too soon. Lu gave birth to Yuanyuan and then to Xiaojia. Their lovely children brought disorder and hardship as well as joy to their lives. When the crib was later replaced by a single bed and the tiny room filled with children's clothes, pots and pans, they could hardly move about. Peace was shattered by their children laughing and crying.

What could an ophthalmologist achieve without keeping

up with foreign developments in the field? Therefore, Lu often sat reading behind a curtain in the room late into the night.

When Yuanyuan began school he had to use their only desk. Only when he had finished doing his homework was it Lu's turn to spread out her notebook and the medical books she had borrowed. Fu came last.

How hard life was!

Lu fixed her eyes on the little clock: One five, one ten, one fifteen. Time to go to work. What should she do? Lots of things needed winding up before she went to the ward tomorrow. What about Xiaojia? Should she call her husband? There was no telephone booth near by and, anyway, she probably could not get him. As he had wasted ten years, better not disturb him.

She frowned, at a loss what to do.

Perhaps she shouldn't have married. Some claimed that marriage ended love. She had naively believed that, though it might be true for some, it could not happen to her. If she had been more prudent, she would not have been weighed down by the burdens of marriage and a family.

One twenty. She must turn to her neighbour Aunt Chen, a kind-hearted woman who had helped on many occasions.... Since she would not accept anything for her services, Lu was reluctant to trouble her.

Still she had to this time. Aunt Chen was most obliging, "Leave her to me, Dr Lu."

Lu put some children's books and building blocks beside Xiaojia, asked Aunt Chen to give her the medicine and hurried to the hospital.

She had intended to tell the nurse not to send her too many patients so that she could go home early, but once she started work, she forgot everything.

Zhao called her up to remind her that Jiao was to be admitted the following day.

Qin called twice asking about the operation and how Jiao and his family should prepare mentally and materially.

Lu was hard put to it to give an answer. She had performed hundreds of such operations and no one had ever asked her that before. So she said, "Oh, nothing special."

"Really? But surely it's better to be well prepared. What if I come over and we have a chat?"

Lu quickly told her, "I'm busy this afternoon."

"Then we'll talk tomorrow in the hospital."

"OK."

When the trying conversation had ended, Lu had returned to her office. It was dark before she had finished her clinic.

Arriving home she heard Aunt Chen singing an impromptu song:

"Grow up, my dear,
To be an engineer."

Xiaojia laughed happily. Lu thanked Aunt Chen and was relieved to find Xiaojia's temperature down.

She gave her an injection. After Fu returned, Jiang Yafen and her husband, Liu, called.

"We've come to say goodbye," said Jiang.

"Where are you going?" Lu inquired.

"We've just got our visas for Canada," replied Jiang, her eyes fixed on the ground.

Liu's father, a doctor in Canada, had urged them to join him there. Lu had not expected them to go.

"How long will you stay? When will you come back?" she asked.

"Maybe for good." Liu shrugged his shoulders.

"Why didn't you let me know earlier, Yafen?" Lu turned to her friend.

"I was afraid that you'd try to stop me. I was afraid I'd change my mind." Jiang avoided her eyes, staring hard at the ground.

From his bag, Liu produced some wine and food and said in high spirits, "I bet you haven't cooked yet. Let's have our farewell banquet here."

9

It was a sorrowful farewell party that evening.

They seemed to be drinking tears instead of wine. To be tasting the bitterness of life instead of delicious dishes.

Xiaojia was asleep, Yuanyuan watching TV next door. Liu raised his cup, eyeing the wine in it, and said with feeling, "Life — it's hard to tell how life will turn out! My father was a doctor with a sound classical education. As a child I loved old poetry and longed to become a writer, but I was fated to follow in his footsteps, and now over thirty years have gone. My father was extremely circumspect. His maxim was 'Too much talk leads to trouble'. Unfortunately I didn't take after him. I like talking and airing my views, so that landed me in trouble and I got bashed in each political movement. When graduated in '57, by the skin of my teeth I missed being labelled a Rightist. In the 'cultural revolution', it goes without saying, I was flayed. I'm Chinese. I can't claim to have high political consciousness, but at least I love my country and really want China to become rich and strong. I never dreamed that now that I'm nearing fifty I'd suddenly leave my homeland."

"Do you really have to go?" Lu asked gently.

"Yes. Why? I've debated this with myself many times." Liu shook the half-full cup of red wine he was holding. "I've passed middle age and may not live many years longer. Why should I leave my ashes in a strange land?"

The others listened in silence to this expression of his grief at leaving. Now he suddenly broke off, drained his cup and blurted out, "Go on, curse me! I'm China's unfilial son!"

"Don't say that, Liu. We all know what you've been through." Fu refilled his cup. "Now those dark years are over, the sun is shining again. Everything will change for the better."

"I believe that." Liu nodded. "But when will the sun shine on our family? Shine on our daughter? I can't wait."

"Let's not talk about that." Lu guessed that Liu felt impelled to leave for the sake of his only daughter. Not wanting to go into this, she changed the subject. "I never drink, but today before you and Yafen leave I want to drink to you."

"No, we should drink to *you*." Liu put down his cup. "You're the mainstay of our hospital, one of China's up-and-coming doctors!"

"You're drunk," she laughed.

"I'm not."

Jiang, who had been keeping quiet, now raised her cup and said, "I drink to you from the bottom of my heart! To our twenty-odd years of friendship, and to our future eye-specialist!"

"Goodness! You're talking nonsense! Who am I?" Lu brushed aside this compliment.

"Who are you?" Liu was really half tipsy. "You live in cramped quarters and slave away regardless of criticism, not seeking fame or money. A hard-working doctor like you is an ox serving the children, as Lu Xun said, eating grass and providing milk. Isn't that right, Old Fu?"

Fu drank in silence and nodded.

"There are many people like that, I'm not the only one," Lu demurred with a smile.

"That's why ours is a great nation!" Liu drained another cup.

Jiang glanced at Xiaojia sound asleep on the bed, and said sympathetically, "Yes, you're too busy attending to your patients to nurse your own little girl."

Liu stood up to fill all the cups and declared, "She's sacrificing herself to save mankind."

"What's come over you today, boosting me like this?" Lu wagged a finger at Fu. "You ask him if I'm not selfish, driving my husband into the kitchen and turning my children into ragamuffins. I've messed up the whole family. The fact is, I'm neither a good wife nor mother."

"You're a good doctor!" Liu cried.

Fu took another sip of wine, then put down his cup and commented, "I think your hospital is to blame. Doctors have homes and children like everyone else. And their children may fall ill. Why does no one show any consideration for them?"

"Fu!" Liu cut in loudly. "If I were Director Zhao, I'd first give you a medal, and one each to Yuanyuan and Xiaojia. You're the ones victimized to provide our hospital with such a fine doctor...."

Fu interrupted, "I don't want a medal or a citation. I just wish your hospital understood how hard it is to be a doctor's husband. As soon as the order comes to go out on medical tours or relief work, she's up and off, leaving the family. She comes back so exhausted from the operating theatre, she can't raise a finger to cook a meal. That being the case, if I don't go into the kitchen, who will? I should really be grateful to the 'cultural revolution' for giving me all that time to learn to cook."

"Yafen said long ago that your 'bookworm' label should be torn off." Liu patted his shoulder and laughed. "You can study one of the most advanced branches of science for space travel, and put on a stunning performance in the kitchen — you're becoming one of the new men of the communist era. Who says the achievements of the 'cultural revolution' were not the main aspect of it?"

Fu normally never drank. Today after a few cups his face

was red. He caught hold of Liu's sleeve and chuckled, "Right, the 'cultural revolution' was a great revolution to remould us. Didn't those few years change me into a male housewife? If you don't believe it, ask Wenting. Didn't I turn my hand to every chore?"

This embittered joking upset Lu. But she could not stop them. It seemed this was now the only way to lessen their grief at parting. She forced herself to smile back at her husband.

"You learned to do everything except sew cloth shoesoles. That's why Yuanyuan keeps clamouring for a pair of gym-shoes."

"You expect too much," said Liu with a straight face. "However thoroughly Fu remoulds himself, he can't turn into an old village woman carrying a shoe-sole around everywhere!"

"If the 'gang of four' hadn't been smashed, I might really have carried a shoe-sole to the criticism meetings in my institute," said Fu. "Just think, if things had gone on like that, science, technology and learning would all have been scrapped, leaving nothing but sewing cloth shoe-soles."

But how long could they keep up these wry jokes? They talked of the springtime of science since the overthrow of the gang, of the improved political status of intellectuals although they were underpaid, of the difficulties of middle-aged professionals. The atmosphere became heavy again.

"Old Liu, you have lots of contacts, it's too bad you're leaving." Fu roused himself to slap Liu on the back. "I hear home helps get very well paid. I'd like you to find me a place as a male domestic."

"My leaving doesn't matter," Liu retorted. "Just put an ad in that new paper *The Market*."

"That's a good idea!" Fu adjusted his thick-rimmed glasses. "The advertiser is a university graduate with a mastery of two foreign languages. A good cook, tailor and washerman, able to do both skilled and heavy work. His health is sound, his temper good, he's bold, hard-working and willing to accept criticism. And, last of all, his wages can be settled at the interview." He laughed.

Jiang was sitting quietly, neither eating nor drinking. Watching them laugh, she wanted to join in but could not. She nudged her husband.

"Don't talk like that, what's the point?"

"This is a widespread social phenomenon, that's the point." Liu made a sweeping gesture. "Middle age, middle age. Everyone agrees that middle-aged cadres are the backbone of our country. The operations in a hospital depend on middle-aged surgeons; the most important research projects are thrust on middle-aged scientists and technicians; the hardest jobs in industry are given to middle-aged workers; the chief courses in school are taught by middle-aged teachers. . . ."

"Don't go on and on!" Jiang put in. "Why should a doctor worry about all that?"

Liu screwed up his eyes and continued half tipsy, "Didn't Lu You say, 'Though in a humble position I remain concerned for my country?' I'm a doctor no one has ever heard of, but I keep affairs of state in mind. Everyone acknowledges the key role of the middle-aged, but who knows how hard their life is? At work they shoulder a heavy load, at home they have all the housework. They have to support their parents and bring up their children. They play a key role not just because of their experience and ability, but because they put up with hardships and make great sacrifices — as do their wives and children."

Lu had listened blankly. Now she interposed softly, "It's a pity so few people realize that." Fu, who had been speechless, filled Liu's cup and declared cheerfully, "You should have studied sociology."

Liu laughed sarcastically. "If I had, I'd have been a big Rightist! Sociologists have to study social evils."

"If you uncover them and set them right, society can make progress. That's to the left not the right," said Fu.

"Never mind, I don't want to be either. But I really am interested in social problems. For instance, the problem of the middle-aged." Liu rested his elbows on the table, toying with his empty cup, and began again, "There used to be a saying, 'At middle age a man gives up all activities.' That was true in the old society when people aged prematurely. By forty they felt they were old. But now that saying should be changed to 'At middle age a man is frantically busy!' right? This reflects the fact that in our new society people are younger, full of vitality. Middle age is a time to give full play to one's abilities."

"Well said!" Fu approved.

"Don't be in such a hurry to express approval. I've another crazy notion." Liu gripped Fu's arm and continued eagerly, "Looking at it that way, you can say our middle-aged generation is lucky to be alive at this time. But in fact we're an unlucky generation."

"You're monopolizing the conversation!" protested Jiang.

But Fu said, "I'd like to hear why we're unlucky."

"Unlucky because the time when we could have done our best work was disrupted by Lin Biao and the 'gang of four'," Liu sighed. "Take your case, you nearly became an unemployed vagrant. Now we middle-aged people are the ones chiefly responsible for modernization, and we don't feel up to it. We haven't the knowledge, energy or strength. We're overburdened — that's our tragedy."

"There's no pleasing you!" laughed Jiang. "When you're not used, you complain that your talents are wasted, you live at the wrong time. When you're fully used, you gripe that you're overworked and underpaid!"

"Don't you ever complain?" her husband retorted.

Jiang hung her head and did not answer.

All Liu had said had given Lu the impression that he felt impelled to leave not entirely for his daughter's sake, but also for his own.

Once more Liu raised his cup and cried, "Come on! Let's drink to middle age!"

10

After their guests had gone and the children were asleep, Lu washed up in the kitchen. In their room, she found her husband, leaning against the bed, deep in thought, his hand on his forehead.

"A penny for them, Jiajie." Lu was surprised he looked so depressed.

Fu asked in reply, "Do you remember Petöfi's poem?"

"Of course!"

"I wish I were a crumbling ruin. . . ." Fu removed his hand from his forehead. "I'm a ruin now, like an old man. Going bald and grey. I can feel the lines on my forehead. I'm a ruin!"

He did look older than his age. Upset, Lu touched his forehead. "It's my fault! We're such a burden to you!"

Fu took her hand and held it lovingly. "No. You're not to blame."

"I'm a selfish woman, who thinks only about her work." Lu's voice quivered. She couldn't take her eyes away from his forehead. "I have a home but I've paid it little attention. Even when I'm not working, my mind is preoccupied with my patients. I haven't been a good wife or mother."

"Don't be silly! I know more than anyone how much you've sacrificed!" He stopped as tears welled up in his eyes.

Nestling up against him, she said sadly, "You've aged. I don't want you to grow old...."

"Never mind. 'If my love green ivy would be, she'd tenderly entwine around my lonely head.'" Softly he recited their favourite poem.

In the still autumn night, Lu fell asleep against her husband's chest, her lashes moist with tears. Fu put her carefully on the bed. Opening her eyes she asked, "Did I fall asleep?"

"You're very tired."

"No. I'm not."

Fu propped himself up and said to her, "Even metal has fatigue. A microscopic crack is formed first, and it develops until a fracture suddenly occurs."

That was Fu's field of research, and he often mentioned it. But this time, his words carried weight and left a deep impression on Lu.

A dreadful fatigue, a dreadful fracture. In the quiet of the night, Lu seemed to hear the sound of breaking. The props of heavy bridges, sleepers under railways, old bricks and the ivy creeping up ruins... all these were breaking.

11

The night deepened.

The pendent lamp in the room having been turned off, the wall lamp shed a dim blue light.

Before her eyes flitted two blue dots of light, like fireflies on a summer night or a will-o'-the-wisp in the wilderness, which turned into Qin's cold stare when she looked carefully.

Qin, however, had been warm and kind when she summoned Lu to Jiao's room the morning he entered the hospital. "Sit down please, Dr Lu. Old Jiao has gone to have his ECG done. He'll be back in a minute."

All smiles, she had risen from an armchair in a room in a quiet building with red-carpeted corridors reserved for high cadres.

Qin had asked her to sit in the other armchair, while she went over to the locker beside the bed and got out a basket of tangerines, which she placed on the side table between the chairs.

"Have a tangerine."

Lu declined. "No, thank you."

"Try one. They were sent to me by a friend in the south. They're very good." She took one and offered it to her.

Lu took it, but held it in her hand. Qin's new friendliness sent a chill down her spine. She was still conscious of the coldness in Qin's eyes when they had first met.

"What actually is a cataract, Dr Lu? Some doctors told me that an operation is not suitable for all cases." Qin's manner was humble and ingratiating.

"A growth which progressively covers the eyeball, destroying the sight." Looking at the tangerine in her hand, Lu explained, "It can be divided into stages. It's better to have the operation done when the cataract is mature."

"I see. What happens if it isn't done then?"

"The lens shrinks as the cortex is absorbed. The suspensory ligament becomes fragile. The difficulty of the operation increases as the lens is liable to be dislocated."

Qin nodded.

She had not understood nor tried to understand what she had been told. Lu wondered why she had bothered to ask questions. Just passing time? Having started her ward duty only that morning, she had to familiarize herself with the cases of her patients and attend to them. She couldn't sit there, making small talk. She wanted to check Jiao's eyes if he returned soon.

Qin had more questions for her. "I heard there was an

artificial lens abroad. The patient needn't wear a convex lens after an operation. Is that right?"

Lu nodded. "We're experimenting on that too."

Qin inquired eagerly, "Can you put one in for my husband?"

Lu smiled. "I said it's still at the experimental stage. I don't think he'd want one now, do you?"

"No." Of course she didn't want him to be a guinea-pig. "What is the procedure for his operation?"

Lu was baffled. "What do you mean?"

"Shouldn't you map out a plan in case something unexpected crops up?" As Lu looked blank, she added, "I've often read about it in the papers. Sometimes surgeons form a team to discuss and work out a plan."

Lu couldn't help laughing. "No need for that! This is a very simple operation."

Disgruntled, Qin looked away. Then she turned back and pressed her point patiently with a smile, "Underestimating the enemy often leads to failure. This has happened in the history of our Party." Then she got Lu to describe certain situations which could cause the operation to fail.

"One has to think twice about patients with heart trouble, hypertension or bronchitis. Coughing can create problems."

"That's just what I feared," Qin cried, striking the arm of her chair. "My husband's heart isn't good and he has high blood pressure."

"We always examine the patient thoroughly before an operation," Lu consoled her.

"He has bronchitis too."

"Has he been coughing lately?"

"No. But what if he does on the operating-table? What shall we do?"

Why was she so anxious, Lu wondered, looking at her watch. The morning was almost gone. Her glance fell on the white lace curtain hanging beside the French windows and tension gripped her when the footsteps approaching the door moved away again. After a long time, Jiao, a blue and white dressing-gown round his shoulders, was helped in by a nurse.

Qin commented, "It's taken you a long time!"

Jiao shook Lu's hand and flopped down exhausted in the armchair. "There were lots of examinations. I had a blood test, an X-ray, and an ECG. The staff were all very kind to me. I didn't have to wait my turn."

He sipped the cup of tea Qin handed him. "I never thought an eye operation involved so many tests."

Lu read the reports. "The X-ray and the ECG are normal. Your blood pressure's a bit high."

Qin piped up. "How high?"

"150 over 100. But that doesn't matter." Then she asked, "Have you been coughing recently, Vice-minister Jiao?"

"No," he answered lightly.

Qin pressed, "Can you guarantee that you won't cough on the operating-table?"

"Well. . . ." Jiao was not so sure.

"That's important, Old Jiao," Qin warned him gravely. "Dr Lu just told me that if you cough, the eyeball can fall out."

Jiao turned to Lu. "How can I be certain I won't cough?"

"It's not that serious. If you are a smoker, don't smoke before the operation."

"OK."

Qin pressed again. "But what if you should cough? What will happen?"

Lu laughed. "Don't worry, Comrade Qin. We can sew up the incision and open it again after he stops coughing."

"That's right," said Jiao. "When I had my right eye operated on, it was sewn up and then opened again. But it wasn't because I coughed!"

Curiosity made Lu ask, "Why then?"

Jiao put down his cup and took out his cigarette case, but put it away again remembering Lu's advice. With a sigh he related, "I'd been labelled as a traitor and was having a difficult time. When the sight went in my right eye I had an operation. Soon after it started, the rebels came and tried to force the surgeon not to treat me. I nearly choked with indignation, but the doctor calmly sewed up the incision, threw the rebels out and then removed the cataract."

"Really?" Stunned, Lu asked, "Which hospital was that?"

"This one."

A coincidence? She looked at Jiao again to see whether she had seen him before, but could not recognize him.

Ten years ago, she had been operating on a so-called traitor when she had been interrupted by some rebels. That patient's name was Jiao. So it was he! Later, the rebels from Jiao's department, collaborating with a rebel in the hospital, put up a slogan claiming that "Lu Wenting betrays the proletariat by operating on the traitor Jiao Chengsi".

No wonder she hadn't recognized him. Ten years ago, Jiao, sallow and depressed, dressed in an old cotton-padded coat, had come to the hospital alone as an ordinary patient. Lu suggested an operation and made an appointment, which he kept. When she began operating she heard the nurse saying outside, "No admittance. This is the operating theatre."

Then she heard shouting and noises. "Shit! He's a traitor. We're against treating traitors."

"We won't allow stinking intellectuals to treat traitors."

"Force open the door!"

Jiao, indignant, said on the operating-table, "Let me go blind, doctor. Don't do it."

Lu warned him against moving and quickly sewed up the incision.

Three men charged in, while the more timid ones hesitated at the door. Lu sat there immobile.

Jiao said the doctor had thrown them out. As a matter of fact, Lu had not. She had sat on the stool by the operating-table in her white gown, green plastic slippers, blue cap and mask. All that could be seen of her were her eyes and her bare arms above the rubber gloves. The rebels were awed perhaps by her strange appearance, the solemn atmosphere of the operating theatre and the bloody eye exposed through a hole in the white towel covering the patient. Lu said tersely from behind her mask, "Get out, please!"

The rebels looked at each other and left.

When Lu resumed work, Jiao told her, "Don't do it, doctor, they'll only blind me again even if you cure me. And you may get involved."

"Keep quiet." Lu worked swiftly. When she was bandaging him, all she had said was, "I'm a doctor." That was how it had happened.

The rebels from Jiao's department, coming to the hospital to put up a big-character poster denouncing her for curing a traitor, had created quite a sensation. But what did it matter? She was already being criticized for being a bourgeois specialist. These charges and this operation had not left much impression on her. She had forgotten all about it, until Jiao had brought it up.

"I really respect her, Dr Lu. She was a true doctor," Qin sighed. "Pity the hospital kept no records then. I can't find out who she was. Yesterday I expressed my wish to Director Zhao to have her operate on my husband." Lu's awkward expression made her add, "I'm sorry, Dr Lu. Since Director Zhao has confidence in you, we will too. I hope you won't let him down. Learn from that doctor. Of course, we've a lot to learn from her too, don't you agree?"

Lu had no alternative but to nod.

"You're still young," Qin said encouragingly. "I heard you haven't joined the Party yet. You must strive for it, comrade."

Lu told her frankly, "I don't have a good class background."

"That's not the way to look at things. You can't choose your family but you can choose what you do with your life." Qin was eloquent and enthusiastic. "Our Party does pay attention to class origins, but not exclusively. It's your attitude that counts. When you draw the line between yourself and your family, get close to the Party and make contributions to the people, then the Party will open its doors to you."

Lu crossed the room to draw the curtain and examined Jiao's eye. Then she told Jiao, "If it's all right with you, let's do the operation the day after tomorrow."

Jiao answered briskly, "All right. The earlier the better."

It was already after six when Lu took her leave. Qin hurried out after her. "Are you going home, Dr Lu?"

"Yes."

"Shall I arrange for Jiao's car to take you?"

"No, thank you." Lu declined with a wave of her hand.

12

It was almost midnight, the ward was very quiet. A single wall lamp cast a pale blue light on an intravenous drip, from which the medicine was dropping, as if the only sign of Dr Lu's life.

Fu, sitting at the side of the bed, stared blankly at his wife. It was the first time that he had sat alone with her since her collapse, probably the first time that he had looked at her so intently for the past dozen years.

He remembered that once he had fixed his eyes on her for

a long time, and she had asked, her head on one side, "Why do you look at me like that?" Sheepishly he had turned his eyes away. That was when they were courting. But now she could neither move her head nor speak. Vulnerable, she was unable to raise a protest.

Only then did he notice that she looked surprisingly frail and old! Her jet-black hair was streaked with grey; her firm, tender skin, loose and soft; and there were lines on her forehead. The corners of her mouth, once so pretty, were now drooping. Her life, like a dying flame, was petering out fast. He could not believe that his wife, a firm character, had become so feeble overnight!

She was not weak, he knew that well. Slim in build, she was in fact fit and strong. Though her shoulders were slight, she silently endured all hardships and sudden misfortunes. She never complained, feared or became disheartened.

"You're a tough woman," he had often said to her.

"Me? No, I'm timid. Not tough at all." Her answer was always the same.

Only the night before she had fallen ill, she had made, as Fu put it, another "heroic decision" that he should move to his institute.

Xiaojia had quite recovered by then. After Yuanyuan had done his homework, the children went to bed. At last there was peace in the small room.

Autumn had come, the wind was cold. The kindergarten had asked parents for their children's winter clothes. Lu took out the cotton-padded coat Xiaojia had worn the previous year, ripped it apart, made it bigger and sewed on a new pair of cuffs. Then she spread it out on the desk and added a layer of new cotton padding.

Fu took his unfinished article from the bookcase and, hesitating for a brief second beside the desk, sat down on the bed.

"Just a moment," Lu said without turning her head, hurrying, "I'll soon finish."

When she removed the coat from the desk, Fu remarked, "If only we could have another small room. Even six square metres, just big enough for a desk."

Lu listened, lowering her head, busy sewing. After a while, she hastily folded up the unfinished coat and said, "I've got to go to the hospital now. You can have the desk."

"But why? It's late," he queried.

She said, while putting on her jacket, "There will be two operations tomorrow morning and I want to check how the patients are. I'll go and have a look at them."

She often went to the hospital in the evening in fact. So Fu teased her, saying, "Though you're here at home, your heart's still in the hospital."

"Put on more clothes. It's cold," he urged.

"I won't be long," she said quickly. With an apologetic smile, she continued, "Two funny patients, you know. One's a vice-minister. His wife's been worrying to death about the operation and making an awful fuss. So I must go to see him. The other's a little girl. She told me today that she had a lot of nightmares and slept badly."

"OK, doc!" He smiled. "Get going and come back soon!"

She left. When she returned he was still burning the midnight oil. Not wanting to disturb him, she said after tucking up the children's quilt, "I'm going to bed first."

He looked round, saw she was in bed and again buried himself in his papers and books. But soon he sensed that she had not fallen asleep. Was it perhaps the light? He bent the lamp lower, shielded the light with a newspaper and carried on with his work.

After a while, he heard her soft, even snoring. But he knew that she was faking. Many times, she had tried to pretend she slept well, so he could feel at ease studying late. In fact he had long since seen through her little trick, but had no heart to expose it.

Some time later, he got to his feet, stretched and said, "All right! I'll sleep too."

"Don't worry about me!" Lu said quickly. "I'm already half asleep."

Standing with his hands on the edge of the desk, he hesitated, looking at his unfinished article. Then he made up his mind and said, closing all the books, "I'll call it a day."

"How about your article? How can you finish it if you don't make full use of your nights?"

"One night can't make up for ten years."

Lu sat up, threw a sweater over her shoulders and said in earnest, her head against the bed board, "Guess what I've been thinking just now?"

"You oughtn't to have thought of anything! Now close *your* eyes. You'll have to cure other people's eyes tomorrow."

"It's no joke. Listen, I think you should move into your institute. Then you'll have more time."

Fu stared at her. Her face was glowing, her eyes dancing. Obviously she was very pleased with the idea.

She went on, "I'm serious. You've things to do. I know, the children and I have been hampering you."

"Come off it! It's not you...."

Lu broke in, "Of course it is! We can't divorce. The children need their father, and a scientist needs his family. However, we must think of some way to turn your eight working hours into sixteen."

"But the children and the housework will all fall on you. That won't do!"

"Why not? Even without you, we can manage."

He listed all the problems, to which she answered one by one. Finally she said, "Haven't you often remarked that I'm a tough woman? I can cope. Your son won't go hungry, your daughter won't be ill-treated."

He was convinced. So they decided to have a try the next day.

"It's so very difficult to do something in China!" Fu said undressing. "During the war, many old revolutionaries died for a new China. Now to modernize our country, again our generation has to make sacrifices though hardly anyone notices it."

He kept talking to himself like this. When he put his clothes on the back of a chair and turned to get into bed, he saw that Lu had fallen asleep. With a faint smile on her face, she looked pleased with her proposal, even in her dreams.

But who would imagine their trial would fail on the very first day?

13

The operations were successful, though Lu's private plan failed.

That morning when she had entered the ward ten minutes early as usual, Dr Sun was already there waiting for her.

"Good morning, Dr Lu," he greeted her, "We've got a donor's eye today. Can we fit in the corneal transplant?"

"Excellent! We've got a patient who's anxious to have the operation done as soon as possible," Lu exclaimed in delight.

"But you already have two operations scheduled for this morning. Do you think you can manage a third?"

"Sure," she replied, straightening up as if showing him that she was perfectly capable.

"OK, it's settled then." He had made up his mind.

Holding the arm of Jiang, who had just arrived; Lu headed for the operating theatre. She was in high spirits, walking with a spring in her step, as though on an outing.

The operating theatres of this hospital, occupying a whole floor, were large and impressive. The big characters "Operating Theatre" in red paint on the beige glass door were striking. When a wheeled stretcher bearing a patient was pushed through this door, his relatives remained outside, anxiously looking at the mysterious, perhaps even frightening place, as if Death were lurking about inside.

But in fact, the operating theatre was a place of hope. Inside, the walls along the wide corridor were painted a light, agreeable green. Here there were the operating theatres for the various departments. The surgeons, their assistants, anaesthetists and theatre nurses scurried to and fro lightly. No laughter, no chatter. This was the most quiet, most orderly area of the large hospital, into which more than a thousand patients poured every day.

Vice-minister Jiao was brought into one of these theatres, and then put on a high cream-coloured operating-table. His head was covered by a sterilized white towel. There was an olive-shaped hole in it revealing one of his eyes.

Lu already in her overall sat on a stool near the operating-table, her gloved hands raised. The height of the stool was adjustable. Lu, being small, had to raise it whenever she operated. But today, it had already been adjusted. She turned and glanced at Jiang gratefully, realizing she had done it.

A nurse pushed the surgical instrument table nearer to Lu. The adjustable plate was now placed above the patient's chest, within the surgeon's reach.

"Shall we start now?" Lu asked watching Jiao's eye. "Try to relax. We'll first inject a local anaesthetic. Then your eye will feel numb. The operation won't take long."

At this, Jiao suddenly cried out, "Steady on!"

What was wrong? Both Lu and Jiang were taken aback. Jiao pulled away the towel from his face, striving to raise his head. He inquired, pointing at Lu, "It was you, Dr Lu, who operated before on my eye?"

Lu quickly raised her gloved hands lest he touch them. Before she could speak, he went on emotionally, "Yes, it was you. It must have been you! You said the same words. Even your tone and intonation are the same!"

"Yes, it was me," Lu had to admit.

"Why didn't you tell me before? I'm so grateful to you."

"Never mind. . . ." Lu could not find anything else to say. She cast a glance at the towel, beckoned the nurse to change it. Then she said again, "Shall we start, Vice-minister Jiao?"

Jiao sighed. It was hard for him to calm down. Lu had to say in a commanding tone, "Don't move. Don't speak. We'll start now."

She skilfully injected some novocaine into his lower eyelid and began the operation. She had performed such operations umpteen times, but every time she picked up her instruments, she felt like a raw recruit on the battlefield. Lu held out two tapering fingers to pick up a needle-holder which looked like a small pair of scissors. She fixed the needle to the instrument.

"What's the matter?" Jiang asked softly.

Instead of answering, Lu held the hook-shaped needle up to the light to examine it.

"Is this a new one?"

Jiang had no idea, so they both turned to the nurse.

"A new needle?"

The nurse stepped forward and said in a low voice, "Yes, a new one."

Lu had another look at the needle pin and grumbled, "How can we use such a needle?"

Lu and some other doctors had complained many times about the poor quality of their surgical instruments. However, faulty ones appeared from time to time. Lu could do nothing about it. When she found good scalpels, scissors and needles, she would ask the nurse to keep them for her for later use.

She had no idea that all the surgical instruments had been replaced by new ones that day, but unfortunately there was a bad needle among them. Whenever such things occurred, Lu's good-natured face would change, and she would reprimand the nurse. The young nurse, though innocent perhaps, could not defend herself. There was nothing to say in the circumstances. A blunt needle not only prolonged the operation, but also increased the patient's suffering.

Frowning, Lu said quietly, so that Jiao could not overhear, "Bring me another!"

It was an order, and the nurse picked out an old needle from a sterilizer.

The theatre nurses respected Lu, while at the same time being afraid of her. They admired her skill and feared her strictness. A doctor's authority was established through his scalpel. A good ophthalmologist could give a blind man back his sight, while a bad one might blind him permanently. Lu had no position, no power, but through her scalpel she wielded authority.

The operation was almost complete, when Jiao's body jerked suddenly.

"Don't move!" Lu warned him.

"Don't move!" Jiang repeated quickly. "What's the matter?"

"I . . . want to . . . cough!" a strangled voice sounded from under the towel.

This was just what his wife had feared would happen. Why choose this moment to cough? Was it psychological? A conditioned reflex?

"Can you control it for a minute?"

"No. I . . . I can't." His chest was heaving.

There was no time to lose! Lu hurriedly took emergency measures, while calming him down, "Just a second! Breathe out and hold your cough!"

She was quickly tying up the suture while he exhaled, his chest moving vigorously as if he would die of suffocation at any moment. When the last knot was done, Lu sighed with relief and said, "You can cough now, but not too loudly."

But he did not. On the contrary, his breath gradually grew even and normal.

"Go ahead and cough. It won't matter," Jiang urged again.

"I'm awfully sorry," Jiao apologized. "I'm all right now. Carry on with the operation, please."

Jiang rolled her eyes, wanting to give him a piece of her mind. A man of his age should know better. Lu threw her a glance, and Jiang bit back her resentment. They smiled knowingly at each other. It was all in the day's work!

Lu snipped off the knots and started the operation again. It continued without a hitch. Afterwards Lu got off the stool and sat at a small table to write out a prescription, while Jiao was moved back on to the wheeled stretcher. As it was being pushed out, Jiao suddenly called to Lu, like a kid who has misbehaved, his voice trembling slightly.

Lu stepped over to him. His eyes had been bandaged. "Anything I can do?" she stooped to ask.

He reached out, groping. When he caught hold of her hands, still in their gloves, he shook them vigorously. "I've given you much trouble on both occasions. I'm so sorry. . . ."

Lu was stunned for a brief moment. Then she consoled him, looking at his bandaged face, "Never mind. Have a good rest. We'll take off the bandage in a few days."

After he was wheeled out, Lu glanced at the clock. A forty-minute operation had lasted an hour. She took off her white gown and rubber gloves and immediately donned another.

As Lu turned to let the nurse tie the gown at the back, Jiang asked, "Shall we continue?"

"Yes."

14

"Let me do the next operation," Jiang begged. "You take a short rest, then do the third."

Lu shook her head and said smilingly, "I'll do it. You're not familiar with Wang Xiaoman. The child's scared stiff. We became friends during the last few days. Better leave her to me."

The girl did not come into the operating theatre on a wheeled stretcher, but was almost dragged in. In a white gown, which was a bit too large for her, she was reluctant to go anywhere near the operating-table.

"Aunt Lu, I'm scared. I don't want the operation. Please go and explain to my mother."

The sight of the doctors and nurses in such strange clothes terrified her. Her heart was pounding, as she tried to wrench away from the nurses, pleading with Lu for help.

Lu walked towards the table and coaxed her with a grin, "Come on, little girl. Didn't you promise to have this operation? Be brave! There's nothing to fear. You won't feel any pain once you've been given some anaesthetic."

Xiaoman sized up Lu in her funny clothes and gazed at her kind, smiling, encouraging eyes. Then she climbed up on to the operating-table. A nurse spread a towel over her face. Lu motioned the nurse to tie up her hands. As the little patient was about to protest, Lu said, perching on the table, "Xiaoman, be a good girl! It's the same for all patients. Really, it won't take long." She gave her an injection of the anaesthetic while telling her, "I'm giving you an injection and soon your eye will feel nothing at all."

Lu was both doctor, devoted mother and kindergarten nurse. She took the scissors, forceps and other instruments which Jiang handed to her while keeping up a running commentary for the benefit of the girl. When she severed the straight muscle which caused the squint, Xiaoman's nerve was affected and she became nauseous.

"You feel a little sick?" Lu asked. "Take a deep breath. Just hold on for a minute. That's better. Still sick? Feeling any better? We'll finish the operation very soon. There's a good girl!"

Lu's words lulled Xiaoman into a trance while the operation continued. When she had been bandaged and wheeled out of the room, she remembered what her mother had told her to say, so she called out sweetly, "Thank you very much, aunty."

Everyone burst out laughing. The minute hand of the clock on the wall had just moved half an hour.

Lu was wet with sweat, the perspiration beading on her forehead, her underwear soaking. Wet patches showed under her armpits. She was surprised at this because it was not hot. Why had she perspired so profusely? She slightly moved her numb arms, which had ached from being raised for the duration of the operation.

When she removed the operating gown again and reached out for another, she suddenly felt dizzy. She closed her eyes for a minute, shook her head several times and then slowly eased one of her arms into a sleeve. A nurse came to help her tie the gown.

"Dr Lu!" the nurse exclaimed suddenly. "Your lips are so pale!"

Jiang, who was also changing, turned to look at Lu. "Goodness!" she said in astonishment. "You do look very pale!"

It was true. There were black rings under her eyes, even her lids were puffy. She looked a patient herself!

Seeing that Jiang's startled eyes remained fixed on her, Lu grinned and said, "Stop fussing! It'll soon be over."

She had no doubt that she could carry on with the next operation. Had she not worked like this for years?

"Shall we continue?" the nurse queried.

"Yes, of course."

How could they afford to stop? The donor's eye could not be stored too long, nor the operation be delayed. They had to go on working.

"Wenting," Jiang stepped over to Lu and suggested, "Let's have a break for half an hour."

Lu looked at the clock. It was just after ten. If they postponed it for half an hour, some colleagues would be late for lunch, while others had to rush home to prepare a meal for their children.

"Continue?" the nurse asked again.

"Yes."

15

Doctors of this and other hospitals who were undergoing further training thronged the door talking to Lu. They had got special permission to see her operate.

Uncle Zhang, helped by a nurse, clambered on to the operating-table, still talking and laughing.

The table was a bit too small for him and his feet and hands dangled over the sides. He had a loud voice and talked incessantly, joking with a nurse, "Don't laugh at me, girl. If the medical team hadn't come to our village and persuaded me to have this operation, I'd rather die than let you cut my eye with a knife. Just imagine! A steel knife cutting into my flesh, ugh! Who knows if it will do me some good or not? Ha! Ha!..."

The young nurse tittered and said softly, "Uncle, lower your voice, please."

"I know, young lady. We must keep quiet in a hospital, mustn't we?" he still boomed. Gesticulating busily with one hand, he went on, "You can't imagine how I felt when I heard that my eye could be cured. I wanted to laugh and, at the same time, to cry. My father went blind in his old age and died a blind man. I never dreamed that a blind man like me could see the sun again. Times have really changed, haven't they?"

The nurse giggled while covering him with a towel. "Don't move again, uncle!" she said. "This towel's been sterilized, don't touch it."

"All right," he answered gravely. "Since I'm in hospital, I should obey the rules." But he was trying to raise his strong arms again.

Worrying about his restlessness, the nurse said, holding a strap, "I'll have to tie your arms to the table, uncle. That's the rule here."

Zhang was puzzled, but soon chortled. "Truss me up, eh?" he joked. "OK, go ahead! To be frank, lass, if it were not for my eyes, I wouldn't be so obedient. Though blind, I go to the fields twice a day. I was born a lively character. I like to be on the go. I just can't sit still."

This made the nurse laugh, and he himself chuckled too. But he stopped immediately when Lu entered. He asked, cocking up his ears, "Is that you, Dr Lu? I can recognize your steps. It's funny, since I lost my sight, my ears have grown sharp."

Seeing him full of beans, Lu could not help laughing. She took her seat, preparing for the operation. When she picked up the precious donor's cornea from a phial and sewed it on to a piece of gauze, he piped up again, "So an eye can be replaced? I never knew that!"

"It's not replacing the whole eye, just a filmy membrane," Jiang corrected him.

"Can't see the difference." He wasn't interested in details. With a sigh, he continued, "It needs much skill, doesn't it? When I return to my village with a pair of good eyes, the villagers'll say I must have met some kind fairy. Ha! Ha! I'll tell them I met Dr Lu!"

Jiang tittered, winking at Lu, who felt a little embarrassed. Still sewing, she explained, "Other doctors can do the same."

"That's quite true," he agreed. "You only find good doctors in this big hospital. No kidding!"

Her preparations over, Lu parted his eyelids with a speculum and said, "We'll start now. Just relax."

Zhang was not like other patients, who only listened to whatever the doctors said. He thought it impolite not to answer. So he said understandingly, "I'm perfectly all right. Go ahead. I don't mind if it's painful. Of course, it hurts to cut with a scalpel or a pair of scissors. But don't worry about me. I trust you. Besides. . . ."

Jiang had to stop him, still smiling. "Uncle, don't talk any more."

Finally he complied.

Lu picked up a trephine, small as a pen cap, and lightly cut out the opaque cornea. Cutting a similar disc of clear cornea from the donor's eye, she transferred it to Zhang's eye. Then she began the delicate task of stitching it with the needle-holder. The suture was finer than a hair.

The operation went smoothly. When she had finished, the transplanted cornea was perfectly fixed on the surface of the eye. But for some little black knots, one could never tell it was a new cornea.

"Well done!" the doctors around the operating-table quietly exclaimed in admiration.

Lu sighed with relief. Deeply touched, Jiang looked up at her friend with feeling. Silently, she put layers of gauze over Zhang's eye. . . .

As he was wheeled out, Zhang seemed to awaken from a dream. He became animated again. When the wheeled stretcher was already out of the door, he cried out, "Thanks a lot, Dr Lu!"

The operations had ended. As Lu was pulling herself to her feet, she found her legs had gone to sleep. She simply could not stand up. After a little rest, she tried again and again, till she finally made it. There was a sudden pain in her side. She pressed it with her hand, not taking it seriously for it had occurred before. Engrossed in an operation, sitting on the little stool, for hours at a time, she was aware of nothing else. But as soon as this operation had ended, she felt utterly exhausted, even too tired to move.

16

At that moment, Fu was cycling home in haste. He had not intended to return that day. Early that morning, Fu, at his wife's suggestion, had rolled up his bedding, put it on his bicycle carrier and taken it to his office to begin his new life.

By noon, however, he was wavering. Would Lu finish her operations in time? Imagining her dragging herself home to prepare lunch for the children, he suddenly felt a pang of guilt. So he jumped on his bicycle and pedalled home.

Just as he turned into their lane, he caught sight of his wife leaning against a wall, unable to move.

"Wenting! What's wrong?" he cried out, leaping off to help.

"Nothing. I'm just a bit tired." She put an arm round his shoulder and moved slowly towards home.

Fu noticed that she was very pale and that beads of cold sweat had broken out on her forehead.

He asked uneasily, "Shall I take you to hospital?"

She sat down on the edge of the bed, her eyes closed, and answered, "Don't worry. I'll be all right after a short rest."

She pointed to the bed, too weak to say anything. Fu took off her shoes and coat.

"Lie down and get some sleep. I'll wake you later."

He went to boil some water in a saucepan. When he came back to fetch noodles, he heard her say, "We ought to have a rest. Shall we take the children to Beihai Park next Sunday? We haven't been there for more than ten years."

"Fine. I'm all for it!" Fu agreed, wondering why she should suddenly want to go there.

He gave her an anxious glance and went to cook the noodles. When he returned, food in hand, she had already fallen asleep. He did not disturb her. When Yuanyuan came home, the two of them sat down to eat.

Just then, Lu began groaning. Fu put down his bowl and rushed to the bed. Lu was deathly white, her face covered in sweat.

"I can't fight it," she said in a feeble voice, gasping for breath.

Frightened, Fu took her hand asking, "What's wrong? Have you any pain?"

With a great effort, Lu pointed to her heart.

Panicking, Fu pulled open a drawer rummaging for a pain-killer. On second thoughts, he wondered if she needed a tranquillizer.

Though in great pain, she was clear-headed. She signed to him to calm down and said with all her remaining strength, "I must go to hospital!"

Only then did Fu realize the seriousness of her illness. For more than ten years she had never seen a doctor, though she went to the hospital every day. Now she was obviously critically ill. As he hurried out, he stopped at the door and turned to say, "I'll go and get a taxi."

He rushed to the public telephone on the corner. He dialled quickly and waited. When someone answered, he heard a cold voice saying, "No taxis at the moment."

"Look, I've got a very sick person here!"

"Still, you'll have to wait half an hour."

Fu began to plead, when the man rang off.

He tried to call Lu's hospital, but no one seemed to be in the office of the Ophthalmology Department. He asked the operator to put him through to the vehicle dispatch office.

"We can't send you a car without an official approval slip," was the answer.

Where on earth could he track down the hospital leaders to get an approval slip?

"But this is urgent! Hello!" he shouted into the receiver. But the line had already gone dead.

He phoned the political department which, he thought, ought to help him out. After a long time, a woman picked up the receiver. She listened patiently and said politely, "Would you please contact the administration department?" Recognizing his voice, the operator demanded impatiently, "Where exactly do you want?"

Where? He was not sure himself. In a begging voice, he said he wanted to speak to anyone in the administration department. The telephone rang and rang. Nobody answered.

Disappointed, Fu abandoned the idea of finding a car. He headed for a small workshop in the lane making cardboard boxes, hoping to borrow a tricycle and trailer. The old lady in charge, hearing of his predicament, sympathized with him, but unfortunately could do nothing, for both her tricycles were out.

What was to be done? Standing in the alley, Fu was desperate. Sit Lu on the bicycle carrier? That was impossible.

Just then, Fu saw a van coming. Without much thought, he raised his hand to stop it.

The van came to a halt, and the driver poked his head out, staring in surprise. But when he heard what was happening, he beckoned Fu to get into the van.

They went straight to Fu's home. When the driver saw Lu being dragged towards the van supported by her husband, he hurried to help her get into the cabin. Then slowly he drove her to the casualty department of the hospital.

17

She had never slept so long, never felt so tired. She felt pain all over her body as if she had just fallen from a cloud. She had not the slightest bit of strength left. After a peaceful sleep, her limbs were more relaxed, her heart calmer. But she felt her mind go blank.

For years, she had simply had no time to pause, to reflect on the hardships she had experienced or the difficulties lying ahead. Now all physical and mental burdens had been lifted. She seemed to have plenty of time to examine her past and to explore the future. But her mind had switched off; no reminiscences, no hopes. Nothing.

Perhaps it was only a dream. she had had such dreams before. . . .

One evening when she was only five, a north wind had been howling. Her mother had gone out, leaving her alone at home. Soon it was very dark and her mother had not returned. For the first time, Lu felt lonely, terrified. She cried and shouted, "Mama...mama...." This scene often appeared later in her dreams. The howling wind, the door blown open by a sudden gust and the pale kerosene lamp remained vividly in her mind. For a long time, she could not tell whether it had been true or a dream.

This time, it was not a dream but reality.

She was in bed, ill, and Jiajie was attending her. He looked flaked out too. He was dozing, half lying on the bed. He would catch cold if not awakened. She tried to call him, but no sound came out of her mouth. There was a lump in her throat choking her. She wanted to pull a coat over him, but her arms did not seem to belong to her.

She glanced round and saw she was in a single room. Only serious cases were given such special treatment. She was suddenly seized by fear. "Am I. . . ?"

The autumn wind rattled the door and windows. Darkness gathered, swallowing up the room. Lu felt clearer after a cold sweat. It was real, she knew, not a dream. This was the end of life, the beginning of death!

So this was dying, no fear, no pain, just life withering away, the senses blurring, slowly sinking, like a leaf drifting on a river.

All came to an end, inevitably. Rolling waves swept over her chest. Lu felt she was floating in the water. . . .

"Mama. . . mama. . . ."

She heard Xiaojia's call and saw her running along the bank. She turned back, reaching out her arms.

"Xiaojia . . . my darling daughter. . . ."

But waves swept her away, and Xiaojia's face grew vague, her hoarse voice turned into sobbing.

"Mama. . . plait my hair. . . ."

Why not plait her hair? The child had been in this world for six years, and her one desire was to have pigtails. Whenever she saw other girls with pigtails adorned with silk ribbons, admiration overwhelmed her little heart. But such requests were ignored. Mother had no time for that. On Monday morning, the hospital was crowded with patients and, for Lu, every minute counted.

"Mama. . . mama. . . ."

She heard Yuanyuan's calling and saw the boy running after her along the bank. She turned back, stretching out her arms.

"Yuanyuan . . . Yuanyuan. . . ."

A wave swept over her. When she struggled to the surface, there was no sign of her son, only his voice in the distance.

"Mama...don't forget...my white gym shoes...."

A kaleidoscope of sports shoes whirled around. White and blue sneakers, sports boots, gym shoes, white shoes with red or blue bands. Buy a pair for Yuanyuan, whose shoes were already worn out. Buy a pair of white gym shoes and he would be in raptures for a month. But then the shoes disappeared and raining down were price tags: 3.1 yuan, 4.5 yuan, 6.3 yuan....

Now she saw Jiajie chasing after her, his running figure mirrored in the water. He was in a great hurry, his voice trembling as he called, "Wenting, you can't leave us like this!"

How she wished that she could wait for him! He held out his hand to her, but the ruthless current raced forward and she drifted away helplessly.

"Dr Lu...Dr Lu...."

So many people were calling her, lining the banks. Yafen, Old Liu, Director Zhao, Dr Sun, all in white coats; Jiao Chengsi, Uncle Zhang and Wang Xiaoman in pyjamas. Among the other patients, she only recognized a few. They were all calling her.

I oughtn't to leave. No! There are so many things I still have to do. Xiaojia and Yuanyuan shouldn't be motherless. I mustn't bring Jiajie more sorrow. He can't afford to lose his wife so young. I can't tear myself away from the hospital, the patients. Oh no! I can't give up this miserable, yet dear life!

I won't drown! I must fight! I must remain in the world. But why am I so tired? I've no strength to resist, to struggle. I'm sinking, sinking....

Ah! Goodbye, Yuanyuan! Goodbye, Xiaojia! Will you miss your mother? In this last moment of my life, I love you more than ever. Oh, how I love you! Let me embrace you. Listen, my darlings, forgive your mummy who did not give you the love you deserved. Forgive your mummy who, time and again, refrained from hugging you, pushing away your smiling faces. Forgive your mummy for leaving you while you're still so small.

Goodbye, Jiajie! You gave up everything for me! Without you, I couldn't have achieved anything. Without you, life had no meaning. Ah, you sacrificed so much for me! If I could, I would kneel down before you begging your pardon since I can never repay all your kindness and concern. Forgive me for neglecting you. I often thought I should do something more for you. I wanted to end my work regularly and prepare supper for you. I wanted to let you have the desk, hoping you would finish your article. But it's too late! How sad! I've no time now.

Goodbye, my patients! For the past eighteen years, my life was devoted to you. Whether I walked, sat or lay down, I thought only of you and your eyes! You don't know the joy I felt after curing an eye. What a pity I shall no longer feel that....

18

"Arrhythmia!" the doctor monitoring the screen exclaimed.

"Wenting! Wenting!" Fu cried out, fixing his eyes on his wife, who was struggling for breath.

The doctors and nurses on duty rushed into the room.

"Intravenous injection of lidocaine!" the doctor snapped an order.

A nurse quickly injected it, but before it was finished, Lu's lips went blue, her hands clenched, her eyes rolled upwards.

Her heart stopped beating.

The doctors began massage resuscitation. A respirator was applied to her head, which made a rhythmic sound. Then a defibrillator went into operation. When her chest was struck by this, her heart began to beat again.

"Get the ice cap ready!" the doctor in charge ordered, the sweat on his forehead.

An ice cap was put on Lu's head.

19

The pale dawn could be seen outside the window. Day had broken at last. Lu had lived through a crucial night. She now entered a new day.

A day nurse came into the room and opened the windows, letting in fresh air and the birds' merry singing. At once the pungent smell of medicine and death was dispelled. Dawn brought new hope to a frail life.

Another nurse came to take Lu's temperature, while a medical orderly brought in breakfast. Then the doctor on duty dropped in on his ward round.

Wang Xiaoman, still bandaged, pleaded with a nurse, "Let me have a look at Dr Lu! Just one peep."

"No. She nearly died last night. No one's allowed to see her for the time being."

"Aunt, perhaps you don't know, but she fell ill because she operated on me. Please let me go and see her. I promise not to say a word to her."

"No, no, no!" The nurse scowled.

"Oh please! Just one glance." Xiaoman was close to tears. Hearing footsteps behind her, she turned and saw Old Zhang coming, led by his grandson.

"Grandpa," she rushed to him, "will you have a word with this aunt? She won't let me...."

Zhang, with his eyes bandaged, was dragged over by the little girl to the nurse.

"Sister, do let us have a look at her."

Now with this old man pestering her too, the nurse flared up, "What's the matter with you people, fooling about in the wards?"

"Come off it! Don't you understand?" Zhang's voice was not so loud today. He went on humbly, "We've a good reason, you know. Why is Dr Lu ill? Because she operated on us. To be frank, I can't really see her, but to stand beside her bed for a while will calm my nerves."

He was so sincere that the nurse softened and explained patiently, "It's not that I'm being mean. Dr Lu's seriously ill with heart trouble. She mustn't be excited. You want her to recover very soon, don't you? Better not disturb her at the moment."

"Yes, you're quite right." Zhang sighed and sat down on a bench. Slapping his thigh, he said regretfully, "It's all my fault. I urged her to do the operation as quickly as possible. But who would've thought . . .? What shall I do if anything happens to her?" He lowered his head in remorse.

Dr Sun hurried to see Lu too before starting his work, but was stopped by Xiaoman.

"Dr Sun, are you going to see Dr Lu?" she asked.

He nodded.

"Will you take me along? Please."

"Not now. Some time later. OK?"

Hearing Sun's voice, Zhang stood up and reached out for him. Tugging Sun's sleeve, he said, "Dr Sun. We'll do as you say. But can I have a word with you? I know you're extremely busy. But I still want you to listen to what's been bothering me."

Sun patted Zhang on the shoulder and said, "Go ahead."

"Dr Lu's a very good doctor. You leaders ought to do your best to cure her. If you save her, she can save many others. There are good medicines, aren't there? Give her them. Don't hesitate. I hear you have to pay for certain precious medicines. Lu's got two children. She's not well off. Now she's ill, I don't expect she can afford them. Can't this big hospital subsidize her?"

He stopped, holding Sun's hands, slightly cocking his ear towards him, waiting for his answer.

Sun had a one-track mind. He never showed his feelings. But today he was moved. Shaking Zhang's hands, he said emotionally, "We'll do everything possible to save her!"

Zhang seemed satisfied. He called his grandson to come nearer, and groped for a satchel which was slung across the boy's shoulder.

"Here are some eggs. Please take them to her when you go in."

"It's not necessary," Sun replied quickly.

This put Zhang's back up instantly. Gripping Sun's hands, he raised his voice, "If you don't take them to her, I won't let you go!"

Sun had to accept the satchel of eggs. He decided to ask a nurse to return it and explain later. As though guessing what was in Sun's mind, Zhang continued, "And don't ask someone to bring them back."

Forced to acquiesce, Sun helped Zhang and Xiaoman down the stairs.

Qin accompanied by Director Zhao, approached Lu's room. "Zhao," the woman talked while walking, rather excitedly, "I was like a bureaucrat. I didn't know it was Dr Lu who had operated on Old Jiao. But you should have known, shouldn't you? Luckily Jiao recognized Lu. Otherwise we'd still be in the dark."

"I was sent to work in the countryside at that time," Zhao replied helplessly.

Shortly after they had entered the room, Sun arrived. The doctor on duty gave a brief report of the emergency measures taken to save Lu the previous night. Zhao looked over the case-history, nodding. Then he said, "We must watch her carefully."

Fu, seeing so many people entering, had stood up. But

Qin, unaware of his presence, quickly sat down on the vacant stool.

"Feeling better, Dr Lu?" she asked.

Lu's eyes opened slightly but she said nothing.

"Vice-minister Jiao has told me all about you," Qin said warmly. "He's very grateful to you. He would have come himself if I hadn't stopped him. I'm here to thank you on his behalf. Anything you fancy eating, anything you want, let me know. I can help you. Don't stand on ceremony. We're all revolutionary comrades."

Lu closed her eyes.

"You're still young. Be optimistic. Since you're sick, it's better to accept it. This. . . ."

Zhao stopped her by saying, "Comrade Qin Bo, let her have some rest. She's only just regained consciousness."

"Fine, fine. Have a good rest," Qin said rising to her feet. "I'll come again in a couple of days."

Out of the ward, Qin complained frowning, "Director Zhao, I must give you a piece of my mind. Dr Lu's a real treasure. If you had been more concerned about her, she wouldn't have become so ill. The middle-aged comrades are the backbone of our country. It's imperative to value talented people."

"Right," was Zhao's reply.

Gazing after her receding figure, Fu asked Sun in a small voice, "Who's she?"

Sun looked over the frame of his spectacles at the doorway and answered frowning, "An old lady spouting revolutionary phrases!"

20

That day, Lu was slightly better and could open her eyes easily. She drank two spoonfuls of milk and a sip of orange juice. But she lay with her eyes blank, staring at the ceiling. She wore a vacant expression, as if indifferent to everything, including her own critical condition and the unhappiness of her family. She seemed weary of life.

Fu stared at her in mute horror for he had never seen her like this before. He called her again and again, but she only responded with a slight wave of her hand, as though not wishing to be disturbed. Probably she felt comfortable letting her mind remain suspended.

Time passed unheeded. Fu, sitting at her bedside, had not slept for two nights. He felt exhausted. Dozing, he was suddenly awoken by a heart-rending scream, which shook the whole ward. He heard a girl wailing next door, "Mama! Mama!" and a man's sobbing. Then there came the sound of footsteps as many people rushed to the room. Fu hurried out too. He saw a wheeled stretcher being pushed out of the room, on which lay a corpse covered with a sheet. Then the nurse in white pushing the stretcher appeared. A girl of sixteen with dishevelled hair stumbled out, shaking, and threw herself at the stretcher. Clutching at it with trembling hands, she pleaded, tears streaming down her cheeks, "Don't take it away! Please! My mother's asleep. She'll soon wake up! I know she will!"

Visitors made way for the wheeled stretcher. In silence, they paid their respects to the deceased.

Fu stood rooted amid the crowd. His cheekbones stuck out prominently in his haggard face. His bloodshot eyes began to fill with tears. Clenching his fists, he tried to pull himself together, but shook all over. Unnerved by the girl's shrill cries, he wanted to cover his ears.

"Mama, wake up! Wake up! They're taking you away!" the girl screamed madly. Had she not been held back by others, she would have pulled off the sheet. The middle-aged man following the stretcher repeated, sobbing, "I've let you down! I've let you down!"

His desperate cries were like a knife piercing Fu's heart, as he stared at the stretcher. All of a sudden, as if electrified, he dashed towards his wife's room. He went straight to her, threw himself on the bed. He murmured with closed eyes, "You're alive!"

Lu stirred awakened by his heavy breathing. She opened her eyes and looked at him, but her eyes didn't seem to focus.

He felt a shiver of fear and cried out, "Wenting!"

Her eyes lingered on his face coldly, and this made his heart bleed. Fu did not know what to say or do to encourage her to hold on to life. This was his wife, the dearest person in the world. How long ago was it since he had read poems to her in Beihai Park that winter? During all these years, she had always been his beloved. Life would be unthinkable without her! He must keep her with him!

Poetry! Read a poem to her as he had done then! It was poetry which had helped him to win her before! Today, he would recite the same poem to remind her of sweet memories, to give her the courage to live on.

Half-kneeling beside her bed, he began to recite with tears in his eyes:

"I wish I were a rapid stream,
. . . . . .
If my love
A tiny fish would be,
She'd frolic
In my foaming waves."

The verses seemed to have touched her. She turned her head towards him, her lips moving slightly. Fu leaned over and listened to her indistinct words: "I can no longer . . . swim. . . ."

Choking back his tears, he continued:

"I wish I were a deserted forest,

......
    If my love
    A little bird would be,
    She'd nest and twitter
    In my dense trees."

She murmured softly, "I can no longer . . . fly. . . ."
    His heart ached. Steeling himself, he went on, in tears:

    "I wish I were a crumbling ruin,
    ......
    If my love
    Green ivy would be,
    She'd tenderly entwine
    Around my lonely head."

Tears, blind tears silently poured down her cheeks and fell on the white pillow. With an effort, she said, "I can't . . . climb up!"
    Fu threw himself on to her, weeping bitterly. "I've failed you as a husband. . . ."
    When he opened his tearful eyes, he was astonished. Again she remained with her eyes fixed on the ceiling. She seemed unaware of his weeping, his appeals, unaware of everything around her.
    On hearing Fu's sobbing, a doctor hurried in and said to him, "Dr Lu's very weak. Please don't excite her."
    Fu said nothing more the whole afternoon. At dusk, Lu seemed a little better. She turned her head to Fu and her lips moved as if wanting to speak.
    "Wenting, what do you want to say? Tell me," Fu asked, holding her hands.
    She spoke at last, "Buy Yuanyuan . . . a pair of white gym shoes. . . ."
    "I'll do it tomorrow," he replied, unable to check his tears. But he quickly wiped them away with the back of his hand.

Lu, still watching him, seemed to have more to say. But she only uttered a few words after a long time, "Plait . . . Xiaojia's hair. . . ."

"Yes, I will!" Fu promised, still sobbing. He looked at his wife, his vision blurred, hoping she would be able to tell him all that was worrying her. But she closed her lips, as if she had used up her energy.

21

Two days later, a letter came for Lu, posted at Beijing International Airport. Fu opened it and read:

Dear Wenting,

I wonder if you will ever receive this letter. It's not impossible that this won't reach you. But I hope not! I don't believe it will happen. Though you're very ill, I believe you'll recover. You can still do a lot. You're too young to leave us!

When my husband and I came to say goodbye to you last night, you were still unconscious. We'd wanted to see you this morning, but there were too many things to do. Yesterday evening may be the last time we will meet. Thinking of this, my heart breaks. We've been studying and working together for more than twenty years. No one understands us as well as we do each other. Who would imagine we would part like this?

I'm now writing this letter in the airport. Can you guess where I'm standing at this moment? At the arts and crafts counter on the second floor. There's no one about, only the shining glass counter in front of me. Remember the first time we travelled by air, we came here too? There was a pot of artificial narcissuses with dew on their petals, so lifelike, so exquisite! You told me that you liked it best. But when we looked at the price, we were scared off. Now, I'm before the counter again, alone, looking at another pot, almost the same colour as the one we saw. Looking at it, I feel like crying. I don't know why. Now I realize suddenly, it's because all that has gone.

When Fu had just got to know you, I remember once he came to our room and recited a line by Pushkin "All that has happened in the past becomes a sweet memory." I pursed my lips and said it wasn't true. I even asked, "Can past misfortunes become sweet memories?" Fu grinned, ignoring me. He must have thought inwardly that I knew nothing about poetry. But today I understand. Pushkin was right. It exactly reflects my mood now. It's as if he wrote the line for me! I really feel that all the past is sweet.

A jet has just taken off, its engines roaring. Where is it going? In an hour, I'll be climbing up the steps into the plane, leaving my country. With only sixty minutes to go, I can't help weeping, and my tears wet this letter. But I've no time to rewrite it.

I'm so depressed, I suddenly feel as if I've made the wrong decision. I don't want to leave everything here. No! I can't bear to leave our hospital, our operating theatre, even that little desk in the clinic! I often grumbled that Dr Sun was too severe, never forgiving a mistake. But now I wish I could hear his criticism again. He was a strict teacher. If not for him, I wouldn't be so skilled!

The loudspeakers have just wished passengers bon voyage. Will mine be good? Thinking of boarding the plane in a moment, I feel lost. Where will I land? What lies in store? My heart's in my boots. I'm scared! Yes, scared stiff! Will we get used to a strange country, which is so different from ours? How can my mind be at peace?

My husband's sitting in an armchair brooding. Busy packing the last few days, he had no time to think. He seemed quite firm about the decision. But last night, when he stuffed the last coat into the suitcase, he said all of a sudden, "We'll be homeless from tomorrow!" He's not spoken since then, and I know his mind is still divided.

Yaya was most happy about this trip. She was nervous and excited, and sometimes I felt like hitting her. But now she's standing at the glass door watching the planes landing and taking off, as if reluctant to leave.

"Won't you change your minds?" you asked that night when we were at your place.

I can't answer that question in one sentence. Liu and I have been discussing it almost every day for the past few months. Our minds have been in a turmoil. There are many reasons, of course, urging us to leave China. It is for Yaya, for Liu and myself. However, none of those reasons can lessen my pain. We shouldn't leave, when China has just begun a new period. We've no excuse for avoiding our duties.

Compared with you, I'm a weaker character. Though I had less trouble than you in the past ten years, I couldn't bear it as you did. I often burst out when viciously slandered and attacked. I wasn't stronger than you. On the contrary, it shows my weakness. Better to die than be humiliated, I thought. But there was Yaya. It was surprising that I was able to brazen it out in those days, when Liu was illegally detained as an "enemy agent".

All these are bitter memories of the past. Fu was right in saying, "Darkness has receded, and day has dawned." The trouble is, the evil influence of many years can't be eradicated overnight. The policies of the government take a long time to reach the people. Resentment is not easily removed. Rumours can kill a person. I dread such a nightmare. I lack your courage!

I remember that you and I were cited at that meeting as bourgeois specialists. When we left the hospital afterwards, I said to you, "I can't understand all this. Why should people who have worked hard in their field be crushed? I'll refuse to attend such meetings as a protest!" But you said, "Forget it! If they want to hold a hundred such meetings, let them. I'll attend. We'll still have to do the operations. I'll study at home." I asked you, "Don't you feel wronged?" You smiled and said, "I'm so busy, I've no time to care." I admired you very much. Before we parted, you warned me, "Don't tell Fu about such things. He's in enough trouble himself." We walked a block in silence. I noticed that you looked very calm, very confident. No one could shake your faith. I knew that you had a strong will, which enabled you to resist all kinds of attacks and go your own way. If I had half your courage and will-power, I wouldn't have made such a decision.

Forgive me! This is all I can say to you now. I'm leaving, but I'm leaving my heart with you, with my dear homeland. Wherever I go, I'll never forget China. Believe me! Believe that I'll return. After a few years, when Yaya's grown up and we have achieved something in medicine, we'll come back.

I hope you'll soon recover! Learn a lesson from your illness and pay more attention to your health. I'm not advising you to be selfish. I've always admired your selflessness. I wish you good health to make full use of your talents!

Goodbye, my dearest friend!

Affectionately,
Yafen

22

A month and a half later, Dr Lu had basically recovered and was permitted to go home.

It was a miracle. Ill as she was, Lu, several times on the brink of death, survived. The doctors were greatly surprised and delighted.

That morning, Fu jubilantly helped her put on a cotton-padded jacket, a pair of woollen trousers, a blue overcoat, and wrapped around her neck a long fluffy beige scarf.

"How are things at home?" she asked.

"Fine. The comrades of your Party branch came yesterday to help clean the room."

Her thoughts immediately turned to that small room with the large bookcase covered with a white cloth, the little alarm-clock on the window-sill and the desk....

She felt feeble and cold, though so warmly dressed. Her legs trembled when she stood up. With one hand gripping her husband's arm, the other touching the wall, she moved forward leaning heavily on Fu. Slowly, she walked out of the ward.

Zhao, Sun and her other colleagues followed her, watching her progress along the corridor towards the gate.

It had rained for a couple of days. A gust of wind sighed through the bare branches of the trees. The sunshine extraordinarily bright after the rain, slanted in through th windows of the corridor. The cold wind blew in too. Slowly Fu, supporting his wife, headed for the sunlight and the wind.

A black car was waiting at the steps. It had been sent by the administration department at Zhao's request.

Leaning on her husband's shoulder, Lu walked slowly towards the gate. . . .

Translated by Yu Fanqin
and Wang Mingjie

A Rose-coloured Evening Meal

THE bottles of wine and soda-water are opened. Deep red wine, orange soda-water. The children cheer. Ribbons dance, dimples appear between wrinkled faces, and little black heads next to dignified white hair. The whole family sits round two tables put together. This is their first reunion after a long separation. Has the God of Happiness really come back to the earth? Please join in this Saturday evening's family feast.

"Rose, rose, red rose, the rose in my heart...." A newly bought tape-recorder stands on the brand-new wine cabinet. The soprano seems to be smiling as she sings for this family, her song adding to the festive atmosphere. Ah, no one can do without music, whether in ancient or modern times, whether in grief or joy.

It looks as if he was right to come. Su Hong sits straight by the table, his five-year-old daughter to his left, his wife to his right. The little girl kneeling on her chair is calling, "Granny, I'm going to drink a whole bottle of pop!" Being a child, she feels at home straight away. Who could believe that she's only known her grandmother for one hour. Mum laughs. Kindly, happy old lady, she seems to have dreamed of her grand-daughter calling her. His wife exclaims, "What a fine cook you are, mum! How did you prepare this liver?" Her voice is nauseatingly sweet. Her smile is repulsive. How can she bring herself to say such things? All these years she's never mentioned his family, as if she had no in-laws.

The nightmare's over, a new day has dawned. At last

you've come back from a rugged mountain to a prosperous city, from medieval barbarity to modern civilization. Everybody longs for Beijing: the Summer Palace, foreign films, boating on the Kunming Lake, the marvellous Echo Wall in the Temple of Heaven, the spirit of the Central Committee, Beijing roast duck, hot pickled mustard tubers from Sichuan, endless specialized conferences, a host of traditional performances.... Thousands of people pull strings yet fail to get transferred here, to squeeze their way in. And now you have come back, never mind how. In this revitalized capital the high-rise buildings are growing higher and higher. What does it matter living on the thirteenth floor? There's a lift. How fascinating it is, looking down from the balcony so high in the air at the toylike pedestrians and traffic below. Life, like a flowing stream, can never bring back what it has borne away. It's wisest to look to the future. Prepare for old age! Your children are grown up, you don't have to support them. You can buy a nineteen-inch colour TV in place of your twelve-inch black and white set. Refrigerators and washing machines are on sale everywhere, you needn't go through back doors. That's a good stereo tape-recorder you've bought, with four loudspeakers. You can sit with closed eyes all evening listening to Mozart and Strauss. The lovely music will carry away your cares, even your past nightmares.

"Come on, let's all drink a toast!" Mum's husky voice sounds rather nasal. Is she smiling or tearful? Her hair is grey, how she has aged. He remembers her with abundant jet-black hair and a sweet, mellow voice.

All glasses are held out towards her, each smiling face turns to her. Deep red liquid flows into their crystal glasses. Is this intoxicating wine or healing medicine? "Rose, rose, red rose...."

Father has the top seat. He has aged, his snow-white head

is drooping as if the light music has lulled him to sleep. No, he's awake. His expression is cold. His small eyes under thick eyebrows aren't looking at anyone.

Mum shoots him a sidelong glance, deploring his coldness. She has gone to great pains to prepare this meal for them all, and invited her sons, daughter and grandchildren to this family reunion. This isn't any festival, but the occasion is more worth celebrating. The last twenty Spring Festivals and Mid-Autumn Festivals had been lonely times for them.

His younger sister and her husband have brought their Imp, a beady-eyed child who is fidgeting on his chair like a monkey. Younger Brother's face is shining. Wearing a spruce uniform and snow-white shirt, with his head held high, he is murmuring to his fiancée. A lovely girl, her limpid, unfathomable eyes are lit up like two little flames. Those bright eyes remind him . . . yes, remind him of the girl for ever hidden in his heart. Her last glance at him was so pathetic. "Rose, rose, red rose in my heart. . . ."

"Turn it off!" Father has at last spoken, gruffly, not raising his eyes. He is not behaving like the master of this new flat, not as if this sumptuous meal is to celebrate his rehabilitation after twenty years in disgrace. He seems unaware that he has returned to the field of art, that his paintings are to be exhibited again and *Su Banshe's Art Album* republished. He looks like an old horse exhausted after a long gallop, like an old man so accustomed to isolation that this rowdy party revolts him. No, I'm the only one who revolts him. Mum's laughing, laughing huskily. Turning a deaf ear to his request she's leaving the tape-recorder on to make everybody happy. She wants to create a harmonious atmosphere. Ah, Mum, Mum, how can you recover spilt water, repair a broken mirror, or heal a broken heart?

He's disgusted with me. Curses me. Detests me. I'm this

family's renegade. Persona non grata here. Why did I come? I shouldn't have come. When my daughter heard we were going to see her grandparents, she stared in surprise. "Have I a granny? A grandad?" She had never heard of them. When my wife knew that Mum had phoned, she was quite carried away. What should she wear, what presents should she bring? She bustled about like a typical petty bourgeois. Look how she's messed up her hair, having it waved in tight curls. Look at her broad grin. As if she's been longing to greet her mother-in-law, as if she's entering a new world by coming into this family which is prospering again. It's her fault, all her fault, why did she insist on coming? If she hadn't, I wouldn't be feeling so awkward and irritated.

Is it really all her fault? No, that's not fair. I wanted to come too. After all he's my dad, in his sixties, without much longer to live. Besides, I'm his elder son, once his favourite son. Childhood, carefree childhood, dream-like, golden childhood. The current races down the gorge, small boats struggle upstream, tow-men strain forward, bent double, the setting sun dyes red the glinting river and the boatmen's perspiring faces. Dad, stooping over his big desk, with a few strokes of his brush paints this enchanting picture.

"Honghong, your glass!" Mum is looking after us all. Honghong! He feels like crying. Something has lacerated his bleeding heart.

"Get on with your meal." The gruff voice sounding coldly from the head of the table seems to rap his wrist. Su Hong puts down the glass he has raised. At once he raises his other hand. "Here, mum, let me help myself." He stands up, reaching out and forcing a smile. Good, only his voice is trembling.

Frantic, I glance at my brother on the left and sense the coldness of his look at me. Yes, he should be the favourite son. When they went through hard times, had nothing to eat and were under fire, he was the only one who stayed at their side. Still small, treated as a little cur, he went with them to the mountains. Saved their lives by lugging them a sack of pumpkins from hundreds of *li* away.

All glasses are raised, clinked together. "Here's to your health, dad and mum!" Brother has a pleasing voice, and his fiancée chimes in like a silver bell, "Dad, mum, good health." Sister's voice is shrill, her husband grins. The Imp stands on his chair. "Here's to your health, grandad, grandma." His father has told him what to say. All the other children join in. My daughter smiles too and calls out, showing the gap in her pearly front teeth. "Rose, rose, red rose...."

Su Hong raises his glass too, this heavy glass of wine. Its rim feels cold to his lips. A familiar feeling. What does it remind him of?

Stacks of rice paper, square inkstones, brushes, cinnabar, malachite green, bright red, big ink-slabs. What an enormous inkstone. Two small hands clutching an ink-slab are grinding it hard, Dad's going to paint! "That's my good sonny!" Paintings cover the wall and everyone listens to Dad as he explains different techniques. What fun it is seeing a dove fly suddenly on to a sheet of white paper. A prawn swims over. Plum-blossom blooms. Chrysanthemums scent the air. Dad has a magic brush. He's a real magician. "Honghong, pour Dad a glass of wine." Quick, pour the wine, Dad paints best when he's drinking. Honghong holds the glass carefully, afraid to spill it. Dad always bends down to put the glass to his lips. "Here sonny, have a sip, it's sweet." Yes, it's sweet, honey-sweet childhood. What's sweet is Dad's love, not the wine. Wine is sharp, bitter, choking. When he frowns, shuts his mouth and makes a face, Dad always bursts out laughing and brushes his prickly moustache against his cheeks, then swings him up high in the air. So high that he can touch the ceiling.... Well, those days can never come back. Ever since that fearful time everything has passed away like a flowing stream or like a floating cloud. Father's tenderness has gone never to return. Everything has turned icy cold, father and son seem strangers. He coughs, raises his glass with the noisy laughing people around the table, and takes a sip. The bitter wine fills his heart with bitterness.

He sees shafts of golden light in which thousands of flowers are swirling. In those days his life was full of light and fresh flowers. The secluded college campus, cradle of engineers, future specialists, scholars scaling the heights of science, probationary Party members, both red and expert. Entrancing, dream-like love, limpid eyes, an innocent heart, rose-red cheeks, strolling in the wood by the brook.... Abruptly the earth spins round, his hopes are toppled, the light of life is extinguished. "Your father's a Rightist." "You must stand firm and make a clean break with him." "Make your choice: side with the Party or with a Rightist." Heavens, how could this have happened? What should he do?

"Why are you a Rightist?"

Amid the talk and laughter this question rings in his ears. What a ridiculous thing to ask his father. His father doesn't answer, cannot answer. He dares not raise his eyes to that icy face, but sees his hands trembling on his knees. Mum's husky laugh rings out, but her laugh is close to tears. "Don't ask your father that, Honghong, how can he bear it." Sobbing, she stands in front of the seated figure....

He feels a lump in his throat, tears spring to his eyes, but he must on no account shed them. He stealthily picks up the bottle to refill his glass. Forcing a smile he screws up his face and drinks. "Rose, rose, red rose...." His rose is a beautiful red, not a gaudy scarlet, not a vulgar pink, but a refined tender crimson suffused with faint melancholy. The same colour as this room. A brand-new room. White walls, glittering glass, a newly painted door, bright electroplated furniture. The red rays of the setting sun have dyed everything in their gay rosy light. Everything is new and spotless in this new home they have set up. The old seems to have been swept away by a flood. Why can't the flood scour our souls? To let the past die and embark on a new life. If we could start again from scratch what a fine world this would be.

It can't be done. Printed in black on white paper, he found the answer in the newspaper. "The Rightist artist Su Banshe with his reactionary outlook has an inveterate hatred for the Party and socialism. In his paintings our motherland's sky is overcast, the earth is grey, socialism is like a sinking ship with people at their last gasp struggling in the water or lying panic-stricken on the deck. What vicious insinuations!" That was the conclusion reached. The final verdict.

Of course he had to make a clean break, could never go home again. There was no need to go. It's the people who raised me, the Party that trained me. The Party is my home. Scrap those petty-bourgeois sentiments and be an iron-willed revolutionary.

White chicken, dark brown preserved eggs, deep red liver, pink sausage, green pickles. Mum made these hometown pickles on her return here. So many pairs of chopsticks, so many smiling faces. Toast after toast, senseless laughter, disgusting flattery. What is she laughing at? How can I live with such a petty-bourgeois hypocrite? Have I really slept with her for twenty years? Is this fate or a trick played on me by history? How could I ever have taken up with her?

"Rose, rose, red rose, the rose in my heart. . . ." Where is the rose in my heart? Where has she gone? With her sweet face and graceful figure she was like the goddess scattering flowers in one of Dad's paintings. That painting was burnt when our house was raided.

She ought to be happy for ever. It would be a crime to let the dust defile her or worldly conventions upset her. How could he, a criminal, harm such an innocent girl? Her eyes are misted over, her step is no longer so light. Stop maundering like this and make up your mind to release her. She should be like a dove, free to fly wherever she pleases. Because I love her I want her to be happy.

Love, love, what is love? He had given his "love" to the librarian. In the old library among all those books, she had seemed a little duck quacking away and preening herself, distracting serious students. He had swooped on her like an eagle, sweeping her off her feet. Had taken her everywhere to flaunt his love, even to the one he loved. Give me up, my heart already numbed.

Amazed, fearful, wounded, she wrote him long passionate letters. Her eyes downcast, her lashes covered her eyes brimming over like autumn pools. What a fool he'd been, thinking he'd acted a part successfully when his performance had in fact been so crude. After the graduation ceremony, when the applause had died away, it was time to take leave of his college. No, take leave of his dreamlike youth. She should be standing by the brook under the weeping willows. How many times she had stood there in the moonlight. Yes, she had come. Go quickly to avoid her. But he couldn't. This was their last meeting, the last, last one, to end everything between them. How could they part like this? He went over to her. Gazing into each other's eyes they drew closer and closer together as they walked. Like characters in a Shakespearian tragedy. A tragedy? Yes, it was a tragedy. He longed with one ardent kiss to wipe away all the hurt, the grief in her eyes.

"You shouldn't do this. You're deceiving yourself, deceiving me and her too. . . ."

This staggered him. Why not pour out to her all the

bitterness in his heart? Only she could understand. No, his own wretchedness was enough. Making a clean break hadn't saved him. He had been switched from studying a most advanced, top-secret course. His admission to the Party had been postponed because he "still sympathized with his Rightist father". He wasn't even eligible to teach in the college as an assistant. Where in the wide world was there a place for him? With my fine academic record I must strike out for myself in the sea of life and battle with angry billows. Not knowing where to row my little craft, how can I involve this angel in such danger?

"She and I have already...."

She turned and quickly made off. Then slowed down and stopped to stare at him with her big dreamy eyes, her sad, expectant eyes....

What a ghastly, irretrievable mistake.

Brother is laughing again, his pretty fiancée too. Carefree laughter, piercing laughter. Peacocks like to flaunt their plumage. Girls like to dress up, lovers to laugh. Ah, they're quietly clinking glasses and drinking to their future happiness. Happiness. From ox-carts to locomotives, kites to rockets, homespun to dacron, kindling fire by rubbing wood to space ships, for how many generations has mankind sought for happiness? Ever since Pan Gu created the world and the search will continue till the end of time.

Love, the greatest happiness of all. Selfish love unwilling to be seen by others. He meets their eyes at an inopportune time for them. At once Brother's smile vanishes, his expression freezes. Why is there such contempt on her beautiful face? Why should she despise me? Are you the only ones fit to be in love? My brother must have told her everything.

Laugh, preen yourselves, enjoy the sweet wine of life. You've no right to despise me, what do you know about love? Do you know what sacrifice means? Love and sacrifice go together, that is the only true love. But why think of such things, don't envy them, swallow the bitter wine of your own love. Where is she now? By the Songhua River in the northeast? On the loess steppe of the northwest? For ten years we hovered between life and death, no, surely she's still alive on this smiling earth.

He reaches again for the bottle.

"Don't drink so much!"

A broad white face. All too familiar, yet like the face of a stranger. Looking at him with reproachful, anxious eyes. He pretends to be drunk. Drunkards with their bleary eyes can't see distinctly. Are you my wife? I don't seem to know you.

Yes, they were strange bedfellows. No wonder she was always complaining, nagging. Habit is a fearful thing. Habit made him come home from work every day and park his bicycle under the eaves as his daughter ran out calling daddy. His meals were cooked for him, his clothes washed, his trousers pressed. His wife was not to blame. Why make a scapegoat of her? As time passed he steeled himself, underwent a slight change, and she had known a little happiness. But his heart was like ice, there was a limit to his self-reproach. He was miserly too with his kindness. They lived together, that was all. Everyone must marry and have children, that was only right and proper. Such was life.

"Rose, rose...." Why does this tune go on and on? Probably this tape-recorder has an automatic replaying circuit. To please his fiancée Brother keeps it repeating itself. She is a rose. Of course, the rose in his heart. His road is strewn with the fresh flowers of love, father's love, mother's love, his fiancée's love.... This song is maddening!

"Turn it off," Father calls, finally losing patience. He gets up to drive the soprano out of the room. With the music turned off the room is suddenly quiet. With so many people there why should it seem so empty? Ah, Mum has gone to the kitchen to fetch another dish. She must have queued up for two days to prepare so many

"Duck, duck, a big duck!" The children clap their hands. It's long since he's seen an Eight-treasure Duck, so yellow, succulent, savoury and translucent. "Come on everybody, eat. I forgot how to cook this after all those years." Mum rolls up her sleeves to attack the poor duck with a knife and chopsticks.

"Honghong, have this, it's one of your favourites." She offers him a leg, using a spoon to catch the fat dripping from it. Quickly hold out your plate. Why has Mum become so ceremonious? He remembers her rapping him on the head with her chopsticks. Which year was that? One Spring Festival, when he was wolfing down duck and she didn't want him to over-eat. He loved duck, loved the way Mum cooked it. He always squeezed into the kitchen, beside the table, to watch as she deftly turned and boned the duck, then stuffed it with ham, mushrooms, sticky rice and lilies. Yes, and Job's-tears. With his little hands he stuffed in a handful too. When Mum tried to elbow him aside he refused to go, waiting right there for the duck to be cooked. She scolded, "Greedy guts!"

The duck on his plate is just as well cooked, with all the old ingredients. Where did she manage to find Job's-tears? No doubt in a pharmacy. He looks, but doesn't pick up his chopsticks — how can he eat this? "Life in the family of a bourgeois Rightist imperceptibly corrupted me. I'm going to make a clean break with my guilty family." As a sign of determination he had denounced this duck, yes, seriously. "That wasn't Eight-treasure Duck but Eight-poison Duck." How utterly ludicrous. Because of this Eight-poison Duck he had been four years on probation before being admitted into the Party. How could he stomach this duck served up today?

Dad isn't eating either. His face is dark, his lips quivering. How many sound teeth has he left? He used to have strong white teeth as handsome as Brother's now. "Eating is an art in China. If an artist doesn't know how to eat, he can't be a good artist." He had been criticized for saying this. His paintings fetched high prices, but by the end of each month Mum complained that she had no money to buy rice. Dad was a spendthrift, Mum was a good cook. When he received money he invited his artist friends and drinking friends to one of the well-known restaurants frequented by men of letters, with inscriptions inside written by Guo Moruo. And every few days they entertained guests at home till all the money was spent. His maxim was: "Money is something we're born without, and it can't be taken with us when we die." Dad was very open-handed. Many, many of his former guests had denounced him.

Now he's old, has given up drinking and hasn't much appetite. He's sitting at this feast as if at a meeting where he has to come clean. He's lost his *joie de vivre*, is worn out, looking listlessly at the duck and at the grown-ups and children seated around him. His cold, blank glance sweeps over Su Hong's face with no love in it, no hate either, nothing but a fearsome coldness which seeps into people's bones.

Su Hong hangs his head, staring stupidly at his empty glass, as empty as his heart. Why look at me like that? Am I feeling good? If I hurt you, acting in a way no son should, it certainly wasn't because I wanted to. If you'd bawl me out it would be better than this. But you can't. Your "good sonny" disappeared long ago, pretend he was never born. No, no, not that. . . . I love you with all my heart. Of course I can't say so, I don't want to tell you anything. Things are too snarled up to be sorted out or explained. Who knows how wretched I am? Instead of dwelling on these things I should be smiling. This is a celebration, a special occasion. . . .

"Rose, rose, red rose...." Why do I still hear that song, like a mosquito buzzing by my ears, when the tape-recorder's turned off? I can't drive it away. I know you blame me, know you can never forgive me. When you were sent away for labour reform, Mum notified me that the train left at 9.45. I remember that distinctly. I sat in my office then, watching the second hand creep to "9". I didn't ask for leave to see you off. Didn't I want to go? I didn't dare to. If I'd asked for leave I'd have had to make long explanations.

I hope you've burnt those three letters. I long ago burnt that one you wrote me, burnt it as soon as I got it. But I remember every word in it. "Su Hong, is work keeping you busy? I've been cleared. Your mum and I are both well. Father." You'd written with a fountain-pen, not a brush, though all your previous letters to me had been written with a brush. I wrote back copying phrases from the paper, so that it wouldn't matter who read my letter. I had to be careful. So many people had got into trouble over letters. A year later I wrote to you again. The year after that, when the "cultural revolution" started, I didn't even dare write. I knew you would hold it against me. No, you can't have. Nothing matters to you anymore.

Why does fate play such tricks on us? I shouldn't have gone to Sichuan that year on business. There was nothing to eat on sale, it was terrible. You'd said our native province was "the land of plenty". That its green hills and limpid streams produced men of good taste. For boasting of your good taste you were criticized. You were too ingenuous, too foolish, no wonder they called you a pedant. I hadn't intended to go to that exhibition, but as my boss went I had to. I hadn't expected you to be helping out there. In the corridor I spotted an old stooped workman, a ladder over one shoulder, approaching with a bucket of yellow paint. He was barefoot, his clothes stained with paint of different colours. Stepping out of the way of the ladder I saw that it was you. I wanted to speak but my boss told me to hurry. I went on, meaning to come back later to see you, but I never did. I know you resented that. No, no no, you may have forgotten. So much the better. I wish I could forget.

"Why aren't you eating, Honghong?" Mum's husky laughter. She's extremely observant. Why single me out? I'm someone special here, needing special consideration.

"He's drunk!" My wife chuckles, showing her teeth. What's funny? I only wish I were drunk, too drunk to think or be conscious of anything.

All right, get drunk. The bottle in front of him is empty. He reaches for the one by his sister and fills his glass. Drink up, eat, don't brood or talk. He picks up his chopsticks to help himself to some food. Is it fish? Prawn? Chicken? Duck? This must be what is meant by "eating without tasting". It's fish, set out on a new blue and white oblong porcelain dish. The tasty fish is decorated with three flowers cut out of carrots and Chinese cabbage to add a festive note. Dad liked "beautiful food, beautifully served". Called that art. "The superior man won't eat a fish that has been turned over." He said this at each Spring Festival when Mum brought in a fish and we were all too full to finish it. So we were all "superior men". Superior men? Then why had it taken intellectuals so long to join the ranks of the working class? Live fish frisk on rice paper. Why are there no paintings in this room? We used to have so many. Live fish, live prawns, all gone now. These speculations must come from drinking too much.

"My head aches, I'll leave you to it." His patience exhausted, Dad stands up, pretending to be tipsy. He's not, in fact, as he has drunk very little. A snail retreats into its shell, an old stag struck by an arrow hides deep in the forest. He walks away, stooping, then glances back. His face is dark, his glance cold, he hates me, hates me. I shouldn't have come.

"So your family's reunited." When colleagues say this I have to smile and nod. But they will never know the nature of this reunion. If kinsmen are unkind it's best to have none. You can choose your friends, can ignore the people you meet, but not your family. Life is not a sheet of paper; if you make a mistake you can tear it up and start again. Life is ruthless, a history written in flesh and blood. Nothing written there can be altered or torn up, how fearful.

What are they laughing at? What are they saying? Dance? The dances of the fifties were too slow, to tunes like *Auld Lang Syne*. It's disco in the eighties, can you dance this? I'll show you how. It's the two of them again, my brother and her. Why not dance disco? It's most civilized, you don't even hold hands. Just twist any way you please. After sitting in an office for a week it's good to dance for a while. But I can't do it. Our college parties used to last all night, she was the queen of those dances. Now she probably can't dance either.

With flushed cheeks, puffing, they sit down again. Sister hands them towels to wipe their perspiring faces. Where did she learn her stock of compliments? She must envy them. Is her marriage happy or not? Her husband's much older than she is, inscrutable behind his spectacles. So thin, so greedy. This may be the best meal he's ever eaten. He's eating the fish too. I'm sure he can't dance. Like a good father he's urging the Imp to eat. He seems very fond of Sister. She and Brother are chattering away. They ignore me, pretend to be discussing dancing. What's there to discuss? Let anyone dance who wants to. It won't make the sky fall down. They hate me too. I'm odd man out here.

Sister knows the whole story, she went with them too, being too small to leave them. But a long time ago she married and left them. She seems to have kept in close touch, buying cloth for Mum, sending Brother shoes. Posing as tolerant she greeted me as Elder Brother. I don't need your tolerance. What crime have I committed? Maybe I was afraid, weak. Yes, I admit I'm a weakling. But to start with I really believed I was right. How could I oppose the Party?

I'm not drunk, no one could get drunk on this wine. I inherited a capacity for liquor, I'm quite sober. Mum's sitting down looking limp, on the verge of collapse since Father left the table. She's still smiling, urging everyone to eat, and to put on the tape-recorder. "Rose, rose...." Is there no other cassette? The room's lively again, she doesn't like awkward silences. "Honghong, eat!" With her husky voice Mum's putting on a show; she obviously hates me. Her smile is a sham. That evening she told me, "Su Hong, forget us, and we won't involve you." That's what she said, she can't have forgotten. She hates me.

I shouldn't have come today.

"Rose, rose, red rose, the rose in my heart...."

The song of the rose circles round the room. The rosy sunset comes to rest on the table. Everything is veiled in its refined, deep colour tinged with grief. Where are you, rose in my heart?

Translated by Gladys Yang

A Distracting Sunday

ONE Sunday morning early in May, 1979, the university's Party Secretary Mu Zhijian was seated in an easy chair in his sitting-room reading the papers. Normally his work kept him too busy to do more than glance at the headlines. So each Sunday he read the most important articles published that week. This had been his habit for years.

His three-year-old grandson Ganggang, leaning against his easy chair, grasped his arm in both chubby hands to pester him:

"Can't we go now? Let's go."

"In a minute." Mu made no move, intent on reading the paper.

"You promised to take him to the park for a ride on the aeroplane," put in his wife Wang Lei, looking out from the bedroom. "Hurry up and get going!"

"All right, straight away." Mu put down the newspaper and padded in his slippers to the window. Outside it was a fine spring day. Pairs of birds were hopping and chirping on the jade-green boughs of the tall poplars. He stretched and said to himself with a smile, "Yes, this is just the weather to go to the park."

Before the "cultural revolution", Mu had been the Party Secretary of this university. Still under fifty then, in his prime and full of drive, he was regarded as one of the most promising cadres in higher education. Now that a dozen years had passed and his temples were grizzled, he had come back to his post. Luckily he was still fit and energetic, confident that he could do a good job of work.

"Ha! Grandad's taking me to the park!" crowed Ganggang.

Mu turned to pick up his grandson and at sight of his radiant face rubbed foreheads with him, then put him down and ordered:

"Go and fetch my cloth shoes and we'll leave. Can you do that?"

"Yes!" Ganggang trotted on sturdy legs to his grandfather's bedroom, ducked boldly under the bed and pulled out the shoes. Scrambling up, a big shoe in each small hand, he trotted back again.

Just then from the hall they heard a soft knock on the door. Mu hurried to open it. There stood a man in his sixties. Tall and thin and wearing glasses for near-sightedness.

Seeing Mu Zhijian he clasped both hands in salute.

"It's been a long time, Old Mu."

"So it's you, Old Dai. Come on in, I haven't seen you for years." Mu stepped forward and shook him cordially by the hand, then cheerfully showed him into the sitting-room.

Ganggang resented this unexpected guest, guessing that his arrival meant no trip to the park for him. He pouted, tears in his eyes.

Ignoring his guest for a moment, Mu said coaxingly:

"Go and play with granny, Ganggang, there's a good boy."

"No. I want...."

"Do as you're told. I promise to take you to the park after I've had a talk with this visitor."

Old Dai, or Dai Jiyao, had been a history professor in this college, an expert on Ming history. Driven out during the "cultural revolution", he had now been assigned to the History Research Institute. Perhaps a common failing of all historians is to concentrate on the past rather than the present, or perhaps he had something on his mind which made him ignore the little boy's dismay and plump himself down on a sofa.

Having handed over the pouting child to his wife, Mu brewed a glass of Dragon Well tea for his guest.

"What wind blew you here, Old Dai?" he asked with a smile.

"An ill wind," answered Dai, taking the glass with a nod, his expression not merely solemn but indignant.

Mu had not seen Dai for over ten years. Before that he had known him as a scholar who paid no attention to the outside world. People addressed him as "Master Dai" but behind his back called him a "pedant". Dai had rarely called on him. One summer when his roof leaked, he had preferred to catch the drips in basins rather than complain to the school authorities. Mu had made a self-criticism because of this, saying that he showed too little concern for the living conditions of senior intellectuals. So what ill wind could have blown this "pedant" to his door?

"I've come to find a back door," announced Dai bluntly, to the Party Secretary's astonishment. "I've spent all my life studying history behind closed doors. But now what can I do? You're forced to look for back doors whether you like it or not. It's preposterous, completely preposterous!"

Mu couldn't help smiling. This scholar who didn't know how to find back doors was certainly going about it the wrong way. With his vehemence and righteous indignation he looked not in the least like someone asking a favour. He said soothingly:

"Never mind. Tell me what you want, Old Dai."

"You've a graduating student called Ding Dazhi, haven't you?"

Mu thought and nodded. "Yes."

"He comes from Beijing but was sent to the countryside.

In '76 he was recommended to study here." Dai went on more slowly, "They say, when jobs are assigned, all graduates will be sent back to the province they came from. His father's worried because he's already found a unit in Beijing to take him. And he's got his son's old brigade to agree to release him. He asked me to take this up with you, Old Mu, to get the college to make allowances for him and keep him in Beijing."

Dai kept his head lowered as he spoke, not watching the reaction of his host.

As Mu listened he cast his mind back. Yes, one of the graduating students was called Ding Dazhi. An impressive-looking youngster, very active in school, with wide social contacts outside, but a mediocre student. He had struck Mu as very pushing.

In 1977, when the enrolment system was being overhauled, one student had put up a big-character poster criticizing the system of "recommendations" introduced by the "gang of four" which made it easy to get in through the back door and lowered the standard of the students admitted. He cited the case of a freshman who had ascribed the defeat of the Paris Commune to "failure to learn from Dazhai".* Though no names were named, the whole school knew that it was Ding Dazhi who had made this howler.

Two days later Ding put up a poster too, stoutly denying that he had got into college through the back door. According to him he had been recommended by the poor and lower-middle peasants and approved by the county, commune and brigade — he had documents to prove this. Furthermore he accused the writer of the first poster of attacking the masses in order to side-track the whole investigation.

---

*An agricultural brigade held up as a model for the whole country.

Two days after this the writer of the first poster put up a second. This time he named Ding Dazhi by name, and disclosed that the documents vouching for him had been procured by his father by bribing his brigade cadres.

This enraged Ding Dazhi. Mu's first task on his reinstatement was settling this dispute. It took a whole week and a whole series of meetings to mobilize Party cadres to persuade the two opponents to call a truce and concentrate on denouncing the "gang of four".

Now, to get a Beijing assignment, this Ding Dazhi and his father had once again shown their resourcefulness, finding a unit in Beijing to take him and getting his brigade to release him. They had even recruited honest Dai Jiyao to come and plead their case! What did Ding's father do, to be able to pull all these strings?

Silence fell in the sitting-room. Having stated his purpose in coming Dai had no more to say. Mu puffed at his cigarette, thinking hard.

"Old Dai," he finally said, "this Ding has a bad reputation. He got into college by the back door."

"Really? I didn't know that." Dai leaned back, taking out a handkerchief to wipe his nose, at a loss for words.

"Now he wants to go through the back door again. What kind of behaviour is that?" His eyes on Dai, Mu unconsciously raised his voice. "You taught here for many years, Old Dai. Before the 'cultural revolution' how many graduating students refused the jobs to which they were assigned? Very few indeed. Now some of them openly say they'll go only to Tianjin, Nanjing, Shanghai or Beijing."

"Are there really students like that?" Dai shook his head.

"You're a historian, Old Dai. Today we ought to learn from the first Han emperor and bring order out of chaos to restore stability." Rather carried away, Mu stood up and poured himself some water. Sipping it he added, "When I came back to work here I told the Party Committee several times: To overhaul this college we must reform enrolment and job assignment. That's our only hope. If we don't recruit students on the basis of merit, how can we guarantee the quality of our higher education? If graduates won't take the jobs assigned by the state, what's the use of training them?"

"You're right, quite right." Dai nodded.

Mu sighed then said, "Unfortunately it isn't just up to us. We come under very heavy social pressure."

Dai apologized, "By taking the liberty to call today I've put more pressure on you. But never mind, Old Mu. I was asked to beg this favour. Whether you agree or not is up to you. I don't want to embarrass you."

Out of curiosity Mu asked, "Are you connected with Ding Dazhi's family?"

Dai shook his head. "We're not related, not friends — there's no connection. I haven't a clue as to Ding Dazhi's height, his appearance or character. As for his father, I know even less about him."

"Then who asked you to put in a word for them?"

"It was all the doing of my Minister of the Interior. Actually she doesn't know the Ding family either. But she has a cousin on the paternal side who does. It seems the father works in some commercial department. You know, Old Mu, my only self-indulgence is drinking two ounces of good liquor every day. Somehow Ding's father got to hear of that, and through her cousin my wife got him to keep me supplied. So for the last two years I've never lacked for good liquor. Pah! I've my self-indulgence to blame. Now I'm having to pay for it. Her cousin turned up the other day to persuade me, saying I'm on good terms with you, and you're in charge of job assignment. She insisted I must help. Old Mu, I hate to raise this request, but what else can I do? It's really most provoking!" He pounded his right fist on his left hand.

"Don't get worked up, Old Dai." Mu forced a smile. "Do you know how many requests like this I've had? In the right drawer in my office I've a list of thirty-eight graduating students, all of whom have had people interceding for them or sending official letters asking us to make special allowances for them. You've simply added another name to the list."

"Then what do you mean to do?" asked Dai.

"I've two alternatives." Mu laughed. "One is to stick to principles and not make any exceptions except in line with official policy, no matter whom I offend or whether I lose my post. The other is to turn a blind eye and give the green light, to do them a good turn which will pay me too. We're having a meeting this afternoon to consider the cases of those thirty-eight students, no, thirty-nine students now."

"I do apologize for troubling you." Dai realized that he was in the wrong.

"Never mind, we'll decide after we've talked it over."

"Then I'll go now, Old Mu." Dai turned back at the door to add, "I apologize too, Old Mu, for stopping you taking your grandson out to play."

After seeing him off Mu returned to the sitting-room. The sunshine was still enchanting, the birds still as merry as ever. But this spring scene no longer appealed to him. Those thirty-eight, no, thirty-nine names were preying on his mind. Each had a host of connections. Those connections enmeshed him like a spider's web so that he was unable to move.

He recalled the exposure of Ding Dazhi's entry into college through the back door. His classmate said that his brigade had originally recommended a girl in every way better than Ding. But his father had squeezed her out, using a first-class bicycle as a bribe.

"How abominable." Mu paced his sitting-room. He had

never met Ding's father Ding Qiliang but he pictured him as a smarmy hypocrite. Ding had no doubt had his eyes on him ever since his reinstatement. In order to have his son kept in Beijing, he had ferreted out all the Party Secretary's social connections. Then had chosen Dai Jiyao to breach his defences and made up to Dai by supplying him with good liquor. Spent two years preparing to get through this back door.

"We certainly can't pander to a man like that." Mu stood up. This decision taken, his heart felt lighter. Just then Ganggang clumped in again, calling:

"Aren't we going, grandad? Let's go!"

"We'll go, right away."

Without waiting to be told, Ganggang brought the shoes he had put by the door and watched his grandfather put them on. As Mu stooped to do this, they heard a woman call cheerfully in the hall:

"Are you in, Sister Wang?"

Wang Lei went to meet her, laughing. "Come on in, Sister Li."

This Sister Li was one of the oldest residents in the street. The Li family was said to have lived there for several generations while some Manchu princes had their mansion there. Brought up in a compound occupied by several households, she was dynamic, capable and outspoken. When Mu came under fire and his whole family was outlawed, under a cloud, she had still called to see them. As she said, "I can size up people for myself. Why should I join in the general hullabaloo?" When Mu was sent down to the countryside and his son was working in the provinces, it was kind-hearted Sister Li who had looked after the rest of the family. So they thought the world of her. Mu and his wife called her Sister; their children, Mama Li; and Ganggang, Granny.

Hearing her voice in the hall Ganggang's face puckered. Mu patted his head and said:

"Granny Li wants to talk to your gran, it's nothing to do with us."

Ganggang brightened up. Mu, straightening up, took his hand. But before they could set off Wang Lei brought in Sister Li.

"Old Mu, Sister Li wants to have a word with you."

"Oh?" Mu wondered why.

Ganggang stamped his feet, howling. His grandmother carried him off.

"Sit down, Sister Li, sit down. Tell me why you've come." Mu offered her a glass of tea.

"Comrade Old Mu, there's a family at the east end of our alley called Song. The wife's name is Jin. D'you know them?"

Mu shook his head. Though he'd lived here for scores of years he didn't know the names of all his neighbours.

"Well, it was Sister Jin who told me this. Made my heart bleed. I don't know whether I'm right to butt in or not, but I just had to do something."

What was on her mind? Could she be looking for a back door too? No, honest Sister Li had never tried to pull strings.

"Sister Jin has a nephew...."

Mu wished she would come to the point. And with a sigh she did.

"His name is Ding."

Another Ding! Mu gave a start. Sister Li went on placidly:

"He's called Ding Dazhi, and he's studying in your college. Do you know the boy, Comrade Old Mu?"

Mu simply nodded.

"What a memory you have!" She chuckled. "All these thousands of students and you can remember their names."

"Not all their names. I remember Ding Dazhi." Mu wrinkled his brows with a wry smile. Failing to notice this she went straight on:

"The trouble the Dings had getting that boy into college! Nearly ruined them, it did."

This bewildered Mu.

"Old Mu, wait till you hear the whole story," she continued. "This Ding Qiliang is a small, low-paid cadre under the Bureau of Commerce. His wife has no job and is poorly, so they've always been hard up. Their elder child, a girl, was born with a weak heart. She's stayed in Beijing with a factory job, but keeps having to take time off. Their second child, this Ding Dazhi, went to the countryside in '69. At first he had dozens of classmates in that village, but in less than two years those of them with pull joined the army, found work in factories, went back to town or managed to get into college, leaving just the few youngsters who'd no back door to stew in that mountain gully. Just think, with the others all gone and so far from home, how could the boy settle down there? The old couple were so worried, they asked right and left for help to get him back. In '76, when the colleges took in students, his brigade was given one place. But what use was that to him? You had to be recommended, and who would put his name forward?"

Sister Li paused for breath and sipped her tea, then went on:

"The old couple talked it over and got busy so as not to miss this chance. They sold the old man's watch to raise the fare, and he asked for leave to visit his son's brigade. He went to beg for this favour. There used to be an old saying: A favour's bigger than the sky, it's something only money and pull can buy. Times may have changed, but money still talks and some people won't listen to reason. Who'd help a nobody like Ding Qiliang? He sold his watch, spent all his money and wore himself to a frazzle, doing everything short of kneeling and kowtowing, but he got nowhere. Too bad! As he was leaving, though, the secretary in charge of that village hinted that if he brought them a good bike they'd let his son go. There was nothing for it but to hurry home, sell up everything they had worth any money, then borrow right and left till he'd scraped together the price of a good bike. He delivered it himself. That's how he pushed his son through the college gate."

Mu sat there motionless, stunned. It had never occurred to him that this despicable back-door farce could give rise to tragedies too.

Her hands to her heart Sister Li sighed again and said:

"They got their son home, but the family was head over heels in debt. His mother was so frantic she couldn't get up from her *kang*. Her husband had to go to work and nurse her too, trying to cut down their food budget to save money to pay his debts. Do you know how they managed? For the last two winters they've never dared light the stove, never bought fresh vegetables, only picking rotten cabbages out of the garbage, without even pickles to eat. They really had a hard time. Sister Jin says her brother-in-law has just turned fifty, but he's bald, his teeth have dropped out, his back is bent, and he staggers along looking like a man of seventy. What for? All to find a back door for his son. Think what he's had to put up with!"

Mu's heart had sunk as he listened. He had a mental picture of an old man shuffling towards him, bent under the burden of finding a back door. He seemed to hear this toothless old fellow asking: "Am I to blame? Did I do wrong?"

"Now they're up against it again." Sister Li's voice seemed to be coming from far away. "Now jobs are to be assigned. And it's said the boy will be sent back to where he came from. Won't that be the death of them? They're so frantic they're begging right and left for help. And now, by a stroke of luck, a factory in Beijing is willing to take him, and his brigade has agreed to let him go. It's just up to your college. Somehow they discovered that we're on good terms, so they sent Sister Jin to me. I told them, if the decision is up to Old Mu, there won't be any problem. Old Mu's a high official but doesn't give himself official airs, he's kind to everyone, always reasonable. If I tell him the whole story he's sure to help. Wasn't I right, Comrade Old Mu?"

Mu found it quite impossible to answer. Sister Li put her glass on the table and aired her views:

"My old man tried to stop me, saying this is going through the back door and I shouldn't have anything to do with it. I asked him: Is there no justice in the world? Ha, the children of big cadres can whisk through any back door. One telephone call or one note and everything's fixed. Why should it be so hard for the children of the likes of us to get anywhere? Should the door be closed against them? Old Ding's whole family has come to grief trying to get his son through a back door, shouldn't we help them out? I told him: I'm going to see to this, so don't give me that daft talk."

Mu had no idea what to say. Her reasoning was wrong, but the situation was such. Many of the thirty-eight students on his list had their names there as the result of a telephone call from some high official or a note from some organization. Of course, the fate of those thirty-eight was still undecided; their cases would be discussed at this afternoon's meeting. But, undoubtedly, it was easy for big cadres to make such requests, while people like Ding Qiliang had to sweat blood to do it. In this sense it was certainly unfair.

Sister Li said no more but waited for his answer. Mu felt as if a great weight had sealed his lips. Finally he answered listlessly, almost rudely:

"You'd better be going now, Sister Li."

She glanced up at him, feeling that Old Mu was not as obliging as usual. As she stood up slowly he added:

"We shall be discussing this problem at a meeting this afternoon."

While Sister Li took her leave of Wang Lei, Mu remained sitting on the sofa. He heard them talking in low voices in the hall. In the silence that followed he visualized Ding Dazhi and Ding Qiliang one after the other. It now seemed to him that Ding Dazhi was not pushing as he had once thought. Apparently push was another form of weakness. To survive when injured the weak had to start pushing.

But what could he do for the Dings? Do as they asked? That would be unprincipled, counter to his pledge at the time of his reinstatement. Refuse them? That would certainly be a big blow to them. And if he refused them he should also refuse all the others who wanted to be assigned to big cities. It would be unfair to discriminate.

"Grandad, let's go...." Ganggang was standing before him.

"Right." Mu spoke wearily, as if too tired to get up.

From the hall they heard another knock on the door, and a very familiar voice:

"Young Mu at home?"

It was Vice-minister Gao, Gao Chengzong, who had been Mu's first superior, his first mentor when he joined the revolution. Mu owed much of his knowledge and experience directly to him. Indeed Gao had influenced his whole way of thinking, his working style and even his behaviour.

Mu stood up to open the door, but Wang Lei forestalled him.

"Minister Gao, why hasn't Nini come?" she asked as she ushered him in.

Nini, Gao's only daughter, had always accompanied him to their home in the past. For Gao hoped, without saying so in so many words, that Wang Lei would introduce a young man to her.

"Aha! Nini has a boyfriend now, that's why she hasn't come with her old man." Gao laughed heartily as he shook Mu's hand.

"Oh?" For a second Mu looked sceptical. Then he smiled. "Fine. Congratulations."

As Wang Lei made tea, Ganggang rushed up to Gao to complain:

"Grandad Gao, grandad said he'd take me to the park, but he hasn't."

"Well, that's not right. Let's criticize him." Gao patted the child's head and said to Mu, "Young Mu, this happened so suddenly, don't you think it's rather strange? Haha! It surprised even me. You know, my daughter's twenty-seven this year, and not good-looking. She said she meant to stay single all her life. But it so happened last Sunday that I took her to Yunshuijian, and there she met a former middle-school classmate. The two of them got talking and hit it off so well that we all came back together in my car. Since then they've got on like a house on fire. We really ought to thank the old man in the moon."* He chuckled.

"Splendid," agreed Mu, though still rather sceptical. Nini wasn't just "not good-looking", she was downright ugly besides being blind in one eye. But her demands were so high that although she had asked many people to introduce her a young man, no one had ever found a suitable suitor for her. How had she suddenly formed this attachment?

"Wang Lei! At last that weight has been lifted from my mind," continued Gao jubilantly. "When a girl's grown she should marry. When I couldn't get her off my hands I was worried stiff."

"When shall we drink at their wedding?" asked Wang Lei with a smile.

---

*A mythical match-maker.

"Soon." Gao roared with laughter. "I saw through that talk of hers about staying single. She capitulated at the first encounter."

Mu joined in his laughter.

"By the way, Young Mu, there's something I want you to do for me." Gao turned to him. "This future son-in-law of mine is one of your college's graduating students."

"Yes?" Mu felt a premonition. "What, what's his name?" he stammered.

"Ding. Ding Dazhi."

Ding Dazhi again! This was a stunning blow. Mu leaned back in his chair, speechless.

"Apparently he'll be assigned to the provinces. Under the circumstances, Young Mu, can't you make allowances and keep him in Beijing?..."

Mu didn't hear the rest of Gao's request. He couldn't believe that anyone would rush into marriage like that. Was this a plot, or love? Was it finding a back door or marrying? His mental pictures of the Dings had blurred again. What sort of people were they? Experts at infiltrating through back doors, or pathetic creatures crushed by this burden on them? How could they be considered pathetic creatures?

"What's up? Have you anything against Ding Dazhi?" Gao noticed Mu's silence and his strange expression.

"No, no." Mu shook his head.

"Well then, you fix it!" Gao turned away to tease Ganggang, assuming that there was no more to be said.

Mu pulled himself together. He was tempted to tell Old Gao of his visits from Dai Jiyao and Sister Li. That seemed to him his duty. Yet how could one gain an accurate impression from their mutually contradictory accounts? And if he spoke up what would the consequence be? If Ding Dazhi were blameless, Mu might destroy a young couple's genuine love, which meant so much to Nini, a love she could never hope to find again. But if this were a swindle and he didn't warn them in time, wouldn't she and Old Gao be in for a terrible shock?

"Old Gao, do you think...." Mu beat about the bush. "Do you think Ding Dazhi is really in love with Nini?"

"I don't know what you mean by in love. My marriage was arranged for me by my parents." Gao had suddenly sobered up.

"Why ask such a question, Old Mu?" protested his wife.

Mu ignored her to probe again:

"Old Gao, do you believe Nini will be happy?"

After a short silence Gao answered:

"Until I go to see Karl Marx I think she may be happy."

"What's got into you today, Old Mu?" Wang Lei demanded.

"Young Mu's right," Gao told her, raising one hand. "That had occurred to me too. But he hasn't thought it through the way I have. All right, let's leave it at that. I leave Ding Dazhi's business to you. I must go and report back. The young couple are waiting at home for news." His forehead had cleared and he was laughing again.

Gao left.

Leaning back in his easy chair Mu felt completely disorientated. The conflicting images of the Dings, father and son, now contemptible, now pathetic, were too confusing to grasp. Then he recalled Dai Jiyao's indignation, heard Sister Li's appeal to right a wrong, and Old Gao's hearty laughter. Back-doorism really seemed to have become an irresistible tide, drawing into it so many people, some of them very good comrades. This tide was sweeping down on him, he found it hard to withstand it.

"Grandad, let's go!" cried Ganggang, rushing in.

This cry sounded only faintly in Mu's ears, and was almost at once drowned out by the clamorous babel of the search for back doors. No, he must hold out, not capitulate, Mu resolved. Sure, it was hard, and precisely because it was hard he must summon up all his reserves of strength. He felt as if the eyes of all the staff and students were fixed on him, to see if he would keep the promise he had made after his reinstatement. He felt the eyes of the public on him too, to see if he would live up to what was expected of a Communist and high-ranking Party cadre.

"Grandad, let's go!" pleaded Ganggang.

Mu sprang to his feet and patted the little boy's head.

"Come on!" he said cheerfully. "We'll have a ride on the aeroplane."

"There's no time. Don't you have a meeting this afternoon?" Wang Lei objected.

As he led his grandson out Mu replied:

"There's time. A turn in the park in the fresh air will buck me up for the meeting."

Translated by Gladys Yang

Snakes and Ladders

—or Three Days in the Life of a Chinese Intellectual

Truth becomes fiction when the fiction's true;
Real becomes not-real where the unreal's real.*

1

"HELLO, is that the communal phone on East Jixiang Road? It is? Could you call Wu Tianxiang at Number 53 for me, please? Yes, 'Wu', the way you write the character is...."

"Don't bother with any of that; can't read so I wouldn't know what you're talking about anyway," The woman's voice on the other end of the line boomed. "You're looking for Comrade Wu, second floor, Number 53, right? Tall thin man? Yeah, I know him."

"Yes, that's the one."

"Who are you then?"

"This is the Foreign Literature Research Centre."

"What, foreign? What country?"

"No, you misunderstand me. Don't worry about any of that. Just tell him Yang wants to speak to him. Yang Changming ... Yang as in...."

"All right already. Hang on, I'll call him for you."

---

*The Chinese title of this story, "Truth and False", is taken from these lines that appear in the opening chapter of the classical Chinese novel, *A Dream of Red Mansions*.

Holding the receiver in one hand, Yang Changming picked up a feather duster and flicked idly at the dust on the table.

"Ah, hello?"

Yang dropped the duster and clasping the receiver in both hands he enquired politely,

"Hello, is that Comrade Tianxiang?"

"Speaking." The reply was a shout.

"Yang Changming here."

"What do you want?"

"There's a meeting in the Centre tomorrow morning at nine."

"Haven't we already been notified once?"

"Well, um, yes, but you see this is a particularly important meeting, and Director Ji of the Party Committee Office, has decided to come in person. He instructed me to double-check with everyone."

The man at the other end was silent.

"Comrade Tianxiang, I hope you'll come in a bit ahead of time tomorrow, as you've been appointed to chair the meeting."

"Who, me? But you're the Party Branch Secretary. It's only right and proper that you chair any study session organized by the Party Committee."

Yang was getting nervous and tightened his grip on the receiver, as though this could pressure Wu into complying with his request. He continued in a plaintive tone:

"But Comrade Tianxiang, you are, after all, the head of the Research Centre. And this is no run-of-the-mill political study session; it's a meeting that's been organized to criticize Old Xu's article, so naturally it would be quite inappropriate for me to take the chair."

"Look, I'm willing to take part in the meeting, but I'm not going to run it."

Wu signalled that he was not prepared to discuss the matter any further by hanging up abruptly.

Yang pulled a crumpled handkerchief out of his pocket to wipe the sweat from his forehead. He dialled the next number on his list.

"Hello, is that Zhu Sheng?"

"Yes, who are you?"

"Now don't tell me you don't recognize my voice. It's Yang Changming."

"Oh, I'm sorry. Is there anything I can do for you, Secretary Yang?"

"I wouldn't be calling you if there wasn't. It's about this meeting. You did get the circular, didn't you?"

"Yes, the postal service is quite reliable. So Old Yang, why don't you let me in on the secret: what document are we going to be studying this time?"

"Come off it. You know full well what the meeting's about."

"Well, I support the decisions of the Party's Third Plenum, oh yes, and I uphold the Four Cardinal Principles. You can check it in my file, it's all there."

"You mean to say you really don't know, or are you just pulling my leg? We're going to be studying Director Zhao's speech and discuss that article Old Xu wrote."

"Now what article was that?"

"Come on now, cut it out. Weren't you there when we were informed of what the Provincial Committee thought of it? Why the Director made an explicit criticism of Old Xu's study of Western modernist literature."

"Sorry, my field's Japanese literature. I've never had anything to do with Western modernism."

"All right, Zhu, I know you're at a public phone, so we'd better not waste so much time. But I'll be seeing you tomorrow morning, nine o'clock on the dot. The head of the

Party Office, Ji Zikuan, will be there too, so don't be late. And don't think you can get out of it by skipping the meeting."

"Right you are. You can count on me. As long as I don't get hauled off to hospital all of a sudden, that is."

"That reminds me, could you pass the word on to Shen Zhiye. He's not on the phone."

"Sure, I'll be your messenger-boy."

A wry smile formed on Yang's lips as he replaced the receiver. The conversation had left his mouth dry. He picked up a thermos and gave it a shake: empty. He went out to the boiler room to refill it.

The Provincial Academy of Social Sciences was housed in an ancient cluster of pine-shaded buildings that resembled an old temple (in fact, the place was nicknamed The Temple). It consisted of a number of courtyards which accommodated the various research institutes in spacious rooms, and seemed expressly designed for arcane scholastic pursuits. But long years of neglect had taken their toll on the buildings: the faded vermilion lacquer was peeling off the pillars, many of the tiles on the roofs were broken and some of the walls were on the point of collapse. Chased by the crisp autumn wind, dry leaves swirled aimlessly around the pitted courtyards. The overall effect was one of decay, even decrepitude.

The Foreign Literature Research Centre was one of the recently revived branches of the Academy. Its director had only secured office space for the Centre after lengthy discussions, endless lobbying and open confrontation. Although the solitary office given over to the Centre would have made a cosy canteen with room enough for seven or so tables and chairs, considering this was supposed to be a research facility it was hopelessly inadequate. If the twenty or more research fellows who were attached to the Centre happened to be there at one time, there would be hardly enough mental, let alone physical space, for anyone to do any serious work. As it was now generally accepted that scholastic research could be done on one's own, Wu Tianxiang used his bedroom as his study. With the revival of the Centre the old rules about keeping to office hours were waived, so now no one came to the office except to take part in administrative meetings and political study or to look up material for their own work. Yang Changming usually had the room to himself, which in practical terms meant that he was both receptionist and general dog's body—apart, of course, from being the Party Secretary.

Returning with a full thermos Yang emptied the previous day's tea from his cup. A foul stench issued from the lidded office spittoon, and Yang quickly replaced the cover. He was so worried about the meeting that he went directly back to the phone, having forgotten all about brewing himself a fresh cup of tea.

"Hello, is that Tongtong? This is Yang. Thank heavens at least one of you has a telephone at home. I'm exhausted after chasing the others up on their infernal communal phones all morning."

"You've sure given yourself a tough job."

Qin Tongtong's father was Deputy-Director of the Provincial United Front Department, a post which qualified him for a private phone.

"Tell me, Tongtong, how do you get away with working at home? Looks like you've been taking lessons from the older researchers."

"I've got a doctor's certificate."

"You never seem to have any difficulty in procuring those things. How about getting me a few?"

"Sure. As long as you got some lingering illness in the border construction corps like I did, that is. If you've got eight or nine years of infirmity behind you, I should have no trouble in getting you a certificate allowing you to stay at home either."

"All right, forget it. Seriously though, I'm ringing to make sure you'll be here at nine o'clock tomorrow morning for the meeting."

"I wouldn't dare play truant! What gets me is that no one ever thinks of me unless there's some meeting."

"Don't be silly, Tongtong. By the way, I'm counting on you to help me clean the place up tomorrow morning. Director Ji is going to be here in person . . . ."

"Oh is he now! It's about time he found out what rotten conditions we've got to put up with. It's no wonder people keep clear of the place — there wouldn't be room for *anyone* to work if they all turned up at once."

"Enough of your complaints. Be serious for a moment. The discussion tomorrow is going to be on Xu's article."

"I don't see why I should even bother coming: I couldn't write an article to save my life. They'll never have any reason to criticize me."

"Look, I'm not going to argue with you. Have a look in on Ye Fei for me and remind her about tomorrow. There's no way I can get in touch with her."

2

Ji Zikuan, Director of the Party Office at the Academy, decided not to wait until the following morning to pay the Centre a visit.

"Have you got in touch with all of them yet, Yang?"

He sprang out of his chair to greet the Director.

"Just finishing the last one now."

"Good job."

Ji was in his late fifties, and although he had gone completely grey, he gave the impression of being youthful and energetic. He pulled up a seat with a leather cushion, but noticing that the leather had split revealing old stuffing and unsightly springs, he had second thoughts about sitting down, and stood with his hands on the back of the seat. His eyes wandered around the room aimlessly and he shook his head.

"This place is a disgrace. Just look around you, it's a wreck. Everything's covered in dust. How long's it been since you cleaned up last? I'm surprised things haven't gone mouldy already. And this is supposed to be a centre for research into foreign literature! Well, you certainly could've fooled me. Looks more like a repository for the decadent habits of feudal literati."

"Well, yes, things might not be as spick and span as they could be," Yang offered obsequiously.

"It's not simply a matter of cleanliness, you know. The root of the problem's up here." Ji Zikuan pointed at his temple. "This is the end-result of ideological rot, that's what it is. Look here Yang, you've been a political commissar for years now. You're an old hand, man. You of all people should be on your guard. There's no excuse for letting up on ideological work just because the Party is emphasizing professional ability and practical results at the moment. This business about Xu Minghui's article is not an isolated incident, let me tell you. And if I've said it once I've said it a million times: if intellectuals aren't constantly remoulding their thinking they're sure to start back-sliding. The new policies have only been in place for a couple of years and these eggheads are already as cocky as all get out. I just knew something like this would happen."

Yang Changming nodded in agreement. He had started out as a functionary under Ji Zikuan's direction during the Anti-Rightist Movement in 1957, and he went on working with him during the struggle against Rightist Opportunism.

Ji had been denounced and sacked in the "cultural revolution", and Yang, having been fingered as one of Ji's cronies, lost his job and was forced into the shadows. When Ji was eventually "liberated" they made him the director of political work in the then Revolutionary Committee of the Academy, and once again Yang was made his subordinate. After the "gang of four" was arrested in 1976, Ji's explanation of his politically questionable stance during the last years of Mao was eventually accepted and he was made Director of the Party Office. He wanted to keep Yang on as his aide, but Yang was anxious to get back to the scholastic world he had divorced himself from for the last two decades, so he got himself assigned to the Centre. Ji Zikuan used to feel that Yang had a promising career as a political commissar; but an end had been put to all that by this recent emphasis on research work and expertise.

"I'll let you get back to making those phone calls." Ji waved him on in a patronizing fashion. "I'd like to talk to you about how tomorrow's meeting should be conducted when you've finished."

The next call was to yet another communal phone.

"Hello, could you get me Zhang Wei up at Number 18, please? What? Who am I, did you say? I'm ringing from the Foreign Literature Centre."

The person on the other end started chuckling.

"Um, comrade," the voice said hesitantly, "can you lay your hands on movie tickets?"

"What are you talking about?"

"Aren't you in Foreign Literature? You must get to see lots of foreign movies. So how about scoring me some tickets?"

"You must be joking. The work I do has absolutely no relation to film tickets."

"Come on, don't give me that routine. Didn't they show one over at the Temple last Saturday?"

"Yes. But it had nothing to do with us. And it wasn't a foreign movie either."

Ji Zikuan had been listening with mounting impatience. He looked at Yang with a scowl and blurted,

"Stop wasting your time. Tell him to get Zhang Wei at once."

Yang covered the mouthpiece with his hand and whispered:

"I can't do that. If I rile the man he'll hang up."

Ji turned the other way in a temper.

"All right. How's about I keep a ticket for you the next time we screen a film? Now, would you be so kind as to ask Zhang Wei to come to the phone?"

"Okay, but don't you forget me."

With that he went off to search out Zhang Wei. Yang heaved a sigh of relief.

"You know things are getting a bit absurd when you can't make a telephone call without handing out film tickets."

Ji Zikuan was still frowning. This wasn't the Yang Changming he had known in the past. One of the very reasons political work was so impossibly difficult these days was that functionaries like Yang all too readily joined the non-Party masses in whining about things. It would lead in the long run to cadres losing the popular respect and authority that they needed to get things done. Ji was on the verge of giving Yang a dressing down, but he was forestalled by Zhang Wei's appearance on the other end of the line.

"Comrade Zhang Wei, at last. Yang Changming speaking. Did you get the circular about tomorrow?"

"Ye, ye, yes, I did," Zhang replied with his habitual stutter.

"Tomorrow at nine then. I hope you'll be on time."

"Cer, certain, ly. Um, um, what are we, we, study...."

"Director Zhao's speech. The Party Committee has instructed us to study it thoroughly."

"Oh, that, that means Old Xu's . . . article; or, or also. . . ."

Keeping an eye on Ji Zikuan, Yang explained slowly:

"For the most part it will be a discussion of Xu's article, certainly. However, there is no need to limit it just to that, we can also. . . ."

"None of this we can also business. Tell him you *must*," Ji broke in irritably.

Yang moved the receiver closer to his mouth and corrected himself:

"You should also relate the speech to your own. . . ."

Again Ji Zikuan interrupted to amend his previous directive.

"Get him to prepare something — a statement on how he interprets the questions involved."

Yang parroted the words into the phone.

"Why p-p-pick on me?" Zhang asked plaintively.

"Of course we expect our team to take part in this meeting with enthusiasm. The Party Committee has made it quite clear that they regard our little gathering as being very important. Comrade Ji Zikuan will be attending in person."

"But, but, I. . . ."

Yang had spoken to everyone who could be contacted by phone. The others would have to be reached by word of mouth. His mission accomplished, he leaned back in his chair with a sigh of relief.

"Carrying out ideological work is a painstaking and meticulous job," Ji Zikuan chimed as he pulled up a wooden chair. "You may have told them about tomorrow's session all right, but you've failed to tell them what we're expecting of them. Nor have you got any of them to prepare speeches and statements relating to the discussion. Frankly, I don't see how it can be a success."

"This is the way things are done nowadays. No one lines up pre-arranged speeches anymore."

"What was that?" Ji shot him a doubting glance. "And I suppose you expect to get results by carrying on in this fashion?"

"Well, yes," Yang said after a few moments of thought. "This way no one feels under pressure and people end up saying what they really think. It makes for a far more lively and natural atmosphere. Of course, on the debits side people sometimes go off on a tangent and the main issues may be forgotten."

"My point exactly. What you end up with is an informal get-together at which people gab away heedless of the topic in question. How can such waffle produce concrete results? All you're doing is providing cynics and malcontents with a forum to exchange gossip and gripe." Ji started getting carried away by his own rhetoric. "As I've so often said in the past, we can't even organize a proper political study session anymore. It wasn't like this back in the fifties, when a meeting was a meeting. You'd start out with a problem to solve or a question that required serious discussion and you'd get stuck right into it. None of this namby-pamby twiddle-twaddle. A meeting requires adequate preparation. As Chairman Mao said, don't hold a meeting unless you're fully prepared. How can you organize this meeting without arranging a few speeches; you need a few catalysts to get things moving."

None of this was news to Yang Changming. He was a past master at applying these methods. His fame as a "meeting strategist" was such that the Red Guards had stuck up a poster in the early "cultural revolution" demanding his "black name list" — his personal files on the people who attended his meetings. They were convinced that apart from the usual list of politically reliable people that he was supposed to keep, Yang had also drawn up lists of middle-of-the-roaders and political stragglers. The Red Guards kicked up such a fuss that he seriously contemplated suicide. Even now, years later, the mere mention of the incident made him nauseous.

"Such methods were condemned ages ago," he offered feebly.

"That was due to the abuses of Lin Biao and the 'gang of four'." Ji dismissed Yang's objection self-righteously. "It's fallen on us to rejuvenate the glorious traditions of the Party, and that includes organizing meetings the way we used to. All this fretting is quite unnecessary. Take stock of the situation and get your priorities right, and everything else will fall into place. Now ask yourself, who's politically the most reliable of this bunch? Who needs to be worked on to be brought up to scratch? And who are the troublemakers? These are questions you should keep in mind at all times."

Yang sat there in silence. He felt desperately sad and frustrated. All he could think of was the endless investigations and criticisms he had been subjected to in the "cultural revolution" as a result of the accusations that he "collected dirt on other people" and "acted as a hit-man" for Ji. He'd put up with it all and eventually came to accept it, though somewhat reluctantly. After 1976 he had pushed his application to go back to his original speciality, as far away from political work and the odium that surrounded it as possible. Now after only a few precious years of respite here he was forced into the same old role again. They had him just where they wanted him, and he had no choice but to play the game by their rules.

"Not much left of the morning I see," Ji barked, glancing at his watch. "I want you to go to their homes this afternoon and arrange for a few reliable people to make speeches tomorrow."

3

Where was he supposed to find these "reliable people"?

Yang was mulling over the problem as he wheeled his bicycle out of the main entrance of the Temple.

The Academy was situated on one of the crowded and narrow streets of the old city. Since the introduction of the new liberal economic policies street-side stalls had sprung up all along the small lanes, forcing the pedestrians to squeeze and jostle in the remaining space at the centre of the thoroughfares. The street in front of the Temple was hopelessly clogged with such stalls. But with confusion came advantages: there were stalls where you could repair your shoes, hawkers selling peanuts, watermelon seeds, fried dough twists, fresh seafood, hot sweet potatoes, as well as itinerant artisans making clay figurines, and entertainers displaying their performing monkeys, doing sword dances and the like. Other stalls sported long oblong signs touting their wares as being "of export quality but now offered for sale on the home market", when all they were doing was flogging unwanted old stock. Even state-run enterprises had set up stalls to take advantage of the open-air market.

Yang made slow and unsteady progress down the street, stopped every few steps by the crowds. Faces of every description bobbed before his eyes and pushed past him, and he found the cacophony of sounds distracting. A mere three years ago this lively scene would have been denounced as a "restoration of capitalism". People were more open-minded now, and such stalls and shops really did offer goods and services not provided by state-run businesses. Free markets had become an indispensable part of everyday life, and "liberated" thinking was the key concept behind it all.

But which of the scholars in the Centre could he rely on for the task he had to ask of them?

If he was to apply the up-dated standards of Party work then he ought to consider Qin Tongtong. Despite her flippancy she was not a person to be trifled with. Admittedly, she was forced to waste years in the boondocks and lacked training in a foreign language; if the truth be known she had actually used her father's position as a government heavyweight to get into the Centre. Tongtong always spoke her mind and she had the courage to fly in the face of accepted norms. And you had to admit that events invariably proved her right. She'd had the guts to come out and say that Mao Zedong was guilty of grave excesses even before the Third Plenum, and once in front of the portrait of "the wise Chairman Hua Guofeng" on the office wall she had sneered, "Humph, not another damned personality cult!"

Tongtong was an example of "special privilege". She'd used it to get her present job; but that didn't stop her from lashing out at cadres' perks and privileges. So-and-so's daughter got special permission to get into university though she failed the entrance exams; a Party leader's family had taken possession of a new colour TV under the guise of giving it a "test run"; so-and-so's secretary was in fact some other fellow's son. So on and so forth: she had dirt on them all. The pity of it was that apart from that brutally frank mouth of hers, and an unflappable up-to-date ideology, there wasn't all that much to her. She used doctor's certificates to hide away at home studying English, and whenever she did drag herself into the office, she'd soon slip off to the screening room to watch restricted movies. Was she really the "reliable type" he was after?

"The latest from Shanghai   nylon shirts with turndown collars. Can't get a better buy. Top quality product. Wears well, latest fashion, only sixteen eighty *yuan*. Hurry, hurry, buy now! They'll be snapped up before you know it." A young man in his early twenties was hawking his wares from the back of a flatbed bicycle. He was holding a purplish red shirt in his hands and flaying it about. The vehicle was surrounded by buyers and onlookers. It had all the signs of being one of those operations run by an unemployed youth. Grinning at his customers, the young man looked every bit the merchant. He certainly knew how to wheel and deal.

Reliable political enthusiasts. Who should he approach?

If he were to judge his colleagues' reliability on the basis of their professional ability, then Xu Minghui would be the obvious choice. In the last year alone, Xu had published seventeen papers on literature, mostly in influential Beijing- and Shanghai-based journals. He had also attended two national conferences and been invited to lecture on contemporary Western literature at any number of universities and colleges in other provinces and cities. But he still had to put up with the most wretched living conditions. He and his wife lived in a hopelessly cramped flat and he was scandalously underpaid. He did all of his writing at night locked up in the kitchen using a stool as his desk. Yet you never heard a word of complaint from him. Wasn't that true devotion? As luck would have it, though, Xu was the one who had written the article attacked by Director Zhao which prompted this whole study meeting in the first place. No, Xu wouldn't do; not by a long shot.

From further up ahead came the clamour of drums and cymbals. Children were pushing and shoving to break into the circle of people so they could get to the centre of the excitement. A martial arts or magic show, or perhaps some quack hawking some special medication or elixir. The commotion jogged Yang out of his meditations.

Who should he get to take the lead tomorrow?

Superficial qualities, the words and actions of a fleeting moment, were no indication of a person's reliability. If someone's thinking was too liberated it could become treacherously reactionary. Similarly, a fellow who was too deeply caught up in his research might well take an erroneous path. People had to be judged according to the way they related to the Party. The hallmark of a true supporter of the Party was a willingness to pour out one's heart to the organization. According to this criterion Zhang Wei was his man.

Zhang first applied to join the Party in the 1950s, but he was knocked back because of "overseas affiliations": he had an elder brother in England. They locked him up on account of his brother in the "cultural revolution".

He had applied again in 1976, then again after the Eleventh Party Congress and the Fifth People's Congress; in fact after every major meeting of the Party Central he had made written or verbal reports to the leadership on his ideological status. In each case he would make a point of discussing his new awareness in terms of the Party's latest decisions, frankly revealing his shortcomings and declaring his determination to conform with the Party's requirements. He was the first to speak at every meeting they held and always made a point of relating the questions under discussion to his own case. People like this weren't exactly a dime a dozen. It was just that … well, quite honestly, Zhang was simply too much of a yes-man. He was, not to put too fine a point on it, gutless, and no one in the office held him in very high regard; nor would any of them have anything to do with him. Was he really the best choice?

Yang manoeuvred his bike out of the crush of the crowd. When he passed a street market selling old furniture, he saw himself reflected in the mirrors on the wardrobes lining both sides of the street, and he stopped for a moment to examine himself. He looked worn out; it was hard to believe he was only a little over forty. Where had all those wrinkles come from? His hair was all over the place, and there was a tuft standing up in the back like a duck's tail. His face had an unhealthy pallor and he looked ill. He was a mess. What had become of the sharp and energetic Yang Changming of the past?

He began his career as the student Party Branch Secretary when he was studying Chinese literature at university in the 1950s. He had been a fine-looking and active young man, brimming with confidence, and enthusiastic about political work.

Doubtless this stemmed from the experiences he'd had in his youth. His mother died when he was in his infancy and his father never thought of anything but his work. He had been raised by his stepmother. Although he had never wanted for food or clothing, nor for that matter was he ever mistreated, his home life had been completely devoid of warmth and affection. He had been guilty of the usual excesses of a callow youth, to be sure, but it was the Communist Youth League and then the Party organization that had helped him through. It wouldn't be too far wrong to say that he was suckled at the bosom of the Party, and he reserved for the Party organization all the devotion and love that others give their mothers. He applied to join the Party on graduating from senior high school.

Yang worked unstintingly for the Party. He could still fondly recall his first private interview with a female fellow student in his capacity as Branch Secretary. Her status as a probationary Party member had been revoked because of certain "personal indiscretions", the type of thing that wouldn't have caused much of a stir in the "cultural revolution", and by today's standards they were a mere trifle. But back in those days discipline was far more strict and such misconduct was not condoned.

She wasn't a classmate of his so they'd had very little contact before that. However, in the Party Secretary's presence she willingly laid her heart bare. Confiding in Yang, she analyzed her problems and told him things that she'd probably never even spoken of to her mother. She deeply regretted her moments of weakness, and the Party's rejection had left her obviously distraught.

Yang counselled her not to be so hard on herself. The Party was still hopeful that she would see the error of her ways and eventually return to the fold a new person.

This had caught her completely unawares, and within seconds tears of gratitude and hope were streaming down her cheeks.

That was the first time Yang actually experienced the awesome power of a Party Secretary — his words would have been considered quite unremarkable in normal circumstances, but here they were capable of consoling a wounded spirit and providing the strength to go on living to a person lost in an abyss of despair. This was only possible because he was working for the Party. At that wondrous moment of her breakdown, his vision of the Party was suddenly suffused with an aura of something akin to sanctity. The Party was both sublime yet humble, magnificent yet approachable. She was warmth incarnate, possessed of the sternness of a strict father, yet brimming with motherly love. She was as clear and transparent as crystal, admitting no trace of impurity in or around Her.

Yang graduated from university with high honours and was assigned to stay on and work in the Party Committee's student office. His teachers and classmates made no secret of their disappointment with the fact that such a promising scholar had been forced to abandon his academic interests. Anticipating resistance, the head of the school's personnel department prepared a list of arguments to convince Yang to accept his work assignment. His concerns proved quite unnecessary, for Yang willingly threw himself into the job.

His girlfriend, Lin Peifen, whom he later married, advised him to think things over very carefully before making a decision.

"Your field's literature, don't you think you're going to regret this move in the long run?"

"No way. In fact, literature has a lot in common with political work: they both have mankind as their target. Literature is used to lift people's spirits and improve them. Political work has the same end in mind; it purges and cleanses the innermost recesses of man's soul."

"Come on. You're making the whole thing sound positively lyrical."

"But it's just that; politics is a paean about man. I believe that my interest in political work stems directly from my study of literature. Like literature, politics works to enhance aesthetics, the natural sciences and the study of man. Politics is an art form, and I want to devote the rest of my life to it."

If nothing else his zealousness touched her and so she agreed with his decision to take the job.

Few people could appreciate the personal sense of satisfaction that his work gave him in those first few years. Though he was hardly a supernatural deity bringing succour to mankind, he did provide others with a warm and understanding mentor. He helped instill others with renewed vigour and sense of purpose. He regarded every person in his charge as a mirror in which he could see his own reflection. And he examined what he saw in that mirror constantly in order to improve himself. Yang was tremendously uplifted by the trust that people put in him. It was a feeling not dissimilar to that experienced by a writer who knows he has a supportive audience.

But those halcyon days were to end all too soon. Political events — the Party-induced campaigns with their attendant criticisms, struggles and topsy-turvy development — turned things sour. Yang was right up there in the front line of class struggle. He had no choice; he was permitted no doubts as to the justice of it all. Then came the ten years of the "cultural revolution" and everything that had gone before it was turned on its head. Now it was he who was the object of the denunciations, and he was vilified as a "cat's paw of the reactionary revisionists". The other names they called him — "accomplice to counter-revolution" and the "hit man" — hurt him deeply.

It was then that Yang Changming's faith in political work began to waver. It was an extremely painful process. Yang didn't see any hope for the future until after 1976 when the Party reaffirmed the value of the seventeen years prior to 1966. The process of restitution and reappraisal gained momentum, first with the negation of the struggle against Rightist tendencies which culminated in the massive Anti-Rightist Movement of the late fifties. But it didn't stop there. One political campaign after another, the whole political process which he had formerly viewed as a kind of on-going "holy war", were called into question and then negated. All those condemnations and denunciations of the past were now condemned and denounced in turn. The philosopher's negation of the negation. Once more Yang Changming felt that political work was truly a profound field, poetical and mysterious.

"Go on, throw in that job of yours and get back to literature." His wife was primed to offer a solution to his dilemma.

This time he took her advice. Yang applied for a transfer to the Foreign Literature Research Centre, and it was granted. He'd finally freed himself from the frustrations of political work. But things didn't work out quite as he had expected. They made him the Party Branch Secretary in the Centre, and now that Xu's article was under fire it was his job to deal with it. And to top it all he had Ji Zikuan, an overly serious and uncompromising political commissar, breathing down his neck. Yang found himself caught in the vise of politics once more.

What could he possibly do? He pushed his bicycle past

another market. Dongxiao Street wasn't too far off. Xu Minghui lived there. Yang decided on the spur of the moment to drop in and see him. After all, twenty years in the business had taught him what his priorities should be.

4

A sheaf of writing paper was laid out on the table with an uncapped pen on top of it. An academic journal was lying open to one side. It was the issue that had carried that damnable article.

Xu Minghui was staring blankly at the table. The print on the page swam in front of his eyes, growing larger one moment and then bunching up before melting into a complete blur the next. It seemed as though the page was gazing up at him like the smiling face of a child, but in a flash it dissolved into a dark and forbidding mass. He rubbed his eyes, but it didn't make things any better. He stood up, considered pacing but as the room was too cramped to allow for peripatetics, he turned back to the table and sat down again. He gazed at the paper dumbly.

The notification of the meeting and the follow-up telephone call Xu'd received had set him on edge. But he wasn't the type to be so easily intimidated. Quite the opposite, he was known as an original and independent thinker from his university days, and he'd been popular with his teachers. That's exactly what had tripped him up in the Anti-Rightist Movement. Finally, twenty long and hard years later the Party had approved his rehabilitation. He'd been given his old job back in the Centre, but instead of being cowed, he had since proved himself as loquacious and critical as ever. He never attempted to mask his opinions.

Those twenty years had left their mark, however. He had gone bald and like the Tang Dynasty poet Li Bai, had a predilection for wine. His wife was hopeless at budgeting their money and his colleagues had never seen him in a decent pair of pants. Broken bits of yarn hung like wispy spider-webs from all his sweaters. His jackets always had one or two buttons missing and the ones he had were invariably of different colours. The universal popularity of nylon socks hadn't touched him, and leather shoes never graced his feet. When holes appeared in his cloth shoes he couldn't be bothered to have them repaired. His colleagues called him a stereotypical "man of learning" who gave no thought to his appearance. Such praise caused him nothing but embarrassment. Nonetheless, it was true that he was so involved in his research that he never spared a thought for anything else.

Ironically, it was his dedication that had landed him in trouble. Am I really in the wrong, though, he wondered to himself. No, I refuse to accept it. He pummelled his head with his fist.

Xu jumped up and paced the small room. Taking a couple of steps to the left he bumped into a bed covered in an old sheet; after a few paces to the right he was stopped by a rickety bookcase, the shelves of which sagged under the weight of old magazines and papers. It was a claustrophobic environment. He picked the magazine up from the table and marched out determined to talk things over with Wu Tianxiang, another ex-Rightist and a friend who'd been sent to the same cadre school as Xu.

Wu's flat presented a scene of tranquility and ease, and although the two rooms he and his wife shared were a bit on the small side, they were always immaculately clean and well-ordered. This was all due to Wu's wife, Wen Suyu, a woman with whom he'd recently remarried. Her guilty conscience — the result of her having divorced him at the height of his political ostracism—made her a particularly industrious home-maker.

Xu Minghui as usual walked straight into Wu's study-bedroom.

The room was full of books. Books lining the shelves, books lying open on the desk; a pile next to the pillow, a stack taking up space in the corner of the room. The only decoration on the wall was a famous couplet by Lu Xun written in Wu's own calligraphy,

"Coolly I face a thousand accusing fingers,
Then bow to act as an infant's willing ox."

Within minutes the small room was clogged with cigarette smoke. Xu had seated himself on a folding chair, with Wu opposite in a rattan seat. An ashtray was perched on the corner of the table. Wu smoked on a pipe, Xu puffed at a cigarette; they sat in silence furiously ingesting nicotine.

Although many years his senior, Wu looked some five years younger than Xu. He was in carefully creased beige woollen pants and a flannel top. He had a pair of very clean plastic thongs on his feet and nylon socks patterned in red and black. Like Xu he had been through twenty years of purgatory, though he had suffered more as his wife had abandoned him when his fortunes were at their lowest ebb. Surprisingly, he hadn't given in to self-pity, drunkenness or despair. He had calmly put up with the seemingly endless train of misfortunes that came his way. As a result he looked as young and sharp as ever, the very picture of an accomplished scholar. He'd played the role expected of him in the immense tragedy of the times without it seeming to have affected him either physically or mentally. It was as though he had achieved some sort of enlightenment.

"Look, Tianxiang, I've been told by the Party Committee that I have to make a self-criticism." Xu's measured words broke the silence.

Wu sat listening to the delicate noise of the tobacco crackling in his pipe without saying a word. He shoved a pack of high-quality cigarettes in Xu's direction.

Xu gloomily lit up a cigarette. Leaning back, he blew out a mouthful of smoke.

They'd been colleagues in a provincial university in the fifties. Wu was a lecturer, Xu a tutor. They had both been condemned as Rightists in 1957. Yet they had taken different roads to perdition.

One could argue that Xu was an accidental casualty of the movement. Enthusiastic, outspoken and easily excited, he had been carried away by the Party's call to air one's views and criticize abuses within the Party. Fired by the speeches and applause at the meetings, he wrote a speech entitled *Ten Suggestions on How the Party Could Improve Its Work*. It was roughly based on what everyone else had been saying. Though it made him famous overnight, it also led to his downfall.

Wu Tianxiang was a completely different case. He had courted disaster of his own accord. The whole time of the "airing one's views" movement, he had been in hospital, so he hadn't had any chance to make any "anti-Party pronouncements". But when he got out he was profoundly shocked to find most of his friends and colleagues — including Xu — had been branded Rightists. His bewilderment quickly turned to indignation and, despite his wife's repeated warnings, he made a direct complaint to the leadership. He was immediately denounced as a "self-confessed Rightist".

Xu smoked his cigarette down to the end and squeezed the burning tobacco out of the butt with his nicotine-stained fingers. He looked up at Wu with wide eyes.

"I just can't figure it out. It's our job to introduce foreign literary genres. What possible cause can they have for complaint?"

Wu sat turning his pipe in his hand.

"You *have* read my article?" Xu asked him point-blank.

"Of course I have," Wu eventually responded with a nod.

"Can you tell me just how I've got out of line? We've cut ourselves off from the outside world for so long that we don't know what's going on any more. Since the Third Plenum we've been encouraged to liberate our thinking. I've kept within reason and done my level best to introduce certain Western literary genres in an objective way. I didn't say that our own writers should start apeing them. If you're going to write about such things you've got to go into their background, after all."

He opened the magazine he had brought with him as he spoke and hurriedly flipped to the half-way mark and pointed at a page.

"Take this passage for example. I go to great lengths to point out the historical conditions that gave rise to modernist literature. I state that following the widespread disillusionment among Western intellectuals following the First World War, Western culture entered a period of crisis. Writers in the West felt they couldn't rely on past values, and this led to an anti-traditionalist modernist literature. Following the Second World War things like existentialism, the theatre of the absurd and black humour appeared. Don't you think I've maintained a critical framework by analyzing things in this way?"

Xu became increasingly worked up as he spoke and beads of sweat formed on his bald pate. His eyes bulged like those of goldfish.

"Of course," he continued without giving Wu a chance to reply, "That may have been the very passage which caused offence. But my thesis is that we've only just become aware of modernist literature, and some people dismiss it out-of-hand as decadent, depraved, reactionary, perverted, exotic, obfuscating and absurd, without knowing the first thing about it. In my opinion such unyielding prejudices preclude the possibility of an objective study of the subject. Director Zhao accused me of acting as an apologist for modernism in his speech, saying that I'd accepted foreign standards and taken a dubious political stance. But what problems can they possibly find in what I've written? Am I honestly expected to prove my political reliability by denouncing modernism as garbage? Surely I've been through all that. Those days are supposed to be over."

Wu looked at him questioningly.

"Come on, that was in 1967." Xu dodged Wu's gaze and took another cigarette. "The Red Guards claimed that reactionary bourgeois scholastic authorities had usurped the right to annotate and publish the Chairman's poems. They ordered me to write some exegetical notes on his poem 'Ode to the Plum Blossoms'. I observed that Lu You was a poet of the Southern Song Dynasty who had been pushed aside by the capitulationists in the court for advocating armed resistance towards the Golden Tartars invaders. The Red Guards accused me of attempting an objectivist analysis without adding a revolutionary critique."

"What did they expect you to write?"

"That because Lu was a member of the ruling élite, his opposition to the invaders had to be distinguished from that of the labouring people. They took the view that the power struggle within the ruling class over the policy towards the Golden Tartars was merely a factional dispute — dog eat dog — and added a line to that effect. They also added a heading to my notes: "Kill, kill, kill: annihilate all demons and monsters!" It was absolutely farcical. I kept the book they produced as a memento."

"I bet Lu You would turn in his grave if he knew about all of this." Wu leant back in his rattan chair with a sigh.

"You can't tell me that we should ape the Red Guards in our studies of foreign literature? If so we might as well change our name to something like Centre for the Denunciation of Foreign Literature. It certainly would make things easier for everyone concerned. We could start all our articles with the words 'Kill, kill, kill!' " Xu was working himself into a fury.

Wu put down his pipe and leant forward,

"Come on, take it easy."

Xu's answer was a long sigh.

"I read your article when it first appeared, and I reread it very carefully after Zhao criticized it. In my opinion it is a work of considerable scholastic merit, a significant attempt at helping the average reader gain access to the field of foreign literature. You should be proud of your achievement. Modernist literature is such a vast subject with so many different genres and sub-genres, it's virtually impossible to get a clear idea of what the differences are if you only limit yourself to descriptions of abstract literary theories. One way to approach the subject is to discuss representative works. Now I'm not saying your article is faultless. Don't you think you were a little too generous in your praise of American black humour, for example? Of course, Joseph Heller's *Catch 22* is a significant work, but not all black humour literature is of such high quality. In fact, some of that stuff is downright fatuous. In my opinion your analysis tends to fall down when it comes to such questions."

"You've got a point there," Xu conceded.

"As for Director Zhao's criticisms, you should certainly give them due consideration, but there's absolutely no reason to overreact. People in research work need to be exposed to all schools of thought. I'm actually impressed that he's taken the time to read what you wrote and comment on it. If nothing else, it shows that our government leaders are finally taking an interest in foreign literature. Of course, I don't agree with anything he's said. The way he sees it, foreign literature's there to be criticized, not studied."

Xu finally began to calm down.

"Frankly, the idea of this study session leaves me cold. Yang Changming rang me up this morning to try to talk me into chairing the meeting tomorrow. I refused. I don't agree with the Director's criticisms, how on earth can he expect me to chair this meeting? Take it from me, Xu, what you have to do is remain calm. It's no big deal. This isn't 1957 after all. They're not gunning for 'Rightists' anymore, and there's no way they can make a case against you. People are still confused about what's going on, especially as there are many cases from the past that the Party hasn't got around to resolving yet. All those years of 'leftist' thinking have left their mark on everyone, and that's what I reckon is really behind this study session."

Wen Suyu called out:

"Dinner's ready. Ask Xu to join us, would you?"

"Come on, let's have something to eat," Wu said, taking Xu Minghui by the arm.

5

A plate of rape and dried shrimps, glistening and green, awaited them on the table. It was surrounded by dishes of spicy beancurd, salted peanuts, and a bowl of soup made with pickled mustard tuber and shredded pork. Wen Suyu had applied all of her culinary talents to the preparation of this simple, mostly vegetarian fare and had made an inviting meal of it.

The sight of peanuts delighted Wu.

"This calls for some drink. I've been keeping a bottle of *Wuliangye* for a special occasion."

"Not for me, thanks." Xu obviously wasn't in the mood.

"Come on, just a sip." Wu took a bottle out of the cupboard. "Connoisseurs say this stuff's better than *Maotai*."

Suyu had got the wine cups out in readiness.

"You two sit down and have a drink. I'll go and make some scrambled eggs."

"No need," Xu protested. "The peanuts are more than adequate to nibble on."

Wu poured out two glasses. After a few mouthfuls of the strong wine Xu felt warm and relaxed. He thought of Wu as a mentor and friend. He respected him for his scholarship and strength of character; he also envied Wu's harmonious family life. Now that his wife was back they seemed happier than ever. He was a lucky man. Even Wu's mother, a kindly old lady, had completely forgiven her truant daughter-in-law; and their son who had been separated from them until he was twenty, behaved courteously and respectfully to his elders.

"Now have some of this, Old Xu." Wen returned in her apron holding a plate of scrambled eggs.

"Delicious," Xu said after taking a mouthful.

"I'll have meat stewed in soy sauce in a few days. Hope you'll come back then," Wen beamed. "I've bought a refrigerator on hire-purchase, we're picking it up tomorrow. Now that we have a fridge it'll be easy to make cold meat dishes and sausages. Ideal snacks for drinkers."

"You're certainly making great strides towards modernization," Xu commented enviously.

Wu took a sip from his glass and shook his head. "It was Suyu and the boy's idea. I don't care one way or the other."

"They say it eats up electricity." The old mother spoke up. "Once you've plugged it in the meter keeps going day and night. The bill's going to be astronomical."

This amused the others no end.

"Auntie, don't forget the saying: if you own a horse you can afford a saddle. You don't have to worry about it, your son's got plenty of money."

"What, him?" The old lady became serious. "I know him too well, he spends every cent he gets. This is all thanks to Suyu...."

"Mum!" Wen Suyu spooned out some beancurd for the old thing to keep her quiet.

At first they thought they'd only have a couple of drinks, but before they knew it they'd each had four or five cups. They were still sipping at the wine languorously after the others had put their chopsticks down. Suyu got some more peanuts for them to munch on. Feeling warm, Xu took off his jacket. He looked incredibly dowdy. What had started out as a beige sweater was now an indeterminately grimy shade of grey, and threads of wool hung despondently from the sleeves. On him it looked more like a sack than an item of clothing, but Xu was unaware of his ragtag looks, and tucking the loose threads into the sleeves without a second thought he picked up his cup.

"Old Xu, why don't you let your wife do something about that sweater of yours?" Suyu asked with a laugh.

"You must be joking. She's even lazier than I am," he said after casually inspecting his garment.

"Xu's a scholar and can't be bothered with such trifles. Why don't you put a few stitches in it for him, Suyu?"

"Very well. Let's have you out of it then." Suyu said as she went over to the cupboard to get out her knitting needles.

"I couldn't let you do that."

He managed to resist the onslaught of her generosity for a while, but finally disrobed in defeat. She set to work immediately while the two men continued drinking.

It was at this juncture that Yang Changming walked in

unannounced. He'd been to Xu's house and was told he'd gone drinking at Wu's. Yang had considered waiting for him, but as Xu's wife told him he might be a long time, he decided to have dinner at home and go directly to Wu's.

The scene he happened upon, one of intimate friends in their cups, made him hesitate for a moment. Though he realized he might not be welcomed, he could hardly retreat now, so he walked right into the room with an exaggerated smile on his face.

"Ah, it's you, Old Yang." Wu was the first one to speak. "Have a drink."

Wen Suyu got up hurriedly and asked him to sit down. She was about to get him a cup and some chopsticks when Yang announced that he didn't drink alcohol. It was the first time in his life that he felt abstinence to be a personal failing, one that in the present situation was actually detrimental to his work.

Xu sat there awkwardly with a dumb expression on his flushed face. He looked like someone who had been caught with his pants down.

Yang immediately fell prey to the suspicions that people in his line of work constantly entertain: what was Xu doing here, tonight of all nights? Are they plotting some sort of unified strategy or even an alliance in preparation for tomorrow's meeting? Or is Xu just sounding Wu out to see if he will support him? These thoughts flashed through his mind, more out of habit than anything else, like a conditioned response, and he immediately chided himself about them. The days of political movements were over; no more attacks on individuals would be allowed. He knew that as well as the next man. All he was trying to do here was organize a study session. No reason in the world for people to get together beforehand to discuss their "strategy", or "plan alliances". Xu was not beseiged by troops. What use did he have for such tactical support?

Though he was secretly castigating himself, on the surface Yang appeared quite relaxed and carefree, and he sat down casually.

"Well, what can we do for you?" Wu asked after finishing the wine in his cup.

"Nothing in particular. I just thought I'd drop by on my way home," Yang said glibly, without at first realizing his slip-up: they lived on opposite sides of the city, Wu's house was hardly on his way home. "But I was hoping to have a word with you about this meeting tomorrow," he added hastily.

"I thought we'd settled all that over the phone. I've agreed to take part, but you can chair the thing." Wu picked up his rice bowl and started eating.

Quite right. That was settled over the phone this morning, wasn't it? The room was quiet except for the scraping of spoons and chopsticks on china.

"The Party Committee called for this special session, therefore it's only proper that the Party Secretary chair it," Wu continued after a time.

"That may well be the case," Yang added quickly. "But as our discussion will be centring on Old Xu's article, we need someone familiar with the scholastic niceties to be involved. You know full well that I've only been working in the field for the past year, so I'm out of touch. I'd really appreciate it if you could see your way clear to chair the meeting."

He seemed sincere and humble enough; in fact he was actually telling the truth. Wu stopped eating.

"I'm afraid the criticisms Director Zhao levelled at Old Xu's article have forced things out of the realm of scholastic discussion and straight into the political arena. He stated that Old Xu is guilty of 'uncritically disseminating Western literary theories' and 'slavishly worshipping things foreign while grovelling at the feet of the bourgeoisie'. Criticisms such as these have put an entirely new complexion on things. You said as much yourself just a moment ago."

Yang knew exactly what Wu was referring to. Wu obviously rejected the Director's attack and the suggestion that Xu's article reflected an unhealthy tendency in research work. Xu had been sitting in broody silence throughout this exchange. The atmosphere was, if not openly hostile, then at least decidedly cool. Yang felt positively uncomfortable. His wife, Lin Peifen, had been nagging him lately to stop going around to people's homes to discuss their ideological faults. "Do you honestly believe you're welcome? You do realize that people call you apparatchiks and informers behind your back?" He knew exactly what she was talking about, although he was reluctant to admit it. The hostile reception he had been given tonight was hurtful. It wasn't fair. But what could he say to convince them that there wasn't anything sinister about his visit? It was hopeless.

He knew full well that he should have excused himself at this juncture and brought this unpleasant and patently unproductive meeting to an end; yet years of working for the Party had instilled in him particular doggedness, so he stayed put. It is strange how the otherwise admirable quality of persistence is so often combined with less laudable traits in the personal make-up of Party functionaries. It tends to make them blindly confident and supercilious. You could always tell them apart from the masses by the way in which they automatically expect everyone to make confessions to them and to see everything their way. In the case of certain Party workers — ones like Yang, in fact — commitment to the cause made them determined to overcome all obstacles and achieve positive results at any cost. They are loath to retreat in the face of difficulties or leave things half-done. As Yang was still involved in Party work, he felt duty-bound to do as good a job as possible.

"Perhaps we should continue our little discussion when you've finished eating," he suggested.

After the meal Wu asked Yang to go next door with him. Xu rose to excuse himself. It was obvious what Xu was thinking: I shouldn't hang around here, as they want to talk about the attack on me. Yang tried to keep him from going so they could discuss the matter together, but Xu simply donned his sweater and coat.

"I didn't tell my family I'd be eating out, they might still be waiting for me."

"But your wife knows you're here," Yang reminded him.

"What?" Xu was somewhat taken aback and stared at the cadre. Yang had really put his foot in it, and he tried to explain.

"I was at your place and she told me you were here."

"I see," said Xu laconically.

Yang could have kicked himself. What a botch-up he'd made of things. Only a moment ago he had said he was just dropping by on his way home. Now it was obvious that he'd been on Xu's trail all along. What he'd thought of as innocent lies would only add to Xu's sense of insecurity.

Following these latest revelations the three finally sat down together. Yang tried to think of something that would put Xu at ease.

"Look, all I wanted to see you about was whether you'd prepared a speech for tomorrow."

"Well I haven't," the words dropped like stones from Xu's mouth.

This put Yang in an untenable position. In the usual course of events a Party worker would have forged on according to the hallowed principle that ideological work was a prolonged and tireless struggle. He would have been quite within his rights to ask Xu what he was going to do about it. He could even advise him to get a move on and write something. If he had so desired he could have confronted him then and there and asked him whether he accepted the Director's criticism; following which, and in the light of Xu's reply, he could elucidate the Party's policy on such cases as his. But Yang chose not to delve any further.

"Very well, then. Perhaps you should just listen to what everyone has to say tomorrow and think things over."

Wu had flatly refused to chair the meeting and it was obvious that Xu was not prepared to say anything about it. Yang wasn't getting anywhere. When he'd arrived the two friends had been enjoying a quiet drink together, now the three of them were sitting there in an uncomfortable silence. Never had the old saying "When drinking with a friend one thousand cups seems too little, when speaking with someone uncongenial half a sentence is too much" rung so true, and Yang knew it. He sat there for a decent face-saving interval before excusing himself.

It was a cool evening for early autumn. As he rode home Yang couldn't help wondering why people were now so hostile towards political commissars? Why were they so defensive? It was true that Lin Biao and the "gang of four" had manipulated political commissars and undermined their reputation; but that wasn't all. Political commissars were too used to acting like pedagogues, they harangued people about vacuous principles and were the ones whose job it was to lead the denunciations and criticisms during political campaigns. They had come to think of themselves as superior beings.

He could remember that things were quite different back in the early 1950s. People had a sense of mutual trust and understanding regardless of whether they were cadres, Party members or whatever. There were no barriers between people, nor was there the universal sense of distrust that one experienced today.

When would things be like that again? Yang peddled on in sombre meditation.

Surely the key to the problem was that political commissars had to learn to treat others as equals. People would only open up when they felt they could trust them. But did *he* trust Xu? Not really. Hadn't he suspected that Xu had been concocting some plan with Wu the moment he saw them together? Such instinctive reactions were proof that he still saw himself as an educator and inquisitor, and Xu as one of his subjects.

The realization pleased Yang. In the present political climate his work was particularly difficult, but things were far from impossible. Ideological work in times like these was a valuable and meaningful challenge. It was important to devise new methods for supervising people's thoughts; it was an exciting prospect, and without noticing it he started picking up speed.

6

Yang Changming was in the office by seven thirty the following morning. Putting down his old black artificial leather bag he opened the windows to let in some fresh air. After sprinkling water around he swept the floor, dusted the tables and chairs, emptied the spittoons, filled the thermos flasks and generally made himself useful.

Although in his youth he had been given a citation for cleanliness he hadn't been so energetic around the office for years. Why the sudden burst of energy? Was he fishing for a promotion by playing up to Director Ji? He dismissed the idea with a laugh. He had always regarded such thoughts as being unworthy of himself. The truth of the matter was that he had his back to the wall. Ji was going to be overseeing the session in person and wanted to see positive results. Since both Xu and Wu were obviously at loggerheads with the leadership in the affair, it was extremely unlikely that they were going to take things lying down. Yang was caught in the middle, and he knew it. He wished he could vanish. He certainly hadn't thought of how he could manipulate the situation to his own advantage.

All this not withstanding, it couldn't be denied that he felt a sense of excitement and anticipation that he hadn't known for years. Perhaps his optimism was foolhardy. But he was counting on having learnt enough from past mistakes to take the plunge into political work with renewed confidence.

Yang was feeling elated. He returned from filling the thermoses with hot water to discover that Zhu Sheng had arrived.

"Well, aren't you enthusiastic today!" Yang cried cheerfully.

"No more than usual. When have I ever been late for a study session?" Zhu replied with a grin.

He was dressed in the latest style. A zip-up beige jacket from Shanghai, and matching light tan pants. He also had on a pair of highly polished leather shoes. His hair was heavily greased, but his slightly pasty face was enlivened by spirited eyes. When his thin lips parted in a smile they revealed a set of gleaming white teeth; more often than not those same lips were twisted in a sarcastic smile. The only flaw in this otherwise ideal vision was that Zhu Sheng was disappointingly slight of build, and he tended to appear conceited and cocksure whenever he struck a pose. He must have worked up a sweat riding to the office as his jacket was draped on the back of his chair. He stood there looking particularly flash with the white collar of his shirt folded over the collar of his patterned V-neck sweater.

Yang had always been of the opinion that people engaged in academic research should devote themselves entirely to their work instead of frittering away their energy on dressing up. In this respect he had more time for Xu Minghui than

Zhu Sheng. On the other hand, Zhu was energetic and efficient, intelligent and quick-witted. The others jokingly referred to him as "the young genius from the south". The articles he had published on Japanese literature had been well received; and the previous year he had spent six months at Waseda University in Tokyo as a visiting scholar, returning to China as a member of the new generation of "Japanese literature experts". One did hear criticisms about him being sly and calculating, but he got on with everyone in the Centre well enough, including Yang Changming. Anyway, this morning Yang was feeling buoyant enough to give Zhu the benefit of the doubt. One really should go beyond mere appearances when evaluating a person, he reasoned to himself. On the spur of the moment he took the unprecedented step of voicing admiration for Zhu's clothing.

"That's a very smart sweater you've got on today. Did your wife knit it for you?"

"As a matter of fact she did," Zhu beamed. "I do like to have a new sweater every year."

"Wealthy indeed the man with an able wife." Yang suddenly found himself mouthing an uncharacteristically old-fashioned saying.

"They tell me you have a very talented wife too."

"Nonsense, she's a northerner; no good for anything but making dumplings."

"In itself no mean achievement. Dumplings are a great dish but an incredible bother to prepare. They require a major undertaking at my place."

Yang recalled the happy scene he had broken up at Wu Tianxiang's place last night and realized that he lacked that type of relationship with his charges, or rather colleagues. Surely, he thought to himself, the lack of a social dimension in his relationship with them disadvantaged his work as ideological minder.

"We're excellent dumpling-makers in my house. You must come over for a meal," Yang offered somewhat rashly.

"I'd be delighted. I wouldn't think of passing up an invitation from a host like you." Zhu Sheng was all smiles.

They continued chatting until the others started trickling in. Everyone greeted each other like long-lost friends, enquiring after each other's health and family in the most effusive fashion. Ji Zikuan put in an appearance not long after. The fact that he was carrying his own thermos cup filled with tea in his hands was an indication that he was eschewing the usual role of Important Party Leader today. He made a big thing of putting his cup down and shaking hands with everyone in the room.

Yang Changming was delighted to see how well they all seemed to be getting on. It augured well for the meeting; maybe today wouldn't be as disastrous as he had expected.

Ji finished saying his hellos and sat down. The others fell silent.

"All here, are we?" Ji turned his head to ask Yang.

"All present and accounted for," Yang replied after taking a quick head count, adding courteously, "Would you care to say a few words first, Director Ji?"

"Mmm ... quite inappropriate," Ji said nursing his cup. "Best if you take the floor first. You're the Party Secretary. Just think of me as a fly on the wall."

Yang turned to Wu next, but he waved the offer aside.

"I thought I'd made myself quite clear: you're the boss today."

"Very well, then, I'll just make a few opening remarks. We are holding this special study session today at the suggestion of the Party Committee of our Academy. Although I haven't been in the Centre long, we all know each other; furthermore, I think it's fair to say that we are all aware of the fact that this is the first time the Party Committee has ordered such a study session. That is so, isn't it, Director?"

Ji nodded.

"I can see two reasons why the Committee is taking this particular study so seriously. The main one being that Director Zhao of the Provincial Party Committee has criticized an article by one of our colleagues, as you all know from the document that was read to us previously. I'm sure I don't have to refresh your memories on this point. Another reason, and to my mind a more important one, is that our response to the Director's criticisms was, to say the least, tardy, and we haven't had a serious study session for ages."

Yang stopped for a moment so as to let his words sink in.

"I must take the lion's share of the responsibility for that. I didn't immediately realize the importance of the Director's criticisms. This reveals a low political level and inefficient work style on my part, and I welcome the criticisms of all of you and the Party Committee."

Yang Changming had thought out the particulars of this short statement last night. He knew Xu Minghui was unwilling to accept Director Zhao's criticisms, moreover he was all too familiar with Ji Zikuan's inflexibility. Together it added up to a formula for disaster. If things went wrong his own position would be untenable. To avoid a debacle he had decided to accept some of the blame so as to take the pressure off Xu Minghui. It was an ingenious enough plan. He thought that if he could avoid antagonizing the "masses" in the Centre they might trust him enough so that in the future he would still be able to do some productive ideological work on them and provide political direction for those who required it. If he took the role of chief inquisitor then he would lose their trust altogether.

"The Party Committee has given specific instructions on how we are to direct our study and the methods we should employ," he said, taking a notebook from his pocket. "One: This is not a political compaign and no one is to be denounced. No one is to be attacked, vilified or singled out. Two: Everyone should feel free to speak their mind. Three: Earnest criticism and self-criticism should be encouraged. If necessary the relevant struggle methods may be employed. That's all, isn't it, Director Ji?"

Ji simply nodded.

Closing his book, Yang called on the first speaker to take the floor.

7

As was to be expected the call for speakers led to an uncomfortably long silence.

Political study sessions in the Centre were a little different from most places. Any lengthy period of silence would invariably end up with everyone looking longingly in Zhang Wei's direction. And Zhang, as usual, was their deliverance. He squirmed for a moment in his seat, took a handkerchief from his pocket, wiped his nose and then he broke the silence with that Cantonese voice of his right on cue.

"I'll speak first."

"Excellent." Yang blurted out in great relief. He opened his notebook in readiness.

Qin Tongtong let out a rakish laugh and nodded her head, making her long knotted hair bob. Everyone else sat by in studied silence as if they were anxious to hear what Zhang had to say for himself.

"To b-begin with, I b-b-b-believe, in my opinion, that the-this special s-s-study s-session called by the Provincial Committee, is very, mm, very important." The words didn't come easily. His stutter was never that pronounced in everyday conversation, but whenever he spoke at a meeting he became so worked up and nervous that the stutter ended up being the only thing people took any notice of.

"J-j-j-ust as Com, Com, Comrade Yang ... just now he put our study within a political frame, frame, work, and so I'm-m-m deter, deter, sure to do my best to understand it... take part in this study enthusiastically, re, re, relate the topic under dis-cussion to myself and raise my, my, oh my ideological level."

His painstaking efforts were obvious to all and sundry. Little did Zhang realize, however, that it demanded just as much effort on the part of his audience to keep listening to him. Naturally, none of them gave any sign of discomfort. All except Qin Tongtong, that is, who at this point leaned over and whispered to Ye Fei.

"I get the jitters just listening to the man. If he can't speak properly why doesn't he just keep his mouth shut?"

Ye Fei's lips formed into a barely perceptible smile.

Zhang forged on oblivious of the others.

"My second point. I would like to ex, express my gratitude to the Pa-pa pa-pa Party once more, the Party Central and Chairman Hua, for, for crushing the 'gang of four', and salvaging the Party and the Revolution; thereby sav, sav, saving me too. My brother in England is a bus, businessman. He sent me some money during the difficult years — not much, mind, but enough to get me in trouble in the cult, cult, 'cultural rev-rev-rev revolution'. I was sus, suspected as a spy. Now, every, every, thing's all right, and I'd like to thank the Party organization for clearing my name. I'll never, ever, never, forget it."

This was all stock material from Zhang's repertoire. He would come out with the same tired screed whenever he was called on to speak at a meeting. Those who had been listening attentively, however, would have been able to detect a new note in today's speech. Zhang must have heard the announcement of the Third Plenum in which Party Central had stated that henceforth less emphasis would be placed on the role of the individual, because he'd had the alacrity to change the usual line about "wise Chairman Hua Guofeng crushing the 'gang of four'" to read simply "the Party and Chairman Hua". The other thing was that his nerves had made his stutter worse than ever.

"Point, point three. In light of the Director's speech, I would like to make a self-criticism."

With these words everyone in the room breathed a sigh of relief. Someone got up to top up their tea, another went over to the spittoon to clear his throat, while others started whispering to each other. "What the blazes is he making a self-crit for? No one's attacked him," Tongtong snarled *sotto voce*.

"Thank god for that," Zhu Sheng commented to Shen Zhiye as he moved past him to get some water.

Ji had first listened intently to Zhang's speech which he had thought to be sincere, but all this stopping and stuttering made him lose interest. His ears had pricked up again with great interest at the words "self-criticism".

Similarly Yang Changming was quick to pounce on this, and his pen was poised to take it all down in detail.

"I made a promise to myself to do my utmost as a member of the Foreign Literature Centre, to make my own contribution to the Par, arty, and the peep, peep-hole." Zhang was frozen bolt upright in his seat with his knees pressed close together prissily. He stared straight ahead and continued in all seriousness. "Bee-b-bee, but, 'cause my understanding of Ma-ma-ma Marxism-Leninism is limited, and my study of politics faulty, I haven't been a good research worker."

He coughed and then continued to drone on.

"My field is eighteenth-century F-French literature, and I'm g-gill-guilty of committing an error that Director Zhao so perceptively pointed out in his speech. I too have been g-

grovelling at the feet of the Western boo-b-boo-bourgeoisie.
I've written a paper on Diderot's aesthetics, and now that I
read it over again carefully I realize that in writing about
Diderot, I, I, I sometimes showed approval of his works."

It was a cause of perennial wonderment that the moment
he started talking about French literature, or Diderot,
Zhang's stammer disappeared completely. He proceeded
with surprising fluency.

"In the first place, I crowned Diderot as an outstanding
aesthetic theorist and art critic. I dared claim that he had
made many penetrating observations in the fields of
aesthetics, painting and drama, the sum total of which I
foolishly opined to be an entire system of realistic artistic
criticism. This was a blatant and unprincipled evaluation. In
fact, Diderot was, despite everything, nothing but a slave of
the bourgeoisie. He himself admitted that 'the basis of
beauty is utilitarian'."

Wu Tianxiang was listening noncommittally with his
carved pipe in his hand. Xu Minghui, who was sitting next
to Zhang, was perfectly still, clearly preoccupied with his
own thoughts. It was doubtful that he had taken in any of
what Zhang was saying about Diderot. Zhu Sheng and Shen
Zhiye were so bored that they had been reduced to swapping
scribbled notes. Zhu had written, "Don't worry, Diderot's
gonna take the rap for you. You won't even have to open
your mouth." To which Shen had replied, "First time lucky,
second time sad."

In fact, Qin Tongtong was the only one who was paying
any attention at all; but that was because this was the first
time she'd ever heard of Diderot, and curiosity had got the
better of her.

Meanwhile, Zhang Wei nattered on.

"In my case the crux of the problem was that I was wrong
to make an objective survey of Diderot's theories. To start

with, he sees the true standard for judging a work of art is whether it is a reasonable imitation of nature. He thought that in recreating nature the artist had to make a choice between the possible and the probable elements of his subject matter, and not simply give himself over to flights of fancy and imagination. He was in favour of representing the characteristic elements of an object, not merely copying its accepted appearance. To achieve the heights of imitation he was in favour of artists making a careful observation and study of nature, and he was opposed to ossified formulae. He even went so far as to assert that if an artist didn't have a proper feel for nature, 'then he might as well give up!' "

Ji Zikuan was completely out of his depth by this stage. Although he had read some foreign novels in his youth, he had never ventured anywhere near literary theory. What the blazes was this fellow Diderot on about, anyway? What are the basic flaws in his theory, that's what Ji was interested in. Is this Zhang Wei character really critical of Diderot or was this just some elaborate smokescreen? Maybe he really likes the man.

"I was of the opinion that Diderot had actually applied the materialist theory of cognition to artistic creativity. He discovered the principle that the true beauty of art is its ability to represent objective reality accurately, thus establishing a fairly thorough-going theory on realistic artistic creation. In short, I could well be accused of accepting his theoretical approach."

Ji frowned. Now this must be the heart of the problem. But Zhang still hadn't got down to tin tacks. What he wanted to know was whether Diderot's theories were ideologically acceptable or not. He listened in the hope of finding out where Diderot had gone wrong. "In particular, Diderot was aiming his criticisms at the classicist theories that had flourished in Europe since the seventeenth-century. All that stuff about 'imitating nature' was for them nothing more than a way of representing 'nature' as viewed by the feudal aristocracy. Diderot was very scathing in his writings and he mocked the mannerisms and excessive formalism of the nobility and their affected artistes. He was opposed to...."

By this stage Ji's brow was knotted in incomprehension and frustration. Zhang was exploiting the occasion to promote Diderot. Ji felt sorely tempted to bring the phoney "self-criticism" to an end, but a fear of saying something wrong and making a fool of himself kept him from opening his mouth. He decided to suffer on in silence for a little longer.

Qin Tongtong, on the other hand, was still listening with rapt attention. Previously she had sensed that although the members of the Centre didn't appear to be very impressive they sure knew a thing or two. Today proved it.

Apart from his mouth Zhang still hadn't moved a muscle, though his face was slightly flushed. The flood of words continued unimpeded. The others sat by passively, and it was Ji who finally broke. He had been brooding on how best to bring this agony to an end, and since he had rejected the option of interrupting Zhang in mid-sentence, he whispered something in Yang's ear. Yang scribbled a note and passed it to the speaker.

Having been given official dispensation to stop, Zhang finally put a rein on himself. He raised his head somewhat hesitantly and apologized to everyone,

"Sorry for going on so, I, I, I've wasted so, so, so much of everyone'z-z-z time. Sorry. I'd like to say in conclusion...."

Zhang's old stuttering self was back with them once more.

"Today my self-crit, criticism has been very shall, shall, simple. I'm determined to make a further analysis of my thinking and my article. I sincerely hope that all the c-ca-c-ca-c-comrades present will be so kind as to criticize me. At the next meeting I promise to make a further self, self, self-crit."

8

Zhang Wei's final stumbling words ushered in the most uncomfortable and persistent silence yet. The room was as quiet as a tomb.

Wu Tianxiang was still preoccupied with his pipe, exhaling large clouds of smoke while gazing unblinkingly at the floor. Shen Zhiye was engaged in clipping his nails and appeared so lost in the job that one would have thought that it was the first time he'd ever seen his fingers. At the first hint of discomfort Zhu Sheng had jumped up again to fill his tea mug, and was now carrying the thermos around and topping up everyone else's cups with unprecedented courtesy. Ye Fei was clawing at Qin Tongtong's knitted sweater pretending to study the pattern.

Yang was the only one to make a decisive move. He stopped writing. But this left him as unoccupied as the others, and it wasn't long before he regretted that he'd listened to Ji and cut Zhang Wei's *mea culpa* short: even Zhang's waffle was preferable to this agonizing hush.

"Who's next then, come on." Yang did his best to put a good face on the situation as he looked around the room expectantly. Everyone was doing their utmost to avoid his gaze.

Ji Zikuan threw him a stern and demanding glance, and Yang was reduced to pleading with his passively disobedient group.

"Come on, anything at all. Even a few short sentences would do. It doesn't have to be a speech, off-the-cuff comments will be fine "

More silence.

Ji had had enough of this. He was glaring at Xu, the central figure of the piece. How come *you* don't speak up, eh?

Xu sat there with head bowed as still as a statue.

Ji Zikuan couldn't stand it another minute.

"Come now. Comrade Xu, don't you think it's your turn to say a few words?"

This unexpected move put Yang Changming on edge. Now that the opposing camps were out in the open, anything could happen. What would he do if there was a confrontation?

"Who, me?" Xu asked moving slightly in his seat. "I haven't thought things out yet."

Ji's displeasure was obvious, and Xu added:

"I told Old Yang that I'd need more time to think."

"Yes, I discussed the matter with Old Xu last night, as a matter of fact, and he said he wanted to mull things over a bit more," Yang added anxiously.

There was little Ji could do, and since it was clear no one else was prepared to speak he decided to take the initiative.

"It would appear that not everyone has had the time to make adequate preparation for this meeting, am I right?"

No one answered.

"In any case, given more time I'm sure the quality of what is said will be somewhat improved." Ji's tone was now actually bordering on the conciliatory.

Yang was immensely relieved. He knew Ji too well to think that years of failure had actually taught him anything; and since the leading role of ideological work had been recently reaffirmed, Ji had become as cocksure as he was before the "cultural revolution". Yang was on tenterhooks. He was afraid that Ji would be as severe and authoritative as he was in the past and only further antagonize the people in the centre, putting him in a more difficult situation. Yang did not know what had suddenly resulted in this uncharacteristically soft line. Whatever the case he was very much relieved that a confrontation had been avoided.

"I don't know the first thing about foreign literature," Ji said, pretending to eat humble pie. "We criticized the theory that 'amateurs can't govern experts' back in the fifties, and as we all know in the 'cultural revolution' the whole country was being led by amateurs. In my opinion dialectics can help us solve this dilemma. At present it is universally true that 'amateurs guide the work of experts', we have to live with this fact, but that doesn't mean an amateur can't become an expert too!"

Talk like this might go a long way in fooling the average man in the street, but it was just so much eyewash to the hardened intellectuals in the Centre. Everyone knew full well that Ji's questions were purely rhetorical, and it wouldn't have occurred to any of them to attempt an answer. But now Yang had another reason to be anxious: why was Ji so determined to make an ass of himself like this?

Thankfully Ji decided to change his tack.

"I've come today among you as a student. Just because I've heard of Tolstoy doesn't mean I know anything about foreign literature. I know I've got a lot to learn, and I'm not going to pretend I don't. For example, today I feel I've learnt a great deal from Comrade Zhang Wei's speech, even though it was a bit on the long side. At least now I know about this fellow Doddera, or was it Diderot?"

Everyone sat there politely, meditative but entirely noncommittal, except for Zhang Wei, who had been blushing since his name was mentioned. Daresay he was deeply moved by this sign of recognition on the part of the leadership.

"But getting back to Old Xu's article, I must admit that before now I hadn't read it. Of course, I would not necessarily have realized its problematic nature even if I had read it. I did, however, make a point of studying it after Director Zhao voiced his criticism. Naturally, I agree with his comments whole-heartedly. It is a work that contains problems of a very serious nature. One, I believe that it offers a fairly systematic introduction to the various Western literary genres. Of course, that's what this Centre of ours is all about, isn't it? We're here to study all their isms, genres and such. But as Director Zhao observed so penetratingly, it's all a matter of one's standpoint. This involves the researcher's worldview and perspective, you know. In short it's a question of whether you're going to grovel at the feet of the Western bourgeoisie and slobber all over their literary clap-trap, or are you going to maintain the standpoint, perspective and critical methods of a Marxist?"

Ji picked up his cup and took a noisy slurp.

"Naturally, we have to liberate our thinking, as the Party has demanded of us. We haven't gone far enough in that direction. But there are limits, you know, a person can go just so far! We want to learn from the good points of the foreigners. We need to study and import their scientific and technical achievements and we want to acquire their superior management methods. Party Central has sanctioned this. Nonetheless, what practical need do we have to learn all those surrealisms and such like from the West? We've got the one literary 'ism' we need: that's realism!"

Ji's voice was becoming louder as he was carried away on the wave of his own rhetoric. He sounded just like one of those martial radio announcers. He sneered wrily.

"Just take a look at what's happening all around us. Aren't things bad enough in our society with young people making all this fuss over bellbottom trousers and that Taiwanese popstar Teresa Teng. If people involved in foreign literature aren't careful, they'll introduce all these foreign genres and things and there's no telling what will happen. Comrades, you must consider the consequences of your deeds. It is for this reason that I for one think that Director Zhao's criticisms were both timely and important. It's a warning to us all. The Party Committee of the Academy has wisely taken advantage of the impetus provided by the Director to organize this special study session and to rectify the work style of the researchers in the Centre."

For some reason this statement elicited reactions from everyone. The hint of a smile that had been lingering on Zhang Wei's face disappeared in a flash. Ye Fei cocked an eyebrow out of displeasure, while Zhu Sheng stared at Ji Zikuan in open amazement. The others bowed their heads. Wu Tianxiang puffed away at his pipe, even though it had gone out some time ago.

Ji gave a little laugh and went on.

"Party Central has repeatedly instructed us to carry out the policy on intellectuals, but we have to be constructive about it. If we discover errors in the ranks of our intellectuals, then we must help them with our criticisms. Once a comrade has seen the error of his ways everything will be all right again. Comrade Xu Minghui is a hard worker. Although he's made a serious blunder by writing this article, he can learn his lesson and make up for it next time. There's no need for him to have a guilty conscience, or to feel any resentment. This business at hand shouldn't be regarded as a major unpleasantness; it ought to be seen as a positive lesson, something we can all learn and profit from, not as something bad. Anyway, we're talking here about a contradiction within the people."

He had been looking directly at Xu while he was talking, and now he looked around at the others.

"Just now Comrade Yang Changming conveyed the directive concerning this study session issued by the

Provincial Party Committee, and I would like to say on behalf of the Academy Party Committee that we are in complete agreement with it. Rest assured this is not a new political campaign. We've all suffered too much over the past years to want to start all that up again. There aren't going to be any attacks on individuals or denunciations, you may take my word for it, comrades. I am not going to denounce any of you. After all, I know what it's like to be attacked in a campaign. Nobody welcomes that approach to things; and it doesn't solve any problems either. All we want to do is do a good job and make a contribution to society."

With this he glanced at his watch and took a deep breath.

"I think that's all for today. Now, comrades, I would like all of you to spend the rest of the day thinking very carefully about what I've been saying. And tomorrow I expect to hear what you've come up with. I encourage you to drop in on each other to do a bit of cross-fertilizing; it might prove helpful."

The first morning session was over.

9

Xu sat in his little study for the whole afternoon unable to read or write a word. He had smoked this way through a whole packet of Struggle brand cigarettes.

Xu had lost count of how many times he'd been denounced and forced to write self-crits over the past twenty years. One thing was for sure: in terms of sheer volume he'd written far more material — self-crits and investigations — for his persecutors than scholastic essays. Since the end of the "cultural revolution" and the Third Plenum he thought all that torture was over and that he'd be able to devote himself to his work. Who'd have guessed he was going to put his foot in it again?

With all his experience it would be simple to write another self-crit. He had all the acceptable cliches at his fingertips: "grovelling at the feet of the Western bourgeoisie", "betrayal of the standpoint, views and methods of Marxism", "unprincipled praise for contemporary Western literature"; nothing would be easier than to accept the attack and write up a self-denunciation. At most he'd have to promise to pay more attention to the remoulding of his worldview. Blah, blah, blah. So simple; after all, it was "a contradiction within the people".

He felt utterly dejected.

What was bothering him was that he didn't think there was anything wrong with his article. He'd made a special point of describing the economic environment and historical background that had given rise to modernism. That should have been Marxist enough for them. All right, so he had only made this point in one line, but the article was an introduction to modern literature in the West, not an article to discuss the relationship of literature to society. Do I have to weigh down every piddling little article I write with political poundage before I can be regarded as being reliable?

He was outraged.

What was that Ji Zikuan had said about feeling resentful at being criticized. Well, he was resentful. If not kept in check he could end up feeling downright rebellious, that could be very dangerous indeed. Rebellion . . . no, he didn't mean that at all. He just didn't think it was fair. There was nothing illegal about that. One should not only think about one's positive points, but also about one's limitations and errors. Wu Tianxiang had himself said there were faults in the article. Xu remembered that Wu had pointed out that he had only used good examples of Western works to illustrate his arguments, nothing negative. Of course, there was a lot of rubbish produced by degenerate and black humour writers·

had he been too anxious in presenting their better works? He couldn't deny that his own approach to literature had been influenced by the West. It wouldn't do him any harm to make a few comments on the fact.

He was feeling a little calmer now.

But was there really any need to make a full-blown self-criticism? They could discuss and dispute whatever they wanted. Wasn't there a policy about "Letting a hundred flowers blossom, and a hundred schools of thought contend"? Furthermore, if it was wrong to introduce readers to modern Western fiction in the objective way he had, what was the use of working in foreign literature in the future? Were they supposed to denounce the modernists in the same way they had attacked the Song poet Lu You in the "cultural revolution"?

He was all confused again, and couldn't see any way out of this dilemma.

Just then Zhu Sheng and Shen Zhiye came to pay him a visit.

"What are you doing cooped up here all by yourself, Old Xu? Writing a self-crit?" Zhu Sheng was his usual confident self, with the look of someone who had never had a down.

"I couldn't write a word. I'm completely mixed up."

Xu was grateful to have a short respite from his troubled thoughts, especially as it was provided by a visit from two friends. He busied himself by preparing them some tea, doing his best to make them feel welcome.

"So what are you going to say at tomorrow's meeting?" Shen Zhiye asked in his Sichuan version of Mandarin. He blew at the tea leaves floating on the surface of the water in his cup and before he even took a sip he let out a long sigh.

"What's that for, they haven't named you in their attack?" Xu laughed as he lit up yet another cigarette.

"What's the difference? Ji's made it quite clear that we're

all expected to make a statement." Shen was not given to playing games.

Zhu Sheng was sitting on the edge of the bed with his legs crossed and one elbow resting on the back of the bed.

"We've come to sound you out, Old Xu." Zhu said with an ingratiating smile.

"Sound me out...?"

"Yeah, to see what line you're going to take with them. If we prepare speeches that are too self-critical it'll put you in a real bind. Come on, give us a look at your speech. Do a little of that 'cross-fertilizing' Ji was talking about."

Xu took one look at the supplicating white hands Zhu stretched out to him and gave a sigh.

"I haven't written a word."

There was silence for a few moments then, having recovered his composure, Zhu spoke up.

"There's no big deal. After what we all went through in the 'cultural revolution', one more study session doesn't mean a thing. We can cope with such minor hassles."

"You make it sound easy, but you know you're bluffing." Shen commented coolly. "So what are you going to say when you're facing Ji Zikuan and he demands a statement from you on Xu's article? He won't let you off unless you say something. And you don't want to blurt out a lot of lies against your conscience."

"After all the politics I've been through, I know every trick in the book. You'd be surprised the type of rubbish I can hand them and get away with," Zhu replied confidently.

"It won't work this time," Xu took over from Shen and said in all earnestness. "We're academics, we can't simply abandon our scientific approach and sidestep the questions with a load of sophistry."

Xu's eyes bulged like a hanged man's and his bald head had broken out in a sweat. His scraggy neck was stretched out of his collar as he spoke. This was the way he always looked when in a fighting mood. He was older and professionally more accomplished than his two colleagues. Shen Zhiye held him in high regard, and shook his head in agreement as Xu spoke. Zhu Sheng was reduced to being sarcastic.

"What a bookworm! Don't you think Director Zhao's speech reeks of sophistry? And what about Ji Zikuan's waffle?"

Xu was lost for a reply.

"They don't know the first thing about the science we're talking about, so why take any of it seriously?" Zhu wasn't going to let up.

"Old Yang is steady and factual in his approach." Xu finally found a defence for his unenviable position.

"But he doesn't have any power. Listen, my friend, I don't care what you say, if they make me speak tomorrow I'm going to do my darnedest to skirt the issue."

"What are you going on about, the 'issue' doesn't involve you anyway." Shen Zhiye was amused by Zhu's empty bravado.

He's right, you know, Zhu thought to himself. I'm not the one they're onto this time. He scratched his head, embarrassed that he'd allowed himself to become so carried away. His discomfort passed momentarily and he stuck his hands in his jacket pockets and pushed out his chest.

"Anyway, I know every trick in the book. Skirting issues, fancy intellectual footwork, turning things on their head, spinning a yarn; if all else fails I'll just start admitting all ideological errors I can think of."

Zhu's exaggerated confidence even made the woebegone Xu Minghui chuckle.

"That's what's known as a 'phoney self-crit'."

"And what's wrong with that? Anyway, by now we're all

used to lying. If we weren't, how would we ever have survived the ten glorious years of the 'cultural revolution'?"

Shen Zhiye came to the rescue just as Zhu Sheng's counter-attack was about to overwhelm Xu Minghui's simple defences.

"They never gave you any choice. I heard this joke at a tea house when I was back in Chengdu last year, it'll kill you."

Shen rarely told jokes, but when he did he would always leave his listeners in stitches, while he himself would sit by in absolute seriousness. Everyone liked his jokes, so Zhu Sheng tried to hurry him.

"What's all the rush. It's bad for health at our age." He spoke in slow measured tones, and took a sip of tea before continuing. "It was back in early 1976 at the height of the 'criticize Deng' campaign. They held meetings in all government offices and schools. Everyone, old and young, had to make a speech and express their support for the campaign. They organized a mass criticism meeting in a workshop at this one factory in Chengdu. Over a hundred people were there, all sitting around the machines. Half an hour passed and still nobody would speak up. The person chairing the thing was so desperate that he was tempted to pull people's jaws apart in order to force them to say something. What could he do?

"Well, just as things were getting to the point of being ridiculous, an old worker suddenly slapped his thigh and screamed out angrily: 'My god, Deng Xiaoping. All that talk about him being in charge of the work of the Central Committee, and look what he was really up to. Instead of spending his time on useful things like class struggle, line struggle and key policies, he went around telling everyone to raise more pigs. What a dastardly plot. Pigs, indeed. Big, fat, meaty pigs. Think of that pork made into sweet and succulent, oily food. How poisonous. All that deadly cholesterol. Why, people, who ate any of that stuff would end up with heart disease, high blood pressure, blood clots in the brain and an endless list of illnesses. It just makes me hopping mad to think about it. Isn't that just the most cunning and devilish plot you've ever heard?'

"There was absolute silence in the workshop for a minute or so and then everyone burst out laughing. That was the end of that criticism meeting."

Shen's earthy Sichuan accent made the story sound even funnier. But he concluded in a cold tone of voice:

"Just think of the economic disaster Sichuan was facing back in 1976: why, people, hadn't seen any pork on sale in ages."

"Brilliant! In spurious criticism lies true praise. Good on the old boy." Zhu Sheng was much impressed.

There was a knock at the door, and who should walk in but Ji Zikuan. The three were dumbfounded.

"Director Ji, what perfect timing." Zhu, smiling profusely, offered him a seat.

"We came specially to have a little talk with Old Xu ourselves. You did encourage us at today's meeting to get into a little cross-fertilization. And what a wonderful suggestion it was. We haven't talked with each other like this for years. We've only been here a short time, and Old Xu really ... he said he's prepared to make a proper self-criticism."

"Now that's what I like to hear."

"You can carry on from where we left off. We really should be going."

The two of them bid Ji and Xu a hasty farewell and left.

"How are you feeling now, Old Xu? Come around to our way of thinking yet?" Ji enquired in the most solicitous tone.

Xu's pate was awash in sweat and he started fumbling for words.

"Some of the, um, ah, way, ... However...."

"Tell us all about it at tomorrow's meeting."

"Very, um, very we-e-ell...." Xu seemed to have been affected by the Zhang Wei syndrome.

10

That evening in a number of homes throughout the city....

Pipe in hand, Wu Tianxiang **sat** in his little room, staring blankly into space.

The sound of cheerful chatter came from the next room as his wife and son installed their new refrigerator. From the way they were carrying on you would have thought this was the single most important event in their lives.

"Tianxiang, come out here for a second, would you? See if you like where we've put it." Wen Suyu wanted her husband to share this delicious moment with them.

He joined them, and after standing there a bit nodded in approval. He swallowed a mouthful of the ice water that his son had handed him. It sent a chill down his spine and he returned to his dazed vigil in the rattan chair in the study.

He was still baffled how Xu's article had managed to cause such an uproar.

Yang Changming was up to his elbows in soap suds washing a sheet. He stopped every few minutes to think things over.

"What's on your mind?" Lin Peifen was leaning over her desk, correcting a pile of students' compositions.

Yang pretended he hadn't heard her.

"Still wondering why no one spoke up at the meeting? I know I'd have kept my mouth shut if I was there. Anyway, the readers'll be the ones who deliver the final verdict on that article, not your Party Branch. In the meantime people can say whatever they want to about it. But what's the point of forcing someone to flagellate himself in public over it?"

Yang kneaded the sheet in silence.

"It's high time you quit your job as political commissar. Who needs all that grief?"

Yang kept attacking the sheet.

"You'd do better putting your energies into something constructive like writing articles for magazines and earn some money to buy a washing machine. Then you wouldn't have to face doing the sheets like this when you get home from the office."

Yang had heard enough. He dropped the sheet.

"Can't you keep your mouth shut for a few minutes?"

But she'd had this on her mind too long to stop now.

"Just listen to what people say about political commissars. No one ever has a good word for them. I just don't understand you — haven't you had enough of that flak?"

"All I want is to do something to change people's prejudices." Yang snapped as he wrung out the dripping sheet.

"What?"

Shen Zhiye was sitting at his desk behind the curtain. The television was blaring on the other side. At first he'd thought of having a look to see what was on, but he was far too preoccupied.

What was he going to do tomorrow?

Things looked bad; he'd have to make a statement. The thing was should he say what he was thinking? It was no easy decision. "In spurious criticism lies true praise." That was one way to get around it. Unfortunately, it would require very careful wording, and that meant a lot of work. His thick lips were pressed tightly together and his brow knotted. It was impossible to tell what he was thinking.

About half an hour later he picked up a pen and started writing with broad flourishes of his pen:

1. Support Minister Zhao. Cite importance of political study.

2. Foreign Lit. Centre recently re-established. Correct way to do research. Need to enhance value of research work.

3. Errors in Xu's article (egs.). Also written good articles (egs.).

4. Self-crit: been lax in work. Time mostly spent collecting materials. Haven't written presentable article yet. Regrets, etc.

Even after he'd jotted down this outline, he was unable to rest. On the other side of the curtain the heroine Mu Guiying was launching into an aria on the TV.

"From youth to master the arts of war has been my will,
A million of the enemy I face, and every one I kill."

Remembering that his twelve-year-old son had to get up early for school the next morning, Shen stepped into the other room and charging up to the woman general on the screen bellowed:

"Aren't you in bed yet? Are you going to be able to get up in the morning?"

Qin Tongtong leaned languidly against the side table as she picked up the phone.

"A film? What's it called? 'Callous Heart'? I see enough of those as it is. Count me out."

Ye Fei had adopted a baby girl and treated the child like a fragile treasure. It had a weak constitution and was forever falling ill. In fact, they had just got back from the hospital where Ye had taken the girl for an injection.

"Couldn't you stay at home with her tomorrow?" she petitioned her husband.

"What about you? Isn't that meeting finished yet?"

"No. Everyone has to make a statement."

"Well, careful what you say."

"Don't worry. I'm a terrible speech-maker."

Smiling coyly, she busied herself with the girl's medication and put her to sleep.

The night lamp at the head of the bed was still on. Its gentle light gave Zhu Sheng's meticulously decorated little bedroom a soft, peaceful glow.

Zhu was leaning against the headboard with his legs under the quilt. He looked utterly exhausted. His wife, Gong Xiaoyan, was sitting on a folding chair and leaning against the bed as she worked on a sweater she was knitting for their daughter.

"What lousy luck. Tomorrow'll be another wasted day."

"If you really don't want to go, ask for the day off."

"Never get away with it. What's really bothering me is that I have to make a statement."

"Go in late. If you're late enough you might get out of it altogether."

"Hey, that's not such a bad idea."

But he had to think of a good excuse. Inspiration struck and his face lit up with a cunning smile.

"I'll tell them it wasn't my fault I was late. In fact, I was so worried about showing up on time that I went to bed especially early, and woke up at the crack of dawn. I grabbed a stale roll and hopped on my bicycle. But on my way I witnessed this collision between a bus and a bike on Luoma Avenue. Luckily the cyclist wasn't seriously hurt, though his bike was completely wrecked. Within minutes the place was crawling with traffic police."

Xiaoyan was listening with an amused smile on her face.

"The bus driver said it was the bicyclist's fault while the cyclist claimed the bus had run into him. Neither side would back down and they were soon squabbling vociferously. This huge crowd gathered to watch the commotion. Well, I *would* have to go and get myself involved. I said I'd seen the cyclist ride straight in front of the bus. That was it for me, boy. The police said I was the only eye-witness and I'd have to go down to the station to make a statement. I panicked when I realized I was going to be late, so I started waving my I.D. card around. I told them I had an important meeting to attend and I couldn't afford to be late. They said police business took priority over everything. And the cyclist was insisting that I go with the police as he claimed I'd falsely incriminated him. They didn't give me a choice. I didn't get out of there till two hours later. I might be late, but surely you can see it's not my fault."

Zhu laughed mischievously like a naughty boy with a new prank. At first Xiaoyan had been caught up in his merriment, but suddenly her face fell.

"It'll never work. If that Director Ji of yours calls the police to check your story you'll be in a terrible mess."

She was right, and Zhu knew it. But no sooner had he trashed plan one than he'd come up with a second strategy.

"Okay, here it is. Please forgive me for my tardiness," he was so pleased with himself that he chuckled. "Really it's not my fault. I got up bright and early this morning and started on my way to the office. Who'd have guessed that fate was going to play a little trick on me? I was halfway here when that stupid bike of mine blew a tire. I started looking for a repair shop, but as you probably realize, comrades, our service industries haven't caught up with the actual requirements of our prospering economy. In other words, it took me ages to find one. Then the old boy in charge told me I could pick it up in three days. He couldn't be budged, so I had no choice but to leave the bike with him and catch the bus."

His wife was so engrossed in this tale that she stopped knitting.

"And what a bus ride it was. The crowds were just

incredible. I missed the first three buses because I couldn't squeeze my way on board. But I was so worried about being late that I made a wild plunge for the fourth and after engaging in a tit-for-tat struggle with my fellow citizens I managed to get on. Wouldn't you know it — the bus seemed like it was never going to stop. I signalled to get off as we were approaching the Academy stop, and the conductress gave me this dirty look. 'This is a long-distance bus, mister,' she grunted. I was so anxious I thought I'd drop dead on the spot. It took forever to reach the first stop and when I finally got off I didn't have any idea where I was. The only thing I could do was to catch a bus going in the opposite direction. I managed to squeeze onto one, but by the time I'd returned to where it all began, I was already hopelessly late."

Zhu faked a look of despair and Gong Xiaoyan gave him a playful shove. She remarked with a click of the tongue:

"Foreign literature is the wrong field for you. You ought to be a stand-up comic."

"I suppose you think I like making up lies?" Zhu tossed off his shirt and snuggled under the quilt.

"Why's this meeting got you so frightened?"

"I'm angry more than anything else. Meetings like this are enough to drive a person to an early grave."

"Don't dwell on it," his wife tried to comfort him. "I have a day off tomorrow. Now, I'll tell you what I'll do, I'll buy some nice fish with our ration coupons and make you a lovely lunch so you can relax when you get home. How would that be?"

Zhu was mollified by his wife's tender mercies, and he drifted into dreamland on a cloud of sweet-and-sour fish.

11

The next morning found Yang in the office straightening

things up once more. Today he had Ji for company. Gripping his thermos cup in both hands, the Director addressed Yang cheerfully,

"Keep a tight rein during today's meeting, Yang. Things cannot be allowed to go the way they did yesterday. Discipline was a shambles."

Yang was wiping the table.

"I wonder what they're all thinking?"

"No need to concern yourself." Ji swigged a mouthful of tea; he was brimming with confidence." I paid a little courtesy call on Xu Minghui yesterday afternoon, and I think our tête-à-tête may prove quite beneficial. He told me he intends to make a self-criticism today."

How could that be? Yang was astonished, for no other reason than that he had re-read Xu's article very carefully the previous night and was now more convinced than ever that it contained no serious political errors. What could he possibly say in a self-crit?

It was getting on for nine, and people began filing into the room. Yang noticed that Zhu Sheng was the only one absent. It wasn't like him to be late. Yang looked at the door and wondered if he should wait a bit longer. Just at that moment, Zhu pushed open the door and walked in. He took a look at his watch and chimed:

"Nine o'clock exactly. Right on time." He was grinning as he took his seat.

Yang called the meeting to order.

About half a minute later, Zhang Wei leaned over the table, shoulders hunched, and launched into yet another stumbling statement.

"Yester-ter-terday, I, I was th-thinking over m-my own p-pee-p-problem again. I f-f-feel that yesterday mor-mor-morning I failed to, mm, analyse it d-deeply enough. I, I only criticized m-my pr-praise for D-doo-d-dee-d-Diderot. . . ."

Everyone in the room started tittering at the mention of Diderot, except for Ji that is. Only yesterday, Ji had been quite interested in hearing about Diderot, but now an ugly scowl was creeping over his features.

Whenever he spoke Zhang incessantly watched out for reactions from the leadership. When he noticed Ji's malodorous expression he became even more incoherent.

"I, I, I won't t-t-talk about Di-Di-Diderot t-too-t-dee-to-day. Instead I sh-shall d-discuss an article I wrote s-several years ago in pr-praise of a six-sixteenth sa-century Fr-French writer. . . ."

Yesterday it was the eighteenth century; today he'd gone back even further to the sixteenth. The more he went on, the further away he got. Ji politely interrupted this time-travelling confessional.

"Comrade Zhang, it's highly commendable that you are so eager to make such a thorough examination of your work, however, our time is limited. Other comrades are waiting to speak. Don't you think we should give them the floor?"

"S-sure. . . ." Zhang Wei had no choice but to stop. But his gaping mouth was a sure sign he was giving up the limelight only with the greatest reluctance.

The atmosphere in the room had been fairly light-hearted at the beginning of part two of Zhang's self-flagellation. Today's not going to be so bad after all, Zhu Sheng had thought to himself. Shen Zhiye had been fiddling with the outline stuffed in his pocket and it occurred to him that he might be able to get away without having to use it. Qin Tongtong was quite excited at the prospect of another lesson in French literature. Even Xu, who had been very tense, relaxed somewhat. But things underwent a sea-change the instant Ji cut Zhang short.

"Has everyone prepared something? Let's keep things moving here. Who'll be next?" For some reason Ji had decided to take it upon himself to chair the meeting. And noticing that no one was clamouring for the privilege to be first, he began calling on people.

"Comrade Xu, I believe you have prepared a statement. Can we hear it now?"

Beads of sweat glistened on Xu Minghui's bald head. Wiping them away with a handkerchief, he took out a small notebook and, referring to it constantly, began speaking.

"I've had a number of conflicting thoughts on the subject under discussion these past few days. To come straight to the point, I've been trying to figure out what's actually wrong with my article. Should I be making a self-criticism or a self-defence?"

These opening lines ensured that everyone was listening to Xu in rapt attention. Wu Tianxiang actually removed the pipe from his mouth. A dim, forced smile spread across Ji's face and Yang, who'd caught himself staring dumbly at the speaker, hastily got down to the job of note-taking.

"When I first heard about Director Zhao's remarks, I felt resentful, upset, even annoyed," Xu paused. "I could not see that I'd made any political errors in my article. All schools of literature have their basis in social conditions. I made this point in my essay; this is the Marxist way of looking at things. Just because I chose not to use the derogatory language with which we are accustomed to hearing Western modernist literature reviled, it doesn't mean that I 'worship at the feet of the Western bourgeoisie'. If it is necessary to employ 'cultural revolution' cliches in order to prove one's own ideological steadfastness, then in my opinion there is no point in studying foreign literature at all."

Xu's tone became more vehement as he spoke. The silence was palpable.

"Furthermore, I got a lot of positive feed-back when my article was first published. Middle-aged and younger writers in particular told me that it had opened their eyes to the possibility of learning from their foreign contemporaries. Critics, as far as I know, reacted encouragingly as well. Some even said that it had broken new ground in the study of foreign literature. Of course, I consider this to be an exaggeration."

Zhu Sheng admired Xu's honesty. Yang Changming was too busy taking notes to react. The others listened in awe; Ji was wondering whether this was a session for self-criticism or self-promotion.

"After yesterday's meeting and following a *personal* visit from Director Ji, I've had a change of heart. The criticism of my article has given the Centre a bad name, but more importantly, I'm very upset that my colleagues have been dragged away from their own work to attend these sessions."

Where was this self-criticism heading? Affecting a warm tone, Ji interrupted:

"Comrade Xu, What are your views on the article now?"

"Now?" Again Xu wiped his perspiring pate. "I now feel it contains political errors."

His face turned red as he spoke. His eyes met the perplexed gaze of Wu Tianxiang and quickly turned away.

"My personal opinion is that modernism cannot make any major contribution to the development of our literature. In objective terms, however, what I wrote may have given people the opposite idea, perhaps for no other reason than that I said more in favour of modernism than against it. But I have carefully scrutinized my feelings on the subject and I deny I have ever grovelled at the feet of the Western bourgeoisie. Nonetheless, I do admit the possibility that I may have given people the wrong impression."

Qin Tongtong was exhausted by Xu's circumlocution. These high-powered intellectuals can never say what they mean. It's enough to drive you batty. Zhu Sheng, meanwhile, had been much impressed by Xu's verbal dexterity. Shen Zhiye felt sorry that Xu had been reduced to this and Wu Tianxiang, though surprised at first, was once more meditating on his smouldering pipe. Ji was nodding in appreciation. True, all this stress on the purity of his motives wasn't really the stuff good self-crits are made of; on the other hand, the fact that Xu was willing to acknowledge that the article contained some ideological errors was a step in the right direction. His home call last night had not been in vain.

"In regard to Director Zhao's criticism, I now recognize that it was his way of expressing concern for my ideological well-being. It was both necessary and timely." Xu raced through the next bit. "After a most beneficial session with Director Ji yesterday, I came to realize the detrimental effects my article has had. Director Zhao was quite right to point out the excessive West-worshipping we are witnessing all around us. You can see sideburns and bellbottom trousers everywhere, and unhealthy tendencies have emerged in our literary works as well. It was most inappropriate for me to have made such a sweeping introduction to modernist literature without making a forceful criticism of it at the same time."

Ji nodded again, his head describing a slightly larger arc this time. He wanted to indicate his approval of the laudable development in Xu's argument.

Xu glanced at the notebook in his hand, mopped his sweat and continued.

"How did I come to write such an erroneous article, you may ask? Basically it was because I have been lax in remoulding my world-view. After they removed my 'Rightist' label I wanted nothing more than to concentrate on my work, and I rarely thought about my ideology. As a researcher of foreign literature I am in contact every day with foreign things. 'Red are the hands of he who handles cinnabar and black are they who would go near ink.' If one doesn't pay attention to the remoulding of one's thinking it is all too easy to come under the influence of foreign ideas."

Ji's head bobbed up and down vigorously. It was true after all, a few years of re-education and most of these intellectuals could be saved. The others were completely lifeless. Qin Tongtong, however, whispered to Ye Fei, "What's he saying? Contact with foreign ideas makes you a foreigner!? And he calls himself a senior researcher!"

"I still have some misgivings, however," Xu closed his notebook. "Primarily I'm concerned as to how I'm supposed to write about foreign literature in the future. It won't do to simply consign the lot to the rubbish heap as we did so blithely in the past, without any regard to artistic merit. Yet it's clearly inappropriate to write the way I did, in a relatively objective way. So what are we to do?"

Ji's nodding head slowed down to a nearly imperceptible quiver. Why was the fellow straying into the realm of practicalities? Of course, now that the ideological problem had been resolved one could address more practical matters. Therefore he felt it necessary to signal assent. On the other hand attention would be deflected from the important ideological issues if too many practical questions of this nature were allowed to clutter up the discussion. It was something he'd have to watch out for. Fortunately, Xu brought his speech to a simple close.

"My self-criticism has not been sufficiently soul-searching, and I welcome any criticisms or help my comrades have to offer."

Ji was much relieved that it ended when it did. Although he only rated it as a fair to middling self-crit, in light of the circumstances it was a promising start. Thought-remoulding was a slow process, one couldn't hurry these things.

"Very well, who's next?" Ji wasn't about to relax his efforts now.

12

Now that Xu's speech was out of the way, things went along smoothly, even enthusiastically. Some people made comments to the effect that Director Zhao's criticism was very important and had a great personal impact on their own thinking, while others called for an end to all this fawning on things Western. Someone even harped on about how the kids were dressing nowadays and bitterly denounced those disgraceful foreign films the stories of which were just a pack of lies. Naturally, there were also those who wanted to offer Xu "a little comradely advice". All in all, the meeting progressed in a lively fashion.

Ji spent most of the discussion preening his thick grey hair, occasionally smiling indulgently or butting in with a stray comment or two.

Then to top it all Zhu even volunteered a statement.

"I agreed with what people have been saying about the Director's remarks. His comments were both important and timely. Although he may have only been talking about one article in particular, I believe that what he said has much broader implications, and I feel I have personally benefitted from his speech."

Hearing the usually flippant Zhu carry on in such an orthodox manner the others also became inordinately solemn. Qin Tongtong curled her lip disdainfully.

"Of more immediate significance and value has been the involvement of the Party Committee of the Academy itself." Zhu's expression was drawn and the severity of his mien and serious tone of voice gave the impression that every word that issued from his lips was the product of careful and profound reflection.

"The Centre has only recently resumed operations, and things have been done somewhat hastily. The people working here have been brought in from various other workplaces, and as we all spend most of our time working in our own fields we rarely consult or even communicate with our colleagues. In circumstances such as these it is well-nigh impossible to avoid one-sidedness. So I think it would be highly beneficial for us all to meet more regularly in study sessions like this. Of course, as Old Xu has said, meetings are time-consuming. But if it helps us in our work then I think it's worth it."

Zhu spoke with such apparent sincerity that you could be excused for thinking that he had harboured a burning desire for political meetings all his life. The torrent continued to pour forth unhindered.

"We all must recognize the fact that in pursuing the study of foreign literature we are constantly facing problems of political standpoint and orientation. Since 1976 we have overturned the isolationist policies which kept China a closed country for so long. And ever since the slogan 'let's liberate our thinking' was formulated at the Third Plenum, we have witnessed almost daily changes and innovations on all work fronts. No one doubts the vital necessity of importing foreign technology. And, of course, cultural exchange has its place in the scheme of things, as does the gradual introduction of foreign literature to Chinese readers. The problem of how this is to be done, however, remains a crucial one. We must be quite clear as to what our critical standpoint should be."

Zhu's tone was now not unlike someone who was delivering an academic paper.

"Some comrades are labouring under the misconception that whatever is Western is good. For them the mere words America, Japan and Europe conjure up visions of private cars, refrigerators, superhighways and skyscrapers. It's as though the outside world were a materialist's nirvana. But as we all know, the capitalist world has its decadent side as well. My trip to Japan in April this year provided me with some first-hand evidence of this."

Zhu waxed eloquent as he hit on the subject of his trip to Japan. His audience perked up too. Even Director Ji found himself taking a real interest in what was being said.

"Just take Japanese department stores, for example. All right, everyone agrees that they're out of this world. A team of pretty young women led by the manager bows respectfully the moment you enter the door, chorusing 'welcome to our store' and 'thank you for coming'. There's a motto they use which says: 'The customer is emperor'. It is truly unbelievable. You go into one of those places and they really treat you as if you were an emperor. I'd be telling a lie if I didn't admit it's a great feeling."

Tongtong laughed out loud.

"So what are you trying to tell us, that you've been emperor of Japan?"

"I know it might sound silly, but you'd have to experience it to believe it." Zhu was getting carried away with himself. "On the other hand, being emperor is not as easy as you might think. In the first place, you need money. Even then you can find yourself in a real bind."

"Come off it. Don't think we're all bumpkins just because we haven't been overseas!" Tongtong wasn't going to let him get away with that. "Everyone knows that in capitalist countries if you have money you can do anything."

"I'm not kidding," Zhu retorted. "One time two Japanese friends asked me to join them for a cup of coffee on a rooftop cafe. We took the elevator up to this very posh place, and as I was drinking in the ambience in the reception area we were approached by three very smart-looking fellows who were wearing matching tailored suits. They asked us if we would care to seat ourselves on the left side of the room, with such courtesy as to be bordering on the servile. Then just as we were about to comply, another three men jumped out in front of us. One was grotesquely fat, another comically thin and the third a midget. They were decked out in incredibly garish clothes, like clowns in a circus. They indicated that they wanted us to sit on the right side of the room, bowing and scraping all the while. It turned out that this cafe had two bosses, each of them ran one side; and they'd both hired people to hustle customers for them. The hired hands started fighting over us and they ended up screaming and yelling at each other. To top it all off, the loudspeakers in the place were blaring out this really vile music. I was totally fed up and didn't know what side we ought to choose. I assumed that they were paid per head for every 'emperor' they managed to pull in. If we went over to the left, we'd disappoint the right and vice versa. So there we were, three 'emperors' without a clue as to what we should do.''

"So where did you end up?" Tongtong couldn't restrain her curiosity.

"End up?" Zhu repeated, rubbing his forehead. "I discussed the situation with my two friends and we agreed that they should not let the visit of a Chinese guest exacerbate factional tendencies among the Japanese people. So we decided to employ the principle of 'equal distribution'. I suggested that one of them could treat me to a cup on the left side of the cafe and one on the right. In that way everyone would be kept happy."

His listeners burst out laughing.

"And one of those 'emperors' in particular knew just how to fleece the other two," Shen Zhiye said chuckling.

"You wouldn't believe it," Zhu rushed to his own defence, "but I ended up losing out on the deal."

"You mean they made you pay?" Tongtong was intrigued.

"Do you have any idea how much it costs to eat out in Japan? They'd already treated me to dinner and by the time we got to the cafe they only had enough money between them for three cups of coffee. I had no choice but to pay for the second lot of coffee out of my government-issue pocket-money. I had just enough to cover the bill, but boy was my wife annoyed. She nagged me about it for month. 'Everyone else brings things home from overseas trips. But not you, oh no. Instead of buying something we could use in the house, you spend your time running around drinking dishwater.' You wouldn't believe what a bumpkin my wife is — she literally throws up whenever she drinks coffee! I'm not joking."

By this stage Zhu was completely oblivious of the fact that this was a study meeting, and he illustrated his comments with dramatic gestures and funny faces, much to everyone's delight. A passerby daresay would have thought they were listening to a comic dialogue or something.

As the laughter died down Ji Zikuan finally came to his senses and realized how far Zhu had strayed off the track. None of this had anything to do with the meeting. He wiped the smile off his face. Zhu, on the other hand, had worn himself out with his performance, and he apologized hastily.

"Dear me, I really have gone on, haven't I? I'd better stop here."

Ji gave a curt smile and surveyed the assembly.

"Ah Comrade Ye Fei. Why don't you say something?"

Ye blushed a deep crimson.

"I agree with what everyone has said so far, and have absolutely nothing to add."

13

Shen Zhiye had crumpled the speech outline in his pocket into a little ball as he listened to Zhu's amusing tales of Japan. When Ye Fei finished he began his own statement slowly, but with considerable assurance.

"I have just a few things to say. I want to add my voice to those who have praised the timeliness and importance of Director Zhao's remarks. I also agree that it was timely and necessary for the Academy Party Committee to have taken a personal role in the political study of our Foreign Literature Research Centre."

Having stated his basic though hardly original position, Shen considerately paused long enough to allow Yang to record it in his notebook.

"But the question remains: how should we approach foreign literature research? How should we be writing on the subject? Is it absolutely necessary that we come together to meet, study and hold discussions like this? Now I heartily concur with Director Zhao that we must not grovel at the feet of foreigners. What's so great about foreigners, anyway? After all, they don't have an extra head on their shoulders!"

This remark caused general merriment. Shen lacked Zhu's mischievous sense of humour, and what made people laugh in this instance was not any intentional wit on Shen's part, but rather his ponderous, academic locution and Sichuanese drawl. When the ban had been lifted on the play 'Press-ganged', someone gave him the nickname Headman Shen.

"What's so funny? I'm serious. Foreigners have their strong points, but they also have their weaknesses, you know. We must learn things like science, technology and management from them. If we didn't, we'd be like the proverbial frog at the bottom of the well with absolutely no understanding of the outside world apart from the small patch of sky directly above its head. But at the same time, we must avoid being tainted by them. To imbibe sour milk but think we're drinking cream is another error in dealing with things foreign. One, the frog in the well, is a mistaken leftist way of dealing with things; the latter a rightist capitulationist approach. Both are detrimental to the Party, the nation and the people. Doesn't everyone agree with me that such behaviour should be criticized?"

Shen Zhiye flapped his hands around in imitation of a frog as he spoke and the room exploded in laughter once more.

"I've never been abroad, and I've never wanted to go tramping about in foreign lands. Several days ago, I saw this American football game on TV. You should have seen those American spectators! Their jawbones never stopped moving; they ate throughout the entire game. In my opinion, there's something barbarous about that."

Another wave of laughter swept the room. But Shen continued in all earnestness.

"Nothing funny about what I'm saying here. In my view, those foreigners are real primitives. We Chinese are an orderly people with well-regulated life-styles. We have three meals a day, and only little children eat snacks. From this you can tell who's civilized and who isn't."

"Old Shen, I think you're talking through your hat," Zhu Sheng objected. "How can you judge a civilization on the basis of when its people snack?"

Shen forged on.

"Just listen to what I'm saying. Man's eating habits are a direct reflection of the evolutionary process. It was a great milestone in the progress of human civilization when man started cooking meat, and another when he started sitting down at a table three times a day instead of feeding anytime and anyplace. If you don't believe me, take a trip to the zoo and have a look at the way the chimps and gorillas stuff their faces from morning to night."

The room rocked with laughter again.

Ji tried to draw Shen back to the matter at hand.

"We need not concern ourselves here with the foreigners' level of civilization. Could we limit our discussion to our own affairs?"

"Right, right, our own affairs." Shen continued, "The way some of our own comrades go about fawning all over foreigners is incredibly offensive. As we all know, the Chinese people are generally very obedient. If you hang up a sign saying 'Reception Room for Foreign Guests Only', for example, what Chinese would dare enter? On the other hand, some regulations are quite unreasonable and an affront to our sense of national dignity."

Although Shen was visibly agitated, he had such an even temper that he continued to speak in his usual, slow-paced manner.

"Last year, I was sent to Chongqing on some business. I arrived on the Mid-Autumn Festival. The fact that I was away from home on that day of family reunion made me feel a bit lonely. The people at my hotel told me that in the surrounding villages they had revived the Lantern Festival, and they told me the best place to view the lanterns was on the hill at the Zhang Family Park. I took a bus there, bought an entrance ticket and sauntered in. The wonderfully luminous moon that was hanging in the sky bathed the whole park in a mellow light.

"It had been years since I had paid a visit to my birthplace and the words of the poet came to mind, 'Never has the dew been so luminous as today; nowhere is the moon so round as over one's own hometown'."

Shen's head bobbed with the rhythms of the verse as he recited. Qin Tongtong collapsed on Ye Fei's shoulder in a fit of the giggles.

Shen paid her no heed.

"I advanced up the hill in the garden and discovered that there were already more than a hundred people gathered on the hill-top to view the moon and enjoy the sight of the lanterns below. I found myself a good vantage-point. The lights of the villages in the mountains were reflected beautifully on the rippling waves of the Jialing River."

Yang Changming had stopped taking notes. None of this was suitable for recording.

"But 'short-lived is the beauty of the world', and just as everyone was excitedly waiting for the appearance of the lanterns, a number of men dressed in blue Mao-jackets appeared on the scene and arrogantly began ordering everyone off the hill. At first, no one could work out what had happened. There was even some speculation that the park was on fire. Some fire! One fellow of about thirty finally pushed his way to the front and announced in a righteous tone, 'All right, everyone off! We've got some foreign guests coming to view the lanterns, so get lost and be quick about it. Hear?' "

"What a nerve!" Zhu was beside himself with indignation.

"Exactly! And such a big hill, too. Why several thousand people could have stood there together. Why did the Chinese have to leave? Everyone crowded around that fellow but he refused to listen. He said he was acting on 'orders from above', so we had no choice but to obey. Some people tried to trick their children à la Ah Q, saying, 'Come on, kids. Your old man'll take you down there to watch. Chongqing's such a big city, we can see the lanterns anywhere we go!' Others were quick to remind each other that it was bad luck to come across 'foreign devils' on a festival day. We can't even enjoy ourselves in peace."

"What did you do?" someone asked.

"Me? I was just a bystander. Once the others had all been driven away I hid behind a pine tree at the foot of the hill and waited for the show to begin. Before long several lackeys carrying rattan chairs, teacups and pots came along, followed not long after by two foreigners in the company of three Chinese, chatting merrily as they walked along. These escorts gestured in the most obsequious fashion for the foreigners to ascend the hill. When they got there, they seated themselves and began sipping tea and enjoying the lanterns in complete tranquillity. What an insult for them to have chased away a hundred Chinese just so a couple of foreigners could have a good time. I simply cannot understand how we can tolerate such fawning on foreigners. Can any of you explain why this is allowed to happen?"

Again everyone had completely forgotten what they were supposed to be discussing, though this time it was anger rather than humour that distracted them. Just as Ji was about to do something about this de-railed train of thought, Shen Zhiye slipped in his concluding remarks.

"Thus I feel that Director Zhao's comments on worshipping at the feet of Westerners were both important and timely. They can be taken as advice not only to those of us involved in the study of foreign literature, but also to people in other fields. I, I just wanted to share my understanding of this question with you all. If I am guilty of any errors, I would appreciate it if you would correct me."

14

Shen's speech had a dramatic "ripple-effect" on everyone at the meeting. He had touched on a raw nerve: that of national dignity, and everyone had something to say on the subject. To a man they denounced servility towards foreigners. Some related personal experiences and slights, others repeated stories they'd heard from reliable sources. Yang abandoned all attempts to take notes, and Ji felt that things had got out of control again.

In the heat of the discussion someone singled out the younger generation for being particularly subject to "unhealthy foreign tendencies". They commented that the young were badly brought up and generally failed to make anything of themselves or bring credit to their families. This was a particularly touchy topic with one member of the Centre: Qin Tongtong, and she exploded:

"Okay, let's not start harping on 'young people nowadays', all right? You guys come down on us every time we have a meeting."

"Comrade Qin, Tongtong, don't take it so personally," said the person who had raised the subject. "I wasn't talking about you."

"So what if you were? Sticks and stones may break my bones, but names can never hurt me. Anyway, it's quite the fashion these days to complain about 'today's youth', isn't it? All those handy labels people have invented, the 'fallen generation', the 'lost generation', the 'wounded generation', 'wasted generation', 'faithless generation' — there's a million of them. Everyone bandies them about, but no one ever asks who's to blame? Don't think for one moment that we chose this fate."

Everything had been going so well until this subject reared its ugly head. Ji hastily tried to smooth things over.

"All right, there's no need to dwell on the subject. Tongtong, I think it's your turn to make a statement."

"What am I supposed to say? I've never written anything and anyhow, the criticism wasn't aimed at me. It's none of my business. I'm not involved!" Tongtong was still fuming.

Ji had once been her father's subaltern, though they hadn't seen much of each other in recent years. Whenever Ji visited the family on public holidays or during the festive season, Tongtong would address him as "uncle". In reaction to her present behaviour, he assumed a somewhat condescending and avuncular tone of voice.

"Come now, Tongtong, how can you say it isn't any of your business? You're a member of this study group like everyone else. Although you might only have been involved in administrative matters so far, if you study very hard you too can write articles!"

"Write myself into someone's bad books, you mean!"

Ji had heard on the grapevine that Qin Tongtong was an impudent character, but this was the first time he'd been subjected to one of her outbursts. He could tell from her tone that she could create a very unpleasant scene if he pushed too hard, so he cut her short with a request.

"Now then, why don't you just tell us what you think about the subject of this study session?"

· "What do you want, the truth or more lies?" She was being deliberately provocative.

"The truth, of course. The Party has always encouraged people to speak frankly and honestly."

"Great. That's what I was hoping you'd say. In the first place I don't know any foreign languages, and secondly, I know nothing about foreign literature — after all, I got into this place through the back door...."

"Comrade, no, Tongtong, no one's ever said you got in through the back door," Zhu spoke in his most amicable tone.

"Give me a break. I know how you all talk about me behind my back." She gave a disarming smile and continued as saucily as ever. "I don't give a hoot what you say about me. You have to earn your bowl of rice one way or another. So what if I don't know beans about foreign literature — how many of the people who run this academy know anything about academies?"

This was too much for Ji Zikuan.

"Just hold on a minute. You can't go around making such sweeping generalizations about the leadership."

"Very well, but an awful lot of them are rank amateurs who publically admit they're 'hardened old ignoramuses'. And does Director Zhao know about foreign literature? Can you tell me how many representative works of modernism, surrealism or black humour he's actually read? The truth of the matter is that he probably sits there all day long listening to the reports he gets from the art and literature section of the Ministry. Daresay he took one look at the word 'black' and figured anything associated with that word had to be bad, so he decided to criticize it."

It was left to Ji to protect the good name of the leadership, since no one else would· say a word.

"How can you say that? How do you know that Director Zhao hasn't read Xu's article?"

"Oh come on, everyone knows about Director Zhao," she laughed ironically. "When we were told to discuss the concept that 'practice is the sole criterion of truth' last year, Director Zhao was the one who immediately condemned it as being 'propounded by people with ulterior motives'; 'this is equivalent to defaming the red flag of the Party' he cried, 'it's de-Maoification'. Those were his exact words, but as soon as the Third Party Plenum came out in public support for the slogan, Zhao was forced to admit that he'd never read the articles on the subject in the first place. Isn't that proof of what type of man he is?"

There was a threatening tone in Ji's voice as he asked her:

"Does that mean you disagree with the spirit of Director Zhao's speech?"

Tongtong looked at the gallery of faces and then flashed Ji a smile.

"Now, don't you go accusing me of thought-error. I never said that. Would you write down what I'm about to say, Old Yang? My formal statement is as follows: I completely agree with Director Zhao, and the Party Committee's decision to lead this study session and with, well, with whatever it is that the people upstairs want us to agree with."

Ji could see it was hopeless. He forced himself to smile.

"You're quite the little rebel, aren't you?"

"I wouldn't dare rebel. I was into all of that stupidity ten years ago, but then I didn't know any better. All I got for my troubles were illness and illiteracy. No one could make me rebel today. I've seen it all and no one can fool me anymore."

"Tongtong, I'm afraid you're an ideologically very mixed up young woman." Ji knit his brows and shook his grey head with a sigh.

"Uncle Ji," Qin blurted out and smiled, "Please don't worry about me. I promise not to get into any trouble. I'll try and be a bit more slippery from now on. 'Reveal but a fraction of your thoughts, 'tis unnecessary to speak for real'."

Ji was livid. But there was absolutely nothing he could do about it. He looked at his watch. It was already eleven thirty, time for lunch. If he didn't hurry off to the canteen, all the good dishes would have been snapped up.

"Today's meeting has been a great success, very lively. We'll resume again at nine o'clock tomorrow morning."

15

The meeting over, everyone headed home.

Zhu Sheng, Shen Zhiye and Qin Tongtong were all going in the same direction. They laughed and chatted as they left the Temple. Indeed, there was much to talk about.

"Tongtong, you were great. What an onslaught. Wonderful," Zhu approved heartily.

Tossing her long hair, Qin replied:

"Oh, but you take the cake. How you carried on! From 'emperors' to 'equal distribution', from China to Japan. A nice bit of shadow-boxing, if you ask me."

Shen, who was pushing his bike in front of them, turned around.

"Zhu certainly proved his originality today."

Everyone laughed.

"I was only trying to stimulate the discussion." Zhu glanced slyly at Shen from the corner of his eye. "But the best was that line of yours about foreigners being savages. Brilliant, absolutely brilliant. That was a state-of-the-art condemnation of West-worshipping if I ever heard one!"

Shen gave a dismissive wave of the hand.

"To tell you the truth, I gave quite a lot of thought last night to what I was going to say. I realized that I had absolutely no idea what was expected of us. There was no way I could get out of speaking; and I really didn't want to take it. Thank heavens for Zhu's little talk; it was like a light in the dark."

"But that Zhang Wei really makes me sick," Qin Tongtong butted in. "He's such a toady. This business has nothing to do with him, so what does he think he's doing, mea-culpaing all over the place like that? He's always the first to speak, I don't know what he's trying to prove."

"Chacun a son goût," Zhu replied. "What I can't understand is why he's such a timid creature."

Shen tossed a glance over his shoulder.

"You people don't know Zhang's background. He's had his share of grief. If you ask me, he's still suffering from a persecution complex."

"Yeah, then why does he have to make such a liar of himself?" Qin Tongtong's tone was disdainful.

"You don't know how lucky you've been, little miss," Shen sighed. "No matter what you do or say, no one would dare lift a finger against you. You can even get away with insulting the director. Zhang Wei's hardly in the same position."

"Besides," Zhu added, "he's dying to get into the Party."

"Zhang Wei? Applying for Party membership?" Qin was frankly incredulous. She sneered, "The man's scared of his own shadow. He doesn't have a friend in the world and never dares speak the truth, unless of course it's across the pillow to his old lady."

"Tongtong, really, you shouldn't say such things," Shen spoke earnestly.

"Why's that?"

"When Zhang was declared a 'suspected enemy agent', his wife divorced him. All he has left now is a daughter. It's quite a sad story."

"How tragic!" Qin sighed. "But don't forget, people who deserve to be pitied inevitably have their more unsavoury aspects."

Shen shook his head lugubriously.

"Tongtong, you're such a cynic."

"Me? Look around you, cynicism is the product of the age!" Qin mounted her bike and sped off with a wave. "See you at tomorrow's meeting, oh mighty researchers!"

"She really is a 'liberated woman'," Zhu remarked. "She never has to think twice about what she says and hasn't a care in the world."

Shen laughed drily as he watched her bicycle disappear in the crowd. "Hardly. You're telling me a 28-year-old spinster has no worries!"

"She certainly has a sharp tongue."

"Good luck to whoever ends up with her."

As they unhurriedly pedalled along, Zhu suddenly remembered the sweet-and-sour fish his wife had prepared for him and warmly invited Shen home. Shen accepted and they rode on together towards Zhu's home.

"How do you think this is going to end?" Zhu asked.

"Oh, I think it'll just run its course. Party Central has promised there'd be no more political campaigns or personal attacks on people. Those who were expected to make self-crits had, and those who had to make statements did that too. What do you want?"

"Guess you're right. But if this thing keeps dragging on, we'll never get back to work." Zhu was in the middle of composing a major critique of Japanese historical fiction.

"The only thing we have to worry about is Director Ji. If he's dissatisfied, Yang wouldn't be able to let things lie. They might decide to work on a few people and persuade them to make more speeches in some other meeting."

"Oh no!" Zhu cried out as though he'd suddenly realized something. "No wonder Yang invited me to his house yesterday for dumplings. Do you think he's got me targeted for an ideological workover?"

"Sure," Shen laughed. "He's probably trying to make you into a political activist."

"Anything but that. I couldn't bear it."

"I don't know about that. Here you are inviting me to your home. How do I know you haven't already been assigned to work on me?"

Zhu laughed.

16

Yang had no idea that the others considered the meeting a giant farce. He'd probably have been hurt, too, had he known how cruelly Zhu and Shen were mocking him for his innocent dinner invitation. On the other hand, maybe not.

The hostility he faced now was nothing compared to what he had to put up with when he was first put in charge of ideological work at the Centre.

Not long after he was made commissar, he decided to pay a call on Xu Minghui and his wife. It was snowing, and it was a particularly cold and windy evening. They'd just been rehabilitated and Xu assigned to the Centre; Yang, whose work included looking after the rehabs, was worried that they hadn't yet gotten around to installing a stove for heating. The couple were known to be rather careless homemakers and besides, they were southerners; even if they had installed a stove, they might not know how to use it. Yang piled on several layers of thick clothing and was just heading out of the door when his wife yelled out:

"Where are you going so late?"

"To see Old Xu."

"You really are a considerate one, aren't you?" Her thick lips contorted into a sneer.

Yang couldn't bear to look at his wife's face for one second longer. "I won't be long," he replied, taking off on his bicycle.

Xu lived some four kilometres away. When at last Yang placed a frozen foot on his doorstep, Xu opened the door slightly and gave the visitor a suspicious once-over.

"Well, if it isn't Comrade Yang."

"I've come to see if you've got a stove."

"A stove? Why yes, we do."

They exchanged a few more pleasantries, but Xu didn't invite Yang in. Finally, with an "I'll be seeing you", he closed the door in Yang's face.

Yang was stunned. Xu had literally left him out in the cold and what's more, he didn't seem at all embarrassed by what he'd done; rather, he gave Yang the feeling that he was in the wrong for coming around in the first place.

Riding home with the wind at his back, Yang could have reached his house fairly quickly. But the thought of his wife's fat, jeering face prompted him instead to take a roundabout route by People's Square. He circled the plaza before turning homewards.

"Now then, have you successfully transmitted the warmth of the Party to the hearts of the masses?" Lin was already lying snugly in bed.

Yang shot her a look but refrained from saying anything.

"How much warmth do you have in store for these people?" She spoke sarcastically.

"What I have, I give!" he snapped, feeding a couple of coal briquets into the stove.

"People's hearts are like blocks of ice these days. You really think you can thaw them out? I don't."

"Well I do."

Lin knew they would never see eye to eye on this.

"Why don't you just give up? Besides, your own family might appreciate some of this warmth we've been hearing so much about."

"We're talking about my work!" Yang exclaimed angrily.

"So why take it out on me?"

Yang was so upset he couldn't get to sleep. Only much later, when he got to know Xu better and won his trust did he feel somewhat consoled.

At the time, however, this sort of thing was always happening. Occasionally, Yang's self-confidence was undermined. Then, he'd feel guilty and curse his own weakness.

"This is the retribution of history. I have no right to complain," he often reminded himself. "The first duty of the political worker during this special period of restoring order from chaos is to recover the faith of the masses."

Yang was a creature of habit.

While others did their research and wrote their articles, Yang ran between one bureaucratic office and the next trying to fix things up for the rehabs. He went all out over the most trivial matters. Just to help Wu secure a two-room apartment, Yang must have made more than a hundred trips to various "concerned organizations", pleading, cajoling, pulling every string possible until he managed to produce a set of housekeys for Wu.

When his wife caught wind of this, however, she was mightily annoyed.

"If you're so good at arranging housing, why don't you do something about getting a decent place for your own family?"

It was true that their place was horribly cramped. Once, when his son was six, the boy tried to find his way through the clutter to the bathroom in the middle of the night and ended up cracking his head on the corner of a table. It needed three stitches; his son's forehead was scarred to this day. No wonder his wife was so testy on this subject. Still, it had never occurred to him to include his own family on the list of people for whom he was trying to arrange better accomodation.

Thus it was in the face of mockery and insult from outsiders and taunts and gripes from his wife that Yang was quietly cultivating that little fallow field that was the Foreign Literature Research Centre with the plough of his sincere, red heart.

Yang never allowed himself to be satisfied with his achievements. On the other hand, he felt that ever since the Third Plenum, it was as though a warm spring breeze had blown into the chilly grounds of the Temple. At last, people's thinking had been liberated from the prison of dogmatic Maoism, inter-personal relationships had warmed up a bit and the gulf between the Party and the people was gradually lessening. Naturally, problems continued to pile up. All kinds of new contradictions had arisen. Yang wasn't bothered by this, for if there were no problems or contradictions to tackle, there'd be no point in doing ideological work. The important thing was that people's trust for the Party was returning; their hearts were opening up to the Party. Already, he could feel his work becoming easier.

How ironic that just at this point this nasty business about Xu's article came up and the Academy's Party Office got all tangled up in the affair. If not handled properly, things might really blow up. And then there was Ji — the kind of political commissar who made up in officiousness for what he lacked in amiability. Yang was quite worried that Ji's attitude would harden, totally alienating Xu and the others and creating a real mess. Just the day before, there'd been an awkward stalemate. Thank goodness Ji at least understood that the art of leadership occasionally calls for a little flexibility. By working behind the scenes, he'd avoided a major confrontation today. On the other hand, today's session was nothing to brag about. It had basically been an exhibition of verbal acrobatics: slippery declarations, a united front of protectiveness towards Xu, a far-fetched discussion of practical nitty-gritty dragging the discussion down from its intended theoretical heights to the level of complete nonsense. Was this really what was meant by "animated discussion"? It was like one of those undecipherable, weirdo abstract paintings which leave one's head spinning.

No, that wasn't really the right comparison. There was nothing undecipherable about this particular scene. It was pure realism. What could possibly be more typical of life in the late '70s than the carefully arranged self-criticism in which the speaker appears sincere as all get-out while skirting the topic and speaking as colourfully as possible? True, people were cautiously tiptoeing outside the boundaries imposed by doctrinaire Maoism yet underneath the rainbowed garb of "liberated thought" lurked lingering fear. This isn't how things were supposed to be; it was hardly proof that ideological education had been successful.

What was Ji really thinking? Could he be pleased with himself over the study session which he had chaired personally? Was he happy with what everyone had said?

Yang decided to go and see his boss. He wanted to work

out with him, or at least receive some orders from him on how to handle tomorrow's session.

When Yang arrived, Ji was buttoning his tunic, for he was about to step out to another meeting. He went on dressing as Yang spoke, only replying on his way out of the door.

"As I see it, while one couldn't exactly call today's meeting exemplary, it didn't go so badly either."

"Wu Tianxiang still hasn't spoken."

"He will." Ji laughed confidently and clapped Yang on the shoulder. "Take it easy, Yang my boy. If you've got nothing else on this afternoon, why don't you take the rest of the day off? I've heard that your wife often nags you."

17

With stomachs full, Zhu Sheng and Shen Zhiye cycled over to Wu's place. They were feeling light-hearted, for they'd convinced themselves that the worst was over.

The Wus had just finished lunch as well and mother and daughter-in-law were cleaning up. Sucking on his pipe, Wu stood to one side, being kept busy by a 6-or 7-year-old boy.

"Uncle, let me see your pipe." The little boy wore tight knit pants of light yellow with a white stripe down the side. He was a cutie — clean, chubby and full of fun.

"No, no, it isn't something for children to play with." Wu retreated and held the pipe out of reach.

"Stop annoying your uncle!" The old lady made a pretence of scolding the boy: he was her only grandson and she rarely had a chance to see him.

"Let's go! I wanna draw a picture of you." The kid tugged at Wu's sleeve and tried to drag him into the inner room.

"All right, all right." Wu had little choice but to give in.

"What a little trouble-maker! Just see if I don't chase you right out of the house!" Naturally, the old lady didn't mean a word of it.

Wen Suyu entered laughing.

"Kick him out? But he's such a sweetie-pie! And Tianxiang adores him—look how he obeys his every command."

"Humph. One child is more trouble than a dozen grown men." She was speaking from experience. Still, this time she didn't mean what she said.

The boy marched into the room, scrambled up onto the chair and, kneeling there, yelled for some paper. Wu hastily moved his books and manuscripts out of danger's way and finding a piece of scrap paper, placed it on the desk for the boy, who appeared disgruntled. He refused to budge until he was given a sheet of the good rice paper Wu reserved for calligraphy and painting. Resignedly, Wu dug up an old painting brush.

"Ink!" the boy commanded, affecting the air of a great master.

Wu handed over the ink.

"Sit down! You're not allowed to move."

Wu sat. Unlike your run-of-the-mill portrait artist, who occasionally glances up at the model, the boy concentrated his entire attention on his drawing, all the while delivering a running commentary.

"First, I draw a circle. That's your head. And this is your hair. There's not much of that, so I'll just put in a few lines. These are your eyes. I'll make 'em bigger than they are. Auntie says I've got bigger eyes than you. I'm better looking too! Now, I'm drawing another little circle. That's your pipe and this is the smoke...."

Zhu Sheng and Shen Zhiye arrived just as Wu was in the middle of his "punishment by portraiture". He stood up to greet them.

"Don't move!" screamed his nephew.

"Okay, okay." He resumed his seat.

The guests went over to the desk and examined the picture.

"Ah, an abstract!" Zhu chuckled.

"Watch out kid, you open yourself to criticism when you start playing with modernism," joked Shen.

"What do you mean?"

"Nothing. Get on with it."

The guests plopped themselves down on the modest, hand-crafted sofa. As he was under strict orders not to move, Wu had no choice but to shout to his wife to bring in some tea.

Anticipating the request, she entered with steaming mugs while he was still in mid-sentence and politely placed them on the little tea-table. She brought out a box of sweets as well and then tried to coax the child out of the room. The boy squirmed stubbornly, and flatly refused to leave until the masterpiece was finished. Helpless, Wen Suyu left the room.

The boy waved his brush about as he listened to the grown-ups' conversation, obviously quite pleased with his performance.

"What's your opinion, Wu? What do you think of today's meeting?" Shen asked.

Zhu butted in before Wu had a chance to reply.

"All in all, I think it went pretty well. Everyone spoke up and there was an animated discussion. It met the basic requirements."

Wu sighed.

"But did anybody really say what they meant?"

Peeling the wrapping off one of the sweets, Zhu replied with an indulgent smile, "Assume they did; anyway, 'Within truth lies falsehood.' Or let's say it was all a pack of lies, within falsehood lies a grain of truth. Truth or fallacy, it's all in the realm of fantasy."

"You know, there are times when people just have to lie," Shen added.

The boy stared at them and cried out indignantly:

"Our teachers say you're never supposed to lie."

The adults panicked. Zhu was the first to react.

"And they're absolutely right, my boy. One must never lie. If you lie your daddy and mummy won't love you anymore!"

Wen, who'd been sitting just outside the door, rushed in and bundled the child out of the room.

The men sat in embarrassed silence. Finally, Shen spoke up.

"Little kids mustn't lie, of course. But it's different with adults. Sometimes you can't help it. It's unavoidable."

Wu sighed.

"Party Central has issued a thousand and one directives telling people to stop lying. But we're still surrounded by lies. It's all a triumph of hypocrisy. What will happen to us all in the end if things are allowed to go on like this?"

"Come, come, Wu, don't take things so seriously." Zhu comforted the older man. "Ever since the Third Plenum adopted the principle of 'seeking truth from facts' things have been getting better. So what if we occasionally have to cough up a lie or two; look at it as the unfortunate consequence of special circumstances."

Shen broke in. "Anyway, even with falsehood lies some truth. Provided that the leadership can hear the 'music beyond the strings' or discover the 'meanings within meanings', they will discover the truth beyond the falsehood."

Wu shook his head in disagreement.

When he was younger, Wu was well known in his field for incisive thinking and reasoned arguments. He was also famous, however, for his conceit and arrogance. Some people even accused him of being a 'solitary flower inebriated by its own fragrance'. Shen, for one, was sufficiently overawed by this brief exchange and concluded that Wu was one who saw things more deeply than most. He kept the cynical complaints in check. Zhu, being younger and exuberantly self-confident himself, persisted in offering advice.

"What's more, when we lie, we're not doing so with malicious intent. It's certainly not like in capitalist societies where people wallow in lies and hypocrisy. Politicians, given to deception and rivalry, assiduously avoid the truth. Businessmen are the worst of all, coaxing the money right out of your pocket with all their honeyed words. In those societies, people wear masks all the time. These few little taradiddles of ours, on the other hand, are simply a way of getting by!"

Wu looked up. "So the way you see things, it's all right to lie."

"Maybe not, but it is unavoidable." Zhu was getting worked up. "Anyway, faced with these people like Director Zhao or study meetings like this, you've no choice but to lie."

"This world we live in, with all its speeches, all its meetings is a blend of truth and falsehood. If we can just take truth as the guiding principle and falsehood as a supplementary one, it's not such a bad compromise." Shen looked so earnest that Zhu burst out laughing.

"That's rich! 'Take truth as the guiding principle and falsehood as the supplementary one.' Brilliant."

Even Wu couldn't keep from smiling.

"So what you fellows are trying to say is that I should formulate a 'blend of truth and falsehood'?"

"Oh, I'd hardly be so presumptuous as to tell you what to do," Zhu said. "You're the head of the Centre, a respected scholar and a Party member. We're only the masses; we wouldn't dare advise you to lie."

"It's incredible, isn't it, to think how much things have loosened up," Shen added. "Just three years ago, people would never dare touch on such subjects. Try it and bam, they'd hit you over the head with 'class struggle'. Why don't we just drop it, eh? This series of meetings will be over soon enough. You'll speak tomorrow, Ji will sum up and we can all congratulate ourselves on a successful and victorious meeting!"

Wu filled his pipe and drew on it earnestly, sitting silently behind a screen of smoke.

18

The room was suffused with the soft glow from a tiny desk lamp. A sense of peace reigned and the glass top of the desk was clean and ready for its master to lay out his pen and paper. Wu sat in the lounge chair by the desk, his eyes shut. The cheekbones on his elongated face stood out, his lips were pressed tightly together and the lines on his forehead appeared as though etched with a knife. He looked old and tired as little wisps of fragrant smoke drifted up from his pipe bowl.

While Wu sat there, his thoughts crested and fell like waves in the sea. The events of the past two days replayed themselves before his eyes: every word, gesture and incident of those meetings re-appeared vividly in his mind. There was Ji Zikuan, bossing people about from his lofty heights; Yang Changming with all his well-intentioned anxiety and concern for getting things right; Zhang Wei's stammering and his Diderot; Xu Minghui's tongue-in-cheek *mea culpa*; Zhu's tales of Japan; Shen Zhiye and his moon over the homeland; Tongtong's permed hair tossing this way and that and her perennial comment "what's all this?" . . . It was so much like the crazy montage of a modern Western film, so confusing to the eye, yet, beneath all the razzmatazz, lay an undeniable consistency and meaning.

From the other room came the sound of furniture being

moved. They were clearing a place for the new refrigerator. This was his son's idea. It had been too cramped in the kitchen with it, and besides, it would get dirty too quickly there. Better that they put it in the living room where it could give the place a fashionable look of modernity. His wife was both cheering squad and obedient servant to their son. Their younger son was jumping around enthusiastically, enjoying the fun. The three of them exhibited an enviable, almost frightening amount of energy and interest in this trivial task, one that they had been going at for two hours already.

Wu's mother was the only remaining opponent to the refrigerator. She had balked at the idea of buying the thing from the start. Now, she satisfied herself by showering the others with a stream of invective from the sidelines.

"What's the point of buying this ridiculously cumbersome thing, I ask you? You can't carry it, you can't even lift it. If we had to move house tomorrow, we'd have to sell it."

"Ma, why must you go on about moving all the time?" asked Wen Suyu.

"It's not that I want to move, it's just that we've already had to so many times the very thought gives me the jitters. How many times have we had to move in the last twenty years?! Just think about it. From the flat to the house, from the city to the countryside and back again. We've had to move every time they've had a campaign. And every time we moved, our things end up in a mess. It still kills me to think of that gorgeous wardrobe; the wood was so good. We didn't get even half the price we paid for it when we sold it to the state-run second-hand store."

The door to the outer room was closed and they were speaking fairly softly. Nonetheless, Wu could hear everything they were saying.

The old lady couldn't help fretting, it was true; she still couldn't quite believe that after twenty years of persecution, her son had finally been given the political stamp of approval. When they'd moved into this new apartment she had felt as though it was some impossible dream. Even after her son's "rehabilitation", she never genuinely smiled or laughed, she was so afraid this blissful dream might end abruptly at any minute.

If those with one foot in the grave were so preoccupied with fears for the future, how could the middle-aged, with the road of life stretching ahead of them, not worry as well? It was probably such lingering fear which had prompted Xu, who only a few days ago was contending that he wasn't guilty of any errors, to indulge so energetically in self-flagellation today. And which motivated Zhu and Shen to such buffoonery. They both carried on as though lying was some kind of talisman that could ward off misfortune. They'd urged him to "try it on for size" as well. Wu wondered if he could get away without it.

The old lady still wouldn't let up.

"All right, so we have money now. Let's buy things to wear or eat or at least things that are easily transported. That way, if someone orders us to leave tomorrow, we can. Otherwise, just wait and see, next time there's a political movement. . . ."

"Ma, take it easy," Wen pleaded with her mother-in-law. "There aren't going to be any more mass movements."

"How do you know?" The old lady sighed.

"Grandma, you've got to learn to look ahead. Party Central has promised there won't be any more movements. Don't you believe them?" Their son spoke light-heartedly.

"Did they really say that? Well, I'll be."

My poor mother! I'll do it for her; I'll use that talisman. Since ancient times Chinese have been caught between lies and the truth. Why do I have to take it all so seriously? When you can, tell the truth, when you can't, lie — what's wrong with that? Still, what about my duties as a Party member?

Or as a scholar committed to upholding the truth? The Party has stressed that truth should be upheld. The Party's work can't be built on lies; nor can falsehood lead to real academic achievement.

What am I going to do about tomorrow?

The refrigerator found its final resting place. The door opened, and Wu heard his wife's light footsteps. She knew what had been happening and had heard him talking with Shen and Zhu about it.

At the time of their remarriage they seemed to have reached a silent accord that they'd never bring up the past; they confined their conversations to affairs of the present or future.

What had she come in for? He wasn't in the mood to speak, or even to open his eyes. He didn't want to interrupt his train of thought; he needed peace and quiet.

"You're so tired. Why don't you go to bed?"

The gentle sound of her voice drifted down from somewhere above his head. He forced his eyes open. She was standing in front of him.

"No, I just feel like resting." He closed his eyes.

"Mother is always saying that you go to bed too late."

"Mm."

He heard her pick something up and leave the room. The door closed. He sensed that she had wanted to say something more than that; in fact, he was sure he knew exactly what she wanted to say. She'd said something like it twenty years before.

Wu had just come out of a spell in hospital. Returning to the Academy, he heard that Xu had been declared a "Rightist" along with a number of other young colleagues whom Wu regarded as having great talent. Deeply disturbed, he stayed awake night after night, puzzling over the attack on them. Finally, he decided to appeal on their behalf to the Academy's Party Office.

"Are you crazy?" his wife had screamed at him. "Everyone else is doing their best to stay out of the line of fire and here you are planning to act as cannon fodder!"

"I'm a Party member. According to Party regulations, I've the right to report my opinions to the Party's organs."

"No, please, you mustn't go!" She wept. "Think of the consequences. If you go, you won't just destroy yourself, you'll destroy me and our family as well!"

He hadn't listened. The Party was soon able to announce that it had nabbed the "Big Rightist Wu Tianxiang", just as she'd predicted.

The walls of the Academy were layered with slogans and wall posters written in the most hideously crude characters.

She had wept, their little boy in her arms. He wasn't even six months old.

Wu pleaded with her.

Choked with tears, she cried, "Save our baby!"

Then, he let go of her and collapsed on the ground in despair. To this day, the very thought of this plea made him squeamish.

Those terrible times had finally come to an end. Since their remarriage, they'd been careful not to reopen old wounds; in fact, they'd never even mentioned what had happened twenty years earlier. He never asked her how she'd gotten by.

The fact that she was older and had a middle-age spread were not the only things that had changed about her. She'd become warmer, more considerate, and far more even-tempered. Besides, she'd become quite good at housework, cooking in particular. Each Sunday she'd spend half the day in the kitchen, producing some culinary masterpieces. Each Sunday evening, as the family gathered around the dinner table, Wu would quote from a book he'd once read about fine food being the key to a happy home life.

He, of course, wasn't exactly the boy she'd known in her youth either. As a young man, Wu had been full of energy and enthusiasm, optimistic and cheerful. He'd been eloquent and confident almost to the point of arrogance, as though he could accomplish anything he wanted to by force of will alone. At the time of their reunion it struck her that he seemed older, thinner and dried up. But what really surprised her was his reticence. Though she reminded herself that it was his big mouth which had caused them so much grief in the first place, this troubled her. On the other hand, if he spoke less and concentrated more on his work, living out the second half of his life in peace, well, that wasn't such a bad thing either.

She devoted all her energies to the family and had become a meticulous housemaker. The little bedroom-study with its brand-new bedding and pretty yellow coverlet, the tiny sofa, wall-high bookshelves, new writing desk and unusual little reading lamp were the product of a guilty conscience.

Oughtn't he to betray himself now for her sake as well, for the sake of this hard-bought tranquillity, for the sake of his family? Couldn't he be capable of the same flexibility of mind that had brought his family back together without degenerating into sliminess and figure out how to coast through the study session?

After all, he wouldn't have to tell such a terrible lie. He'd just follow everyone else's example. The lessons of thousands of years of Confucian tradition, the "way of the mean", all boiled down to one thing: you should follow the herd. And then too, one had to consider the "special historical conditions", as well as the importance of "keeping the big picture in mind", "paying strict attention to the requirements of form" and all those other new slogans. Why couldn't he too take his place in the vanguard?

And yet, he just couldn't do it. It wasn't right.

Everyone had suffered enough from lies. Fabricated reports, insincerely motivated political activism, fake exposes, false denunciations and untrue confessions... how many people had fallen into such traps? How many homes had been wrecked? Even now, when the Party strongly advocated the telling of the truth and opposed falsification and hypocrisy, it was still so terribly difficult to tell the truth! They continued to live in a thicket of lies. It seemed as though the heroes of the day lived according to the principle that "You don't utter a word during political meetings, but you can shoot your mouth off in private". The best philosophy for survival appeared to be to keep one's mouth shut and to deny all knowledge of a subject when directly confronted. How could the Party ever improve its work style and create a morally sound social environment if this type of situation persisted?

Twenty years ago, amidst the great hue and cry of political movements, in the face of political campaigns which steamrolled over everything in their path, Wu had shunned lies and dared to speak the truth. He had been a worthy member of the Communist Party. Yet now that the Party had corrected its errors and professed that there would be no more "political movements", he was prepared to stay as silent as a cicada in winter. He was a long way from being a true Communist.

I have faith in the Party, thought Wu. If it weren't for Party Central how could the mistakes of 1957 have been redressed? If it weren't for the Party, would I be where I am today? How can I have anything but trust in the leadership? I must have faith, I must speak out, I won't avoid the issue by lying!

Maybe I'm wrong. It's impossible to completely avoid one-sidedness or subjectivity. But a person can make up for their mistakes. Truth is a moral issue. If nothing else the last twenty years must have at least taught us this.

Wu suddenly opened his eyes. A vivid radiance emanated from them as he sat in the shadows. He rushed over to his desk and took out an inkstone. He began to grind the ink with circular motions of his wrist.

Wu was quite old-fashioned when it came to this sort of thing. When he was serious about something he was writing he never used ready-mixed ink. He felt it to be a slight on the art of calligraphy. The process of grinding ink allowed a person to collect their thoughts and get into the right frame of mind for writing. Thus he focused his concentration on the little column of ink and ground away.

His wife could hear him from the outer room. She was sitting at the square table on which lay some cloth which she'd measured out ready to cut, but somehow she couldn't bring herself to go on. She was restless, disturbed. She couldn't decide whether or not she should go and talk to him. Memories of the past stung her like barbs. It had been so difficult to re-establish their little family; yet did she really think it could be split up again over such an issue? Never had she dared remind herself of the terrible loneliness of those twenty years!

She hesitated. The measured sound of the ink being ground interrupted her meditations. What was he going to write? What did he think he could accomplish? She pushed open the door and went in without another thought.

Wu didn't budge an inch. It was as though he hadn't heard her heavy footsteps or the door opening. She looked at his thin, bent back. He was gripping a large writing brush saturated with ink and writing on a sheet of rice paper.

She stood mute behind him, finally releasing her breath after he'd written two lines of swirling characters on the paper:

"Willing am I to hear unpleasant words, But ne'er shall I betray my conscience."

He turned around and asked softly, "What do you think?"

"Good."

As she spoke the word "good", tears welled up in her eyes, even though she herself couldn't tell whether she was moved or horrified by what he was doing.

He placed his hand on her shoulder and patted it lightly. It was so long since he had shown her any affection that it made her quiver. Tears trickled down her cheeks in transparent streams.

19

"All right, who's going to be first?"

On the third day of the meeting, Ji still took it upon himself to act as chairman.

As usual, Zhang Wei gave the response.

"Yes-yes-yesterday, I th-thought about it again f-for a l-long t-t-time and my l-last two, two self exam-m-minations were very sh-shallow...."

"Comrade Zhang," Ji cut in bluntly, "I don't think we need to hear from you today."

"B-but I, I, I have something impor-portant t-t-to s-say." He was getting worse.

Since Zhang had said it was important, Ji gave in. Zhang leaned forward, concentrating all his energy on squeezing out the following lines:

"I, I, I have m-made up my m-mind over th-the c-course of this stu-study session to use the st-standards of a P-pee-Party m-member to evaluate my-myself. Even if the P-party does not want to rec-rec-rectify me, I want to rec-rectify my-m-myself. If the P-party is not interested in con-conducting a cam-campaign against me, I, I want to con-conduct a cam-campaign against m-myself."

Now this was novel. Some people began sniggering. But

the issue of applying Party standards was so serious and Zhang such a horribly sincere sort of fellow that no one dared laugh out loud.

Fearing that Zhang was about to launch into one of his long-winded jags, Ji broke in.

"Most commendable, Comrade Zhang. It is an excellent idea to use the standards of the Party to judge yourself. As for 'rectification' and 'campaigns', however, well, perhaps there would be a better way of putting that. You are, after all, acting out of your own accord. . . ."

"I'm c-ca-c-completely willing. . . ."

"Well isn't that wonderful!" Ji reacted swiftly. "But if this gets out, other people might get the wrong idea. Best not to use those terms, as I said."

"Th-that-s all r-right. R-really, all I, I wanted to say is th-that I've re-resolved to m-m-make a s-systematic examin-mination of m-my own ideology."

"Good, good, good, good." Ji used a string of "good"s to tie up Zhang's mouth. He looked at Wu Tianxiang. "Why don't we hear from those comrades who haven't spoken up in the last two meetings. Uh, Comrade Ye, you didn't say much yesterday. What do you have to say for yourself?"

Ye Fei's plump face flushed red. Her sparse eyebrows seemed to disappear altogether in a crimson sea. She mumbled, "I agree with what everyone's said so far. I've nothing new to add."

Ji nodded, a smile on his face.

"Then Comrade Tianxiang, I believe it's your turn."

Wu removed the pipe from his mouth and let his gaze roam about the room before nodding back at Ji.

"All right. I'll speak now."

The room quieted down.

"First of all, I ought to criticize myself for not taking a more active interest in this study session. Originally,

Comrade Yang suggested I chair this meeting, but I refused. Why? Frankly speaking, it's because I disagree with the criticism offered by Director Zhao. And from the start I didn't think it necessary for the Academy's Party Office to get directly involved in the affair."

Wu's words came as a complete surprise to everyone in the room. Ji's thick eyebrows shot straight up to his hairline and Yang stared stupidly at Wu, completely forgetting to take notes. Xu's goldfish eyes nearly popped out of his head and Zhang Wei's jaw dropped. Tongtong's ponytail stopped its wagging and those nearly invisible eyebrows of Ye Fei's went high and wide. That supercilious smile of Zhu's was knocked right off his face and Shen Zhiye lowered his head, afraid to meet Wu's eyes.

"I am the head of this Centre and a member of the Communist Party. I could have taken my views to Comrade Yang for discussion, or to the Academy Party Committee or even directly to Director Zhao. All this would have been perfectly in keeping with Party discipline. But I did none of those things, adopting instead a hands-off attitude. I told Yang that I'd come to the meeting, but he'd have to chair it. This was wrong of me. I clearly had strong ideas on the matter, yet I did not raise them with anyone. You could say I dumped the entire burden onto Yang's shoulders. I shouldn't have done this and I want to apologize to Comrade Yang."

Yang's hands trembled and his nose felt ticklish. If it weren't for all the people around, and if it weren't a meeting, and if he hadn't caught sight of the livid expression on Ji's face, he'd have leapt up and grasped Wu's hands in his own. How warm those words had made him feel!

"Second, I'd like to explain why I can't concur with Director Zhao's remarks. Director Zhao admonished us not to 'grovel at the feet of the Western bourgeoisie'. He's right in principle, of course, and I heartily agree. As members of an organisation dedicated to the study of foreign literature, we ought to take this as a relevant piece of advice. We're in contact with foreign literature all day long. If we're not vigilant, it may exert a subtle influence on our thinking. But Director Zhao applied this criticism to Xu Minghui's article, which is, in my opinion, one of the best of its kind!"

Xu lowered his eyes, then his head, until his forehead was nearly parallel with the table.

"What's so outstanding about Xu's work, in fact, is that it applies the concept of seeking truth from facts to the analysis and assessment of contemporary Western literature. It uses neither crude nor simplistic methods nor deprecatory language. If that is what's known as licking the boots of the Westen bourgeoisie then I honestly have no idea how this Centre is supposed to carry out its work."

He paused slightly, as though to calm himself.

The silence was so palpable you could have cut it with a knife.

"Of course, I'm not saying that Old Xu's article is above criticism. As I've told Xu personally, I think that in enumerating the representative works of various Western literary genres he has laid too much stress on those works with social content and artistic value. He has largely ignored works of low standard and I believe this makes for a one-sided picture. I'm sure Old Xu must've had his reasons for this — perhaps he felt that it's more important to introduce works of value. He might be right, too."

With a glance at Xu, he forged on:

"All these are matters open to discussion and deliberation by everyone. So are Director Zhao's criticisms. There's nothing wrong with bringing such ideas up with the author, for criticism is a vital prerequisite for academic pursuits. Without criticism, how can we possibly improve our work?

Unfortunately, Director Zhao did not choose to offer his criticisms in such a context."

Ji turned a pale sickly colour. He'd known of Wu's reputation for arrogance and had heard that he was buddy-buddy with Xu. But since Xu had already made a self-crit, what was Wu doing carrying on like this? Why, he was directing his fire at the Director himself! This was really too much.

"The third point I'd like to make is that right from the start I've been opposed to the handling of this meeting by the Academy's Party Office. These past few days, everyone has been put through the wringer so to speak. People have been tying themselves up in knots trying to come up with the right 'attitude', which is the only reason you hear all this rubbish about support for Director Zhao's criticism and the personal intervention of the Academy Party Office. But what are they really thinking? I'm sure at least half of what's been said in this room has been sheer lies. We are in a realm of half-fantasy, half-truth and it looks to me like there's more fantasy than truth around. First of all, I doubt that Xu meant a word of what he said in his self-criticism. Just two days ago he didn't see anything wrong with what he had written. What transpired in the intervening 48 hours that led so unexpectedly to this wretched self-flagellation?"

Xu's head was so low by this point that only his bald pate was visible. Except for Qin Tongtong, whose thin black eyebrows were raised in a transparent expression of surprise, no one in the room dared meet the speaker's gaze.

"As for whether the other comrades were sincere in what they have said, I don't think I need go into any of that. But there is one point I'd like to make. Ever since the fall of the 'gang of four' and particularly following the Third Plenum, honesty and truth have begun to reappear in the society and in our Centre. There's simply no need to lie anymore. There are no more political campaigns, no more orders of the day from Mao. So why in heaven's name are people still going to all the trouble and grief of lying? Putting a stop to dogmatic Maoism helped liberate our thoughts and, generally speaking, the situation is excellent. But this study session has led to so much tension that we're not doing our work any good at all."

Underneath his steely hair, Ji's face went an even funnier colour and it looked as though he'd aged a few years in the process. He was about to explode. Was Wu implying that he had coerced them into lying? He was so upset that he resolved that after Wu was finished he would make everyone admit whether they'd spoken sincerely or not. But then again, what if. . . .

"I only wish to make the above points. If I've said anything out of place, I hope my comrades will correct me."

The flush faded from Ji's face. He was his usual pale yellow self once more. Tapping on the table with his fingers he hastily brought the meeting to a close.

"Very well then. Wu's statement was extremely forthright. It's good, that, to say what you mean. Today's meeting will end here. We'll inform you when the next session is to be held. Everyone's dismissed."

He picked up his thermos mug and walked out.

20

The moment Ji left, the room erupted with excitement. Some people got stuck into Director Zhao for being too subjective, others blamed Ji for his domineering attitude and a few even carried on about how important it was to stand up for the truth, especially at meetings.

Yang felt slightly euphoric. He mightn't agree with all that was being said, but he was pleased as punch that everyone was so willing to speak like this in front of him. He felt that as a political commissar he'd taken a giant step forward.

"Old Wu, you were terrific. Just great." Zhu stuck up his thumb at Wu. "I was feeling so depressed before you spoke up!"

Tossing her shoulder bag over her arm, Qin Tongtong rolled her eyes.

"What's this? So Zhu's finally decided to align himself with the legions of truth. Where were you all along, eh?"

Shen rushed over, his hands clasped in an old-style martial salute.

"Upright and straight to the point. Truly a man of honour, a man of honour! 'Listening to one speech by a gentleman one learns more than from ten years of reading books.'"

Wu waved aside these effusive compliments and, sticking his pipe in his bag, headed for the door. Yang, who was sitting just across the desk from him, quickly stuffed his notebook into the drawer.

"Old Wu, if this meeting hasn't been conducted properly, it's because I. . . ."

"No one's blaming you. You've got your own problems," Wu cut him off.

Yang sighed and looked more cheerful.

"Still, I ought to have consulted more with Director Ji and explained to him about our work here at the Centre."

"Going to tell on me, I suppose?" Zhu cut in, chuckling.

"Don't fret," Yang replied amicably. "The age of denunciations is over."

One by one, they filed out of the room. Wu discovered Xu waiting for him outside the main gate of the Temple.

Twenty years of sharing the same fate, the same tragedies, had made the two men bosom buddies. They knew each other inside out. One look at Xu's protruberant eyes and Wu knew his old friend wanted to say something.

At first, they walked along in silence, however. Xu stared at the ground, never so much as glancing up at his companion. Just before they reached the bus stop, Wu spoke up.

"Why don't you come over for lunch? We've still got some *Wuliangye*."

"No." Xu looked miserable.

They'd reached the main avenue. Young poplar trees lined both sides of the wide pavement, their leaves catching the sunlight. It was the noon rush hour and the streets were filled with people. Except for Xu and Wu, everyone was rushing home for lunch. The two men strolled slowly along.

Wu had one hand stuck in the pocket of his flannel jacket.

"Say something for pity's sake."

"Old Wu, you...." Xu's voice faltered.

"What is it? What're you trying to say?"

"You oughtn't to have done it."

Wu didn't answer. He slowed down.

"Okay, so you told the truth, but have you thought for just one moment what the consequences might be?"

"Yes, I have," Wu said calmly. "I'm sure it won't bring on any great disaster. On the contrary, I believe it may motivate more people to speak their minds. And this is so important if we are to start working normally again."

"You...." Xu shook his head.

"Yes?"

Xu walked on with a sigh. School had just let out and a flood of noisy school children, little red scarves and pigtails flying, poured out in front of them. They stopped to allow them to pass. Xu turned to Wu.

"It's not that I'm in favour of lying. In fact, my self-crit was sincere. It was an accurate reflection of the contradictions in my head. I admire your courage in saying what you did. But how are they ever going to be able to wrap up this meeting?"

"I hadn't thought of that."

"You should have. You're the director of the Centre."

Wu didn't reply.

"There's a time and a place for the truth," Xu said. "Whether that's in front of so many people in a meeting, or after the meeting in one-on-one sessions, now or later — all this must be decided on the basis of possible consequences."

Wu pondered Xu's words. Had he been presumptuous in speaking up?

They walked along quietly. Apartment blocks still under construction lined the avenue stretching before them. There was also the telegraph office, the foreign trade building, the travellers' hostel, workers' dorms. The arms of a giant crane lifted prefabricated concrete slabs into the sky, raising the wall of buildings even higher. All this building represented a new lease on life for this ancient provincial capital. The symphony of construction noises drowned out the sound of the pair's footfalls.

21

Yang spent the whole night in thought and resolved to see Ji first thing the following day.

"I really don't think we should go on like this."

"What?" Ji snapped. He didn't seem to be in a good mood. His forehead was furrowed and his eyes puffy. Clearly he hadn't had a good night's sleep either.

"I mean, rather than create a situation where no one says what they mean, why don't we encourage people to speak their minds?"

"And who told them to lie?" Ji looked upset.

"Of course, we never forced anyone to lie," Yang said gently. "But the whole atmosphere, the pressure...."

"A suitable amount of pressure is necessary and beneficial

when one's trying to persuade people to abandon mistaken ideas. Comrade Yang, we've been working togehter on and off for some twenty years now. Don't tell me you still haven't grasped this line of reasoning. I'm afraid I must caution you against accomodating yourself to the retrogressive sentiments of the masses. If a political worker lowers himself to the standards of an ordinary citizen, he cannot hope to raise their ideological level!"

He saw that it was going to be a difficult task to convince Ji. But he couldn't just let the matter drop.

"Of course one must avoid stooping to the level of the masses. But when a member of the masses comes up with a sensible opinion, we are obliged to consider it. Besides, Wu isn't just one of the great unwashed, he's an administrative leader and a Party specialist."

Ji's tone was so cold his words fell from his mouth like little ice cubes:

"Are you implying that he has offered a reasonable opinion?"

Yang thought a moment.

"Just take the issue of whether Director Zhao's criticisms were appropriate or not. He may have had a point there."

Ji looked at Yang.

"The question is not the reasonableness of Zhao's criticisms. Rather it is whether or not Wu Tianxiang is going to get away with an attitude which is both unhealthy and that has a very bad influence within the Centre."

22

Three days later, Ji notified people that the meeting would be resumed. When all had gathered in the office, he began.

"Today I wish to sum up. First of all, as a result of this study session, the majority of comrades have raised their level of awareness and come to understand the importance and timeliness of Director Zhao's remarks. They understand that these remarks have not only sounded an alarm bell for us in the Centre for Foreign Literature Research but have a wider relevance as well. We have all also recognized the importance and timeliness of the involvement of the Academy's Party Office. Many comrades have mentioned that because the Centre has not been in operation very long and due to the individual nature of the work, there is a tendency to one-sidedness which might be corrected through better communication. Therefore, it was agreed that it is necessary to get together more frequently in meetings such as this in order to exchange ideas, learn from one another and engage in criticism and self-criticism. Some comrades have enthusiastically proposed making meetings like this a regular practice. An excellent suggestion! I will put it before the Party Committee for their serious consideration. I think we should hold three sessions a week on Monday, Wednesday and Friday afternoons. How does that sound?... Ah, perhaps three a week would be a bit much? In order to ensure that there's still plenty of time for research work we could keep it to twice a week. How about Tuesdays and Thursdays? All right. Yang, Wu, you two work out the details, will you?

"Secondly, during the course of this meeting, Comrade Xu has humbly accepted Director Zhao's criticism of his article and recognized his own errors. He acknowledged that it is dangerous to introduce Western modernism without strongly criticizing it at the same time. He also showed his awareness of the fact that Director Zhao's criticism is in fact an expression of his deep concern, and that it was both necessary and timely. Comrade Xu has promised to write better articles in the future. This is a good attitude. His comment that ever since his rehabilitation he's concentrated on his work to the neglect of remoulding his world view was especially commendable. We take his point on how 'ink rubs off'; anyone who spends all his time immersed in Western literature must guard against the infiltration of the Western outlook into his own thoughts. That Comrade Wu has so carefully examined his own world view shows that his self-criticism was a relatively profound one. Other comrades also mentioned the need to strengthen their own understanding of Marxism, Leninism and Mao Zedong Thought; to further remould their ideology and use the Marxist-Leninist standpoint more effectively in their work. Some comrades reviewed their own works for political errors. Zhang Wei is an example. His serious attitude ought to receive our affirmation and is much welcomed."

The ring of the office telephone cut into Ji's speech. Qin Tongtong picked up the receiver. "Hello?" She handed the phone to Yang. "Your wife."

Yang frowned.

A sharp high-pitched sound emitted from the receiver. It was impossible, however, to make out what was being said. Impatiently, Yang whispered, "I'm in the middle of a meeting."

At this point, his wife raised her voice so much that everyone in the room heard the rest of the exchange.

"Well when you're through, pick up some steamed bread rolls. There's nothing to eat in the house."

"All right, all right."

She wasn't finished.

"And don't hang around gabbing till all hours. Come straight home."

Everyone pretended they hadn't heard. Hastily, Yang hung up the phone and picked up his pen. Ji carried on talking.

"Third, in the course of this study session, quite a few

comrades have acknowledged that there's a serious problem of standpoint and direction in foreign literature research. They have raised many valuable suggestions in respect of the goal of such research and how to do one's work so as to best serve the people, our own cultural field and the four modernizations. Our comrades have at this meeting probed deeply into the genesis of Western modernism, showing it to be the product of the decay of Western society and the profound crisis faced by capitalism. This was well illustrated by anecdotes based on the personal experiences of comrades who've been abroad. Many comrades forcefully criticized the phenomenon of West-worshipping in our own society as well. This all proves that the glorious tradition of linking practice and theory through political study has not only been revived but enhanced.

"Fourth, I want to stress that at this meeting, our comrades have truly 'spoken their minds' achieving a good political atmosphere of centralization and democracy, discipline and freedom, unity of will and personal ease of mind. Some comrades dared to raise dissenting views and voice their true feelings; this is good. The Party has always encouraged people to speak honestly. It has called upon us to eliminate dishonesty, empty talk and bragging, and to promote the principle of 'seeking truth from facts'. We must encourage this, for we've experienced enough grief stemming from lies and falsehood. All of our comrades must have faith in the Party and the Party Office of the Academy. We resolutely oppose attacking people for what they say or attempts at seeking revenge. The Party has always believed that the majority of intellectuals are good or relatively good. Now that the Party's policy on intellectuals is finally being carried out, opportunities are being created for intellectuals to further realize their unique talents. That is of course true for us here at the Centre as well. Since its re-establishment, our comrades have worked diligently and conscientiously and can boast of many accomplishments. As for mistakes in our work, well, they are part and parcel of things and unavoidable; it is only natural that there are still differing views. Just as the ten fingers of the hand are different lengths, so do people hold different opinions. All we can do is demand of ourselves that we pay attention to our own ideological remoulding in order to achieve a whole-hearted dedication to serving the people and constantly improve our own work.

"A final lesson we've learned is the importance of upholding the Party leadership. The Academy's Party Office can take credit for making this meeting as productive as it was. Furthermore, we've learned the importance of mass participation in political work. It won't do just to rely on Young Yang here and myself. Finally, there's been good co-ordination of political work in the meetings and behind the scenes. Indeed, the most important ideological work can be done outside of the meeting room.

"Of course, there are some drawbacks to the proceedings. The meeting was called too hastily and people weren't given enough time to study the relevant documents. I must take responsibility as well for the slow pace of discussion."

Ji turned to Yang.

"Young Yang, do you have anything to add?"

Yang shook his head. Ji turned to the others.

"Anybody else?"

No one spoke. Ji quickly announced:

"Good. This study session has been satisfactorily concluded. Meeting adjourned!"

1980, Beijing
Translated by Geremie Barmé
and Linda Jaivin

The Secret of Crown Prince Village

1. An Anonymous Letter

Respected Leading Comrades of the County Committee,

The present situation is fine, getting better all the time. The overthrow of the hateful White Bone Monster* and her three minions has pepped up everyone. Hurrah for the brilliance of the Party Central Committee, the great victory of Chairman Mao's revolutionary line. There were things no one dared say before for fear of being arrested or beaten up. But now that Secretary Feng has come to head the County Committee, that's put fresh life into me. This is our second Liberation. We must help the County Committee do a good job. That's why I'm making so bold as to write this letter.

The reason I'm taking time off from my work to write is because Li Wanju, Party secretary of Crown Prince Village has been a double-dealer all along, who only pretends to carry out the orders from above. He has cheated the commune, the County Committee, the Party Central Committee and the masses in a most outrageous way. Last month at your meeting for commune and brigade cadres, you declared Crown Prince Village a model in criticizing the "gang of four" and praised it for going all out for socialism, awarding it another red flag. And Li Wanju made a speech

---

*A man-eating monster in the Chinese classical novel *Pilgrimage to the West*.

boasting about their advanced experience. Crap! He was simply fooling people.

Li Wanju can fool other people, but not me. I know the fellow. He went to junior middle school and has the gift of the gab. The beady-eyed little runt with his wispy moustache is smart enough to size up any situation, and is hail-fellow-well-met with all the villagers. If you go there you're certain to hear young and old sing his praises. Oh yes, the fellow knows a trick or two. Can trim his sails to suit the wind. Nothing stumps him. Everybody for ten *li* around knows him as the man who is always popular and in power. Li can weather any storm.

Secretary Feng, this wasn't the first time he's passed on his experience in our county. He's forever doing it. When Red Guards came he summarized his experience in "supporting the revolutionary young generals". Who dared offend the Red Guards in those days! Like young kings of Hell they turned each village upside down. Killed three of our villagers in one night! Crafty Li Wanju was the only one who managed to suck up to them. He set up two cauldrons just outside the village to supply them with boiled water and big steamed buns, and lined up school kids waving red and green flags to shout slogans of welcome. Brought tears to the Red Guards' eyes. He saw to it that they were well fed and slept on heated *kangs*. Oh, it was easy to fool those half-baked kids. So they had nothing but good to say of him. Into the village from the west they went and out again from the east, as good as gold, not touching a stick of firewood. And the landlords and rich peasants got off scot-free. In other villages no one could stop them from killing off a few landlords and rich peasants, but those in Crown Prince Village came through safe and sound. That's why all the class enemies there support him. Do you call that the correct line?

Well, that's an old story now. The year before last we had

to criticize our respected and beloved Vice-Chairman Deng. They went all out on that. Put up two hoardings as high as a house in front of their pig farm and drew cartoons on them. To debunk Lin Biao and Confucius, they drew Confucius back to front on a donkey. To blast Deng they painted cats, black, white and tabby cats,* absolutely lifelike except they couldn't meow. And guess what they did when the "gang of four" was toppled. They whitewashed over the cats and painted a picture of Monkey King defeating the White Bone Monster. So quick to chop and change!

They say, Secretary Feng, that as soon as you took up office you cracked up Crown Prince Village for grasping revolution and boosting production. What I can't figure out is how they raised their output in each movement. Our county has twenty-odd communes and several hundred brigades. They all joined in those movements, not missing out on one, but their output didn't go up. Only in Crown Prince Village. Forgive me, Secretary Feng, for speaking bluntly. The fact is you've been fooled by Li Wanju. There've been scandalous goings-on there which they hide from outsiders. You can't be blamed for not knowing this as you're new here. Li must have the backing of someone in the County Committee. How else could he stay in power and have such a nerve? I'm letting you into this secret. Please keep it to yourself, and don't hold it against me.

I never had much schooling and my political level is low. The little book learning I had has all trickled out to manure the fields. So please make allowances if I've written anything wrong. I don't mind telling you I'm a funk. Though the gate to your office stands open and there are no sentries there, I'm scared to go in to appeal to you higher-ups. This business has been on my mind day and night, as it affects our whole

---

*Deng was criticized for having said, "Black cat or white cat, whichever catches mice is a good cat."

county. The Central Committee has warned us against lying, boasting and empty talk. Although I'm just a peasant, I feel it my duty to show up Li Wanju. All I want is for you to send a reliable cadre to find out the truth. See whether Crown Prince Village is red or black. If it's red, well and good. If it's black you can deal with it.

Being timid and afraid of trouble, as I said, I'm not signing my real name. Not that I'm afraid of the Public Security Bureau investigating me, but because I don't want to offend Li Wanju. There's no feud between us. He hasn't thrown any child of mine down a well, I can't afford to make an enemy of him. I've sold two eggs in the co-op to buy a stamp, although we've no salt left at home. Honestly, I'm thinking of the public good, not of my private interests

With respectful wishes for the leadership's good health and the early realization of modernization.

A Commune Member
August 2, 1978

2. Secretary Feng's Decision

Secretary Feng Zhenmin of the County Committee read this anonymous letter twice, then lit a cigarette and leaned back against his wicker chair to blow smoke rings. His dark, lantern-jawed face was impasssive. He knit his short black eyebrows. Not having shaved for several days, the grey stubble on his chin made him look extra old and haggard.

It was less than half a year since Feng's appointment as Party secretary of this Qingming County Committee. He had arrived on the day of the Grain Rains towards the end of April. Years of experience had taught him that top priority must be given to farming. The spring sowing must at no cost be delayed. He therefore went straight to the countryside to see to the ploughing and sowing, not returning to the county town till it was finished.

Feng found no difficulty in this task, as he had grown up on the land and worked in the countryside for years after Liberation. He was familiar with the farm work of all four seasons. His problem was that as a result of the "cultural revolution" he did not know the calibre of the cadres in the county, communes and brigades. Opinions about them differed. And how could he direct operations without understanding his officers and men?

In the "cultural revolution" the Qingming County Committee had been scrapped for "peddling the wares of the black Provincial Committee". Its secretary, dubbed a "renegade", had died in prison. Its second in command had not been cleared until after the fall of the "gang". The "new cultural revolutionary committee" set up in 1968 had been instructed to co-opt a revolutionary leading cadre, but there was not one to be found in the whole county. As a last resort they had co-opted Qi Yuezhai, former chairman of the County Committee Office now deputy secretary.

For years Qi had been a conscientious chairman. He had made appropriate arrangements for Feng's arrival and his trips to the different communes. The two of them co-operated closely. Yet, although several months had passed, Feng was still not clear what type of man Qi was.

Tall, lean Qi with his fair complexion had an air of refinement. Some called him well qualified; others, incompetent. Well qualified because he had studied agronomy for two years in the People's University. How many county secretaries in the whole country had such good qualifications? Incompetent because he was indecisive and afraid of trouble — he never seemed able to make up his mind.

Opinions also varied on the role Qi had played since being co-opted on to the new committee. Some considered him as no more than a figure-head, able only to shout slogans or quote Chairman Mao, of no real use but no trouble-maker either. Others maintained that although he looked so flabby he had all along been the power behind the scenes. For in those years the No. 1 had been either an army representative or one of the young rebels. Army representatives had little say, not being familiar with the local conditions; while all the young rebels could do was talk big and hold struggle meetings. It was Qi who really ran things.

Feng was confused by these conflicting views. He had the impression that Qi had a weight on his mind. He had tried several times to have a frank talk with him, but it was very hard. Qi seemed inhibited.

Feng straightened up, glancing again at the letter on his desk. That reference to "backing" in the County Committee — could that mean Qi? Could he be connected with Li?

When they had been preparing for last month's meeting, it had indeed been Qi who commended Crown Prince Village for its exposure of the "gang of four". But it had been Feng's idea to have Li Wanju speak at the meeting. This letter said he had been fooled. In what way? And by whom?

Feng's face was lined, his hair greying, his back rather stooped, but he was actually only fifty-five. Long experience had taught him how to size up cadres. Before that meeting, in a small group discussion, he had heard Li Wanju speak and had not been impressed by his political platitudes which most village cadres could reel off.

What did impress him was Li's confidence, boldness and gusto. He wasn't full of complaints like so many cadres, nor did he sound down-hearted. After all those calamitous years, optimists of this kind were badly needed to give the lead in restoring the village economy.

So Feng had chosen Li to speak at the meeting, hoping he would infect the others with his gusto and get them to put on a spurt. But it didn't turn out like that. Li had talked exuberantly in the small group, but his speech in the meeting was dull and dry, quite pointless.

This wasn't because he was nervous speaking in public. There were some grass-roots cadres who spoke clearly and logically on informal occasions but dried up when standing in front of a microphone. Not Li Wanju, however. Having done well in movement after movement, he often spoke in public. Had Feng really been taken in by this man of the day? He bit his lip, inwardly sighing: It's hard for a newcomer. Especially when you're on your own, all at sea. Never mind, better follow this up. He picked up his ball-point pen and wrote on the top right-hand corner of the letter:

Comrade Yuezhai,
Please read this letter. I think we might send someone down to investigate. What's your opinion?

Feng Zhenmin
August 15, 1978

3. Deputy Secretary Qi's Dilemma

Qi had in fact read the anonymous letter on the 10th of August when Qiu Bingzhang, chairman of the County Committee Office, had been so struck by it that he delivered it to him in person.

"This is a letter worth studying!" Qiu took off his cap and sat down in front of the desk, scratching his head while Qi read the letter carefully with no expression on his pallid face. When he had finished it Qiu ventured his opinion, "Looks as if this attack on Li Wanju is actually...."

Qi had reached for his mug and slowly removed its lid. Now, instead of sipping the steaming tea, he raised his puffy eyelids to stare at Qiu, making him break off.

Deputy Secretary Qi had been strangely moody of late. He often kept so quiet, looked so lukewarm, that it was hard to guess what he was thinking. Qiu had worked in the County Committee Office for twenty years, and it was Qi who had promoted him to his present post of chairman. His colleagues therefore believed that he knew how Qi's mind worked. But these last few days even Qiu was baffled by him.

Since Qi hadn't shut him up, Qiu scratched his head again and said quietly:

"Seems to me, this is aimed at you."

Qi snorted, then sipped his tea and curled his lip, looking indifferent. Hitching his chair closer to the desk Qiu continued:

"Who's Li Wanju? Secretary of a brigade. Why accuse him of sailing through each movement with flying colours — a red flag? The point is who boosted him? Who's kept him red right up to now?"

Qi had fixed his big eyes on Qiu's fat face and bald head, as if listening intently. Pointing at the letter Qiu said:

"Isn't it clear? Li Wanju had the backing of someone in the County Committee. Who does that mean? Isn't it obvious. . .?" He broke off again.

Qi glanced at the letter as if stung, then turned to look out of the window, his narrow lips clamped together, his face impassive again.

"And look at the timing." Qiu perched himself on the edge of the desk, his head closer to Qi's to whisper, "Why wasn't it written earlier instead of a few months after Secretary Feng's arrival, and soon after he commended Crown Prince Village at that meeting? The letter may not hang together, but it seems to me someone put him up to writing to give Secretary Feng a handle against you."

After so many years in the County Committee Office Qiu had the lowdown on all that had happened there. Though fat and indolent he was quick-witted and shrewd in sizing up the situation. In the "cultural revolution" he had learned by reading between the lines of the press to scent big political changes. Incredible as it might seem, before word of it came down from the Central Committee, from certain changed formulations in the papers he even detected and gave warning of the fall of the "gang of four". Later someone joked, "By smashing the 'gang of four' the Central Committee saved the revolution, saved the Party. By guessing that the gang had been smashed Chairman Qiu saved the County Committee, saved Qi Yuezhai." This had strengthened Qiu's position and given him more confidence to analyse new trends and situations.

The last couple of years' developments had been so rapid that it was hard to keep up with them. Yesterday's fallacies had become today's truths. Yesterday's prisoners had turned into heroes. Opinions that no one had dared to whisper in private could be shouted to raise the roof. Qiu felt he had lagged behind, had less right to speak, and was of little use to Qi these days.

Qi too had realized that he could no longer rely so much on Qiu to grasp the policies of the Central Committee. He wanted to do a good job, but hadn't been able to in the years before the fall of the "gang". The Party secretary at that time had been an invalid. Some said he suffered from a "political illness". Because when it wasn't clear which way the wind was blowing and the political climate seemed abnormal, he took refuge in hospital. Others said he was genuinely ill with heart disease and cirrhosis of the liver. At all events he had been hospitalized for two years and a half, leaving Qi in actual charge of the County Committee. But the situation at that time was precarious with pitfalls right and left. If you fell in you might never climb out again. It was hard to achieve anything.

After October 1976 Qi longed for peace and stability in which to work steadily for a few more years. But it seemed there was still a struggle in the Central Committee. Any reversal now would finish them off. So he grew more cautious than ever, trusting Qiu's analyses. Qiu, however, for all his shrewdness, was also out of his depth. So Qi was reduced to inching along, slowly following instructions from above and trying to keep out of trouble.

Feng Zhenmin's arrival, instead of relieving his mind, made him more anxious than ever. He lost more weight, looked more delicate than before. His colleagues often saw him brooding in silence.

To Qiu's mind, Feng's appointment heralded a restructuring of the County Committee, a "stealthy seizure of power" Although Qi said nothing he had the bitter sense of not being trusted.

He braced himself for an investigation. When Lin Biao and the "gang of four" had been in power, claiming to be the "proletarian headquarters", they had launched a whole series of political movements attacking Premier Zhou and Deng Xiaoping. And county heads had to join in. If called on to account for this now, what could he say? When would it be his turn to be exposed? Sometimes he felt he should take the initiative, but didn't know where to start.

He didn't believe that anyone in their county had been in cahoots with Lin Biao or the "gang of four". If one had to be found, he would surely be the scapegoat. Since he had been put in a leading position, how could he help obeying those fascists' orders? But he hadn't belonged to their camp. Couldn't have sucked up to them even if he'd tried. As for saying the wrong things or making blunders, who didn't make mistakes? On this score he had no misgivings. When

Qiu maundered about his danger he sometimes told him, "If you have a clear conscience you needn't be afraid." Still, for some reason or other he couldn't help worrying. He grew thinner and thinner, more and more depressed.

He had thought that Feng, immediately on his arrival, would set about cleaning up the County Committee. Had sorted out all his notebooks, ready to hand them in as soon as required. But to his surprise the new secretary instead of investigating him concentrated on production, implementing the new economic policy, and clearing up old cases of injustice. On all these matters, moreover, he consulted Qi and the other committee members. He showed no intention of kicking Qi out, and seemed a good man to work with, with a higher political level than his own. But was Feng perhaps biding his time? Waiting till he had a firm foothold here to reshuffle the County Committee?

Qiu kept urging Qi to be on his guard. A former representative of the "County Committee's revolutionary masses", though he had pulled in his horns he still had many sources of information and was always ready to report any number of "new trends", which had to be taken with a grain of salt. He now produced this anonymous letter as if it were a time-bomb — no trifling matter.

"There's something peculiar about this letter." Qiu tapped the red-lined stationery and narrowed his eyes with a shrewd smile. "It's a hotchpotch of colloquial and classical terms, obviously cooked up to conceal the identity of the writer."

"Who do you think wrote it?" If they could track down the anonymous letter-writer, Qi felt it shouldn't be hard to discover his motive and the target of his attack.

"I figure he must be an old fellow, fifty or thereabouts," said Qiu confidently. "He's read some of the classics. Has inside information about the County Committee and Crown Prince Village. And he must have attended that meeting here. I'm sure we can ferret him out."

But instead of following this up, Qi said:

"Give the letter to Secretary Feng to deal with."

"That's no way to handle it!" Qiu was horrified. Had Qi taken leave of his senses giving Feng this handle against him?

But with no word of explanation Qi raised his hand dismissively, indicating that Qiu should take the letter away.

Now this letter had come back with Feng's proposal. Qi sent for Qiu and told him with a smile:

"We'll act on Secretary Feng's instructions."

There was much that Qiu would have liked to say. How could Qi take it so lightly?

"But, Secretary Qi, how can we investigate this?" He scratched his head, very put out.

"The practical way, sending someone down to the village," replied Qi calmly, as if quite unconcerned.

"Who shall we send?"

"You can go."

"Me?"

Qiu stood rooted to the floor, the letter in his hand.

Qi lowered his head over a document. After a while he glanced up and said slowly:

"You've analysed this letter in detail, haven't you? Well then, go and look into the matter."

Qiu stared at him to watch his expression. Pricked up his ears to catch the tone of each word. Finally he nodded reluctantly. Nodded slowly and rhythmically, as if there were more to this than met the eye.

4. The Minutes of a Meeting

Date: August 19, 1978
Place: Crown Prince Village Brigade
Chairman: Chairman Qiu

Present: Wu Yougui (Party Committee member, chairman
          of the brigade's revolutionary committee)
          Xiao Meifeng (Youth League secretary)
          Gui Qiushi (head of the crop team, a demobilized
          soldier)
          Mother Liu (poor peasant working in the pig farm)
          Grandad Ma (poor peasant, head of the pig farm)
          Zhang Guilian (poor peasant working on sidelines)
          Second Sister Lu (poor peasant)
Minutes recorded by Yang Dequan (brigade accountant)

CHAIRMAN QIU: We've called this meeting today to
      hear your views on the work here the last couple of
      years. What's your experience, what mistakes have
      you made? What's your opinion about the County
      Committee? It's nearly two yours since the fall of the
      "gang of four" and the Central Committee has called
      on us to be more democratic, to listen to the masses, so
      just say whatever you please. About your production,
      your difficulties, whether you've done a good job in
      exposing bad characters... anything you like. Wanju's
      gone to a meeting in the commune. Never mind, you
      can criticize him back to back and have less scruples
      about it. Well, let's hear what you have to say.
WU YOUGUI: I'll start. Chairman Qiu has told us to talk
      about our village, so you can bring anything up. Times
      have changed, the rebels are no longer in power; don't
      be afraid to speak out. Get everything off your chests,
      our good points and bad ones. But don't exaggerate.
      Just say what you think of Wanju and our brigade,
      without being afraid of reprisals.
CHAIRMAN QIU: Go ahead, let's not waste time.
MOTHER LIU: Well, I'll make a start, I'm not afraid.
      Chairman Qiu asked about our production and living
      conditions. We're doing fine since the fall of the

"gang". When they ruled the roost they kept us in a tizzy with all those movements and struggles. Didn't give us a moment's peace. Right? And now the County Committee's sent one of its top men here to hold this discussion. That's real democracy. Fine, don't you all agree?

SECOND SISTER LU: That's it! We're doing fine. The "gang of four" were a vicious lot, Lin Biao taking a plane to kill Chairman Mao.

XIAO MEIFENG: What, Second Sister! Lin Biao wasn't one of the "gang". And it wasn't in a plane that he tried to kill Chairman Mao.

SECOND SISTER LU: No? Well, that's what I heard. It's hard to remember after all this time. Talk of a train *and* a plane, that's what muddled me.

CHAIRMAN QIU: Let's keep to the point. Of course, I'm impressed by your strong proletarian feeling and indignant exposure of Lin Biao and the "gang". We can come back to that later. Today let's concentrate on your brigade and on your cadres. Wanju, for instance. To help improve the work.

WU YOUGUI: That's right. Stick to the point. Speak out. No one's going to hold it against you.

MOTHER LIU: Our brigade's doing fine. Our cadres get up early, turn in late, working alongside us. Nothing wrong with them.

WU YOUGUI: You can bring up their faults too.

MOTHER LIU: Who doesn't have faults? In the village I come from the Party secretary has a bad temper — flares up at the least little thing! So people keep out of his way, even on the Spring Festival. He hasn't a friend in the village, yet he has to run the brigade. Our Wanju's different. He's been liked ever since he was a boy. He calls everyone by name, not like some cadres who give themselves stinking airs. He's been that way all these years, polite and pleasant. Whenever he comes to our pig farm he calls me Mother. Has a smile for everyone. Don't the rest of you agree?

GRANDAD MA: There aren't many cadres like Wanju. Not only smart but fair. There are plenty of villagers older than him and he treats us as his seniors. Hasn't made any big mistake all these years — that's not easy. For all he's so young, he knows what's right. I can't say how he treats other people, but he's been very good to me, an old fellow all on my own. When I sprained my back years ago, Wanju gave me a light job as storekeeper, saw to it that I wouldn't go cold or hungry. I've no fault to find with our brigade. I'm all for Wanju.

GUI QIUSHI: I've worked here for two years since being demobbed. I think our brigade has a good leading group. Take Comrade Wanju, he understands production, has a practical approach and a good working style. That's why everybody has confidence in our cadres. And our output of grain and sidelines shows that our village isn't doing badly.

MOTHER LIU: That's a fact. If you don't believe it take a look at all the village around. We deliver more grain to the state, sell more surplus grain. Our model plots are famous. Visitors flock to see them every year. All this comes of having a good leadership. I've no fault to find with Wanju.

SECOND SISTER LU: That's right! Wanju has a good heart. Take the wheat harvest, for instance. The brigade sent everyone in the fields a big fried dough-cake and plenty of mung bean porridge....

MOTHER LIU: Let's stick to the facts, Second Sister.

This is the first I've heard about fried dough-cakes, and I go harvesting each year, so how could it have slipped my mind? Eh, Grandad Ma?

GRANDAD MA: I work in the storehouse, so I wouldn't know.

SECOND SISTER LU: Well, you needn't ask around, Mother Liu. I must have dreamed about it so much that it seemed real to me.

XIAO MEIFENG: Why try to cover it up if you ate dough-cakes? In town the workers on night shift get a snack. So why shouldn't peasants harvesting wheat eat a couple of cakes!

GRANDAD MA: That's right. In the old days when landlords hired extra reapers, they had to give them good meals to get them to work.

CHAIRMAN QIU: Let's not discuss that now. Stick to your brigade and its cadres.

ZHANG GUILIAN: Even in the chaos of the "cultural revolution" our side-line group kept going, all thanks to Wanju. The commune blasted him for that several times. Wanju has the brigade at heart, no doubt about it. That's all I have to say.

XIAO MEIFENG: Chairman Qiu, I'm not clear why you've called this meeting. Do you mean to make Wanju a model or promote him to the county...?

WU YOUGUI: Why ask, Meifeng. This has nothing to do with your Youth League. Just tell us your opinion of Wanju....

XIAO MEIFENG: I've nothing to add to what the rest have said.

CHAIRMAN QIU: Let me ask you: Did your village "criticize Deng"?

MOTHER LIU: You mean Vice-Chairman Deng? Never! What an idea! With Wanju in charge, Chairman Qiu, our village has kept straight. I remember the rally we had in front of the primary school. Wanju stood on the steps and said: All's well now, Vice-Chairman Deng has taken over. He wants us to raise more pigs and grow more grain. We must work with a will. Wanju came to the pig farm to tell me to raise more big fat pigs. And so I did. People have come from the county to see my pigs! No, our village never criticized Deng!

GRANDAD MA: I don't remember. Working in the storehouse I don't attend all the meetings. There was a time when we had one almost every day. Oh yes, I did hear that a poster had been put up about black cats and white cats.....

MOTHER LIU: Don't talk such rubbish, grandad! There were two criticism hoardings in front of the pig farm, but who ever bothered to read them. Not long ago a beauty was posted up there. You can go and see it for yourself, Chairman Qiu. Cats and dogs, that's ancient history. Take it from me, our village was never against Vice-Chairman Deng. Don't the rest of you agree?

SECOND SISTER LU: That's a fact. We heard Vice-Chairman Deng was under fire, but we had nothing against him. Why should we bash him? We never did. Now Chairman Qiu has come all the way from the county and gone to the trouble of calling this meeting. So we should speak out. We did have two criticism hoardings. Did better than other villages. If you don't believe that, go to Lai Family Grave. They didn't put up a single board — couldn't afford to buy one! And we had some splendid cartoons, all so lifelike. Everyone liked those cats. We had a White Bone Monster too, double-faced. A pretty face in front, a skull behind....

ZHANG GUILIAN: That was to debunk the "gang of four". Second Sister.

GUI QIUSHI: I was in the army during the campaign to
"criticize Deng" so I don't know what happened here.
With all the political pressure then, stands to reason
our village must have joined in. At least made a show
of it.

MOTHER LIU: How would you know, Qiushi, all those
years you were away. Now the county's sent to check
up. On a serious business like this we can't talk wildly.
Our village never debunked Deng. Isn't that true?

XIAO MEIFENG: What I say is: Since the county wants
to check up we should tell the truth. Our village did
criticize Deng. We criticized lots of big shots. As soon
as their names came out in the papers we joined in the
criticism. When the Party Branch gave the lead, our
Youth League Branch went into action. We were the
ones running that criticism column. But now it's over
two years since the fall of the "gang", none of us had
any connection with Jiang Qing, and the "gang" did
nothing for us, we weren't in cahoots — so why come
to investigate us? We weren't even in with the rebels in
the county or the commune. Why pick on us?

CHAIRMAN QIU: You've got me wrong. This is not an
investigation. Just a discussion at which you can air
your views. Wanju's been your secretary for so long,
why shouldn't the county hear you opinion of him?

XIAO MEIFENG: Whatever you say I can't see the point
of this meeting, or why you're collecting material on
Li Wanju. Has he done something wrong? Has
someone informed against him? Chairman Qiu wants
us to discuss him behind his back. I don't like the
sound of that. Why behind his back? And why has
nobody come from the commune? Did they put you up
to this? Maybe you don't know, Chairman Qiu, that
the commune has it in for our village, calls us an

independent kingdom, swears at Wanju for not obeying its orders. That's common knowledge. So why not announce what dope you've got, Chairman Qiu? What investigation can just the few of us make? Better hold a mass meeting, bring everything into the open. If cadres are to be bashed for debunking Deng, all brigade Party secretaries should be ditched. And before them the county and the commune cadres....

WU YOUGUI: You're going too far, Meifeng. The higher-ups often send down to investigate. Why get so worked up about it! All we need do is stick to the facts. We all know what went on in the "cultural revolution". We can't say we took no part in "criticizing Deng", but we didn't bash him hard either. We had our criticism hoarding just like every other village. As I recollect, to criticize Deng all we did was draw two cats.

SECOND SISTER LU: That's right. Every bit as lifelike as Mother Liu's big black cat. Don't you agree, Mother Liu?

MOTHER LIU: I never saw them.

(At noon Chairman Qiu adjourned the meeting till the afternoon.)

5. Second Sister's Hospitalization

Second Sister Lu took Chairman Qiu home to lunch. While she prepared noodles in the outer room he sat chatting with her husband on the *kang* inside. The topic of conversation was still Li Wanju.

"You want to know about Wanju? He's a decent sort. Does a lot for our brigade." Second Brother stroked his wispy beard and chuckled.

Qiu had been sleepy after the morning's meeting but now, revived by strong tea, he hoped to be able to write up one or two of Li's exploits in his report.

"Tell me some of the things he's done," he said eagerly.

Second Brother perked up and replenished Qiu's cup. "This morning the old team leader told my wife to go to the meeting. I don't suppose she was able to talk any sense. I'm the one who really knows Wanju."

His wife called from the other room:

"Just you ask Chairman Qiu if I spoke or not."

With a scornful look in her direction her husband said softly:

"Women have seen too little of the world. I'll tell you a true story to show you what Wanju's like. In the autumn of '62 my wife had a bad turn. She mightn't have pulled through if not for him."

"Bah! Stale news, why rake that up? Making me look a fool!" Second Sister had come in to wipe the table and lay two places.

"You looked a fool; Wanju showed the stuff he's made of." Her husband turned to Qiu. "She was rolling all over the *kang* with belly-ache. I was frantic, didn't know what to do. Wanju happened to call and saw the state she was in. 'Take her to the county hospital,' he said. But I'd no money — that was in the hard years when everyone was half-starved. Wanju knew what to do though. Said, 'She's in a bad way — let's go.' As I couldn't let her die on the *kang*, while he went for a cart I told her to get ready."

Second Brother shot a sidelong glance at the door and pursed his lips, exclaiming scornfully:

"Women! Know what? She couldn't bear to lose face. After all that thrashing about on the *kang*, she didn't want to look a sloven. So up she crawls to wash and comb her hair, then ransack her cases for a change of clothes as if she were going home as a new bride. Was there any call for that?"

Second Sister came in with a bowl of fried bean sauce, another of garlic cloves, which she put on the table. She chuckled:

"No call for it? A chance in a lifetime to go to town — why shouldn't I look my best?"

Qiu nodded in amusement.

"She was groaning and whimpering all the way to town," her husband went on. "But as soon as we got to the hospital she piped down. And when the doctor asked was the pain very bad, she went and said, 'Nothing much!' What a time to choose to pose as a heroine! So they made her out a prescription and sent her home."

Second Sister coming in with a dish of cabbage explained:

"I'd never seen the likes before! A roomful of people, all in white coats and white masks, they made me lie on a cot and undo my clothes, then prodded me and listened. Scared me out of my wits, so I couldn't make a sound!"

Qiu was wondering where Li Wanju came in.

"Back home she took off her finery and started groaning again. The medicine had no effect at all," continued Second Brother. "I didn't know what to do. Take her back to hospital? They'd just sent her away. Then Wanju came and found her at her last gasp. 'This won't do,' he said. 'She must be hospitalized.' I asked, 'Will they take her?' He said, 'Leave it to me.' I propped her up more dead than alive, but she still insisted on prinking herself up. Wanju told her, 'Just listen to me. Go as you are and the hospital will take you — I guarantee it. Let's get started.' He brought over the cart again and fetched a big crate for her to sit in. My old woman refused — a question of face again. Wanju said, 'You're not going to market, Second Sister, don't bother about your looks, you're an emergency case.' So we got her on to the cart."

Qiu couldn't resist a smile at the thought of Second Sister in the crate.

"At the hospital gate she wanted to get out and walk. Wanju wouldn't let her. Between us we carried the crate inside. And Wanju whispered to her, 'Go ahead and groan, don't hold back.' She couldn't have kept quiet anyway then. So we carried her groaning through the gate, and Wanju yelled, 'Make way please! We've brought an emergency case!' Folk scattered as if at sight of the God of Plague while we rushed her into the emergency ward. Well, this time it worked! Three doctors arrived in no time to take a sample of blood; then they put their heads together and said her guts were blocked, she must be operated on at once."

In came Second Sister again with two steaming bowls of noodles. She glared at her husband, then said with a smile:

"Tuck in, Chairman Qiu, while it's hot. Don't listen to his nonsense."

Paying no attention Second Brother went on:

"That talk of operating made me frantic. Where was the money to come from? If I sold my house I'd still not have enough. I stood there unable to get out a word. Trust Wanju! He took the hospitalization slip without even batting an eyelid, saying, 'Give her the very best care you can, you must save her!' Then nurses wheeled my old woman off, telling us to pay the deposit. Wanju just slapped his chest saying, 'Right, you attend to the patient. I'm a brigade cadre, I'll see you get your money.' How could he promise that? In those days our brigade was too broke for the accountant to buy a bottle of ink!"

"Then did you pay a deposit or not?" asked Qiu.

"Just listen! Once she'd been wheeled off Wanju wrote an I.O.U. and stuffed it through the window of the admission office. Then he said to me, 'What are you waiting for? Let's go!' We both skedaddled, jumped on to the cart and made off as if the police were after us. Didn't dare go back to the hospital to see her. I was a bit anxious but Wanju said, 'Don't worry, no people's hospital is going to neglect a poor peasant.' And that made sense."

"Didn't the hospital dun you?" demanded Qiu.

"Don't go into that!" Second Sister was now eating noodles herself on the edge of the *kang*. "It was a shame, playing them such a dirty trick. He dumped me there and never showed up again. But those doctors looked after me well. After the operation they gave me medicine. And the nurses took pity on me all on my own, they bought me white sugar and tried to cheer me up."

"Did you pay the hospital later?" Qiu asked again.

"No, no more was said about it." Her husband bellowed with laughter.

"Everything was topsy-turvy with the 'cultural revolution'," she chimed in.

Qiu lowered his head over his noodles in silence. He was thinking: What does this count as? It was a shady business, not something to write up in a report.

6. Minutes of the Meeting (continued)

Present: the same group as this morning.
Minutes recorded by Gui Qiushi.

Chairman Qiu opened by explaining the policy more fully, emphasizing that this meeting was not aimed at any single individual, but at improving the work and fostering democracy in the Party.

Yang Dequan said: This morning, as I was writing the minutes, I had no chance to speak. Now I'll take the initiative and come clean. In the campaign to "criticize Deng" I was the one who drew those two cats. It had nothing to do with Li Wanju. (Xiao Meifeng put in: This isn't a question of initiative or coming clean.)

All the comrades present supported Yang Dequan's statement, as well as Xiao Meifeng's comment.

In summing up, Chairman Qiu approved of what everyone had said, and pointed out that today's meeting had been limited to a small group. We shouldn't talk about it, as that might undermine stability and unity.

(The end.)

7. An Encounter on the Road

In summer Crown Prince River flows green and rippling. Willows shade its banks. Children strip off their clothes and splash about like ducklings in the water.

The road to the county town runs alongside the river. One hand on the handlebars, with the other Qiu unbuttoned his jacket to enjoy the breeze as he cycled swiftly along.

He was thoroughly satisfied with today's investigation. He hadn't had to resort to any ruse, and the meeting had been attended by a good cross-section of representatives chosen by the brigade. He had not covered up for Li Wanju either, and had raised the question of "criticizing Deng" — the most crucial one in the anonymous letter. And so what? They had simply drawn two cats. What was wrong with that? The ex-armyman was right: under such political pressure they had to join in that movement.

What did rather surprise him was Li Wanju's great popularity. As the letter said, "young and old sing his praise". See how loyal Mother Liu had been, so laughably muddle-headed that she wouldn't hear a word against him. That's the way peasants are. If Secretary Feng were to gun for me, who would defend me? No one, I suspect. At most Qi would shoulder a bit of the blame.

The thought of Qi disturbed him. These last few days Qi seemed to be avoiding him. If Qiu spoke to him he pretended not to hear. As if Qiu were in big trouble and he didn't want to be involved. What big trouble could I be in? We simply carried out orders. Qi should know that. But we both feel so insecure, if we came under fire we'd turn and bite each other.

Luckily Li Wanju stood firm. They hadn't got anywhere trying to undermine him. But who were "they"? Who had written that anonymous letter? Someone in the village? Not likely. He had no enemies there. Someone in the county didn't seem likely either. No one there could have written in such detail. Someone in the commune? That was possible. The letter said the commune had it in for Wanju.

As Qiu peddled along he analysed the problem. If the letter came from the county it was aimed not at Li but at Qi. Why should a county cadre be out for the blood of a brigade secretary? If it came from the commune that was a different matter. The commune was bound to resent a brigade boosted up by the county; on top of which Li with his caustic tongue could always be accused of pride and of disobeying the commune leadership. If that was the case, it needn't be taken too seriously.

In his preoccupation Qiu slowed down. Suddenly someone hailed him.

"Chairman Qiu! Where are you off to?"

Qiu started. Looking up, he saw the "accused" Li Wanju.

Li had dismounted about ten paces ahead and was wheeling his bike towards him. He was short, dark and lean. And his sweatstained T shirt disclosed his scrawny arms. His blue cotton pants were rolled up above his knees, revealing his sinewy, hairy legs. There was not an ounce of superfluous flesh on his face, throwing his pointed chin into relief.

Qiu dismounted too and wheeled his bike forward. They stood under the shade of a roadside willow.

"Going back to the county?" Li asked.

"I've just been to your village." Qiu smiled.

"Oh!" Li looked rather surprised. "What's the hurry? Did you want to see me? Come on back to my place."

"No, I've finished my business there."

"Well, can't you stay a bit, it's so seldom you come." Li didn't ask his business.

"Have you been to the commune?"

Li fished out a crumpled handkerchief and mopped his perspiring face.

"To a meeting, yes," he said with a rueful laugh. "One of these days those meetings will be the death of me."

"Wanju, you should keep on better terms with the commune."

Li eyed him sharply, then sighed.

"No way! Their idea of work is holding endless meetings. Twenty a month, at least. I'm not like them: after each meeting I've loads of work in the village. Do meetings grow grain? Can I spend all my time in meetings? A few days ago we decided to send an old Party member to their meetings, but when they caught on they made a scene. 'Is that Li Wanju of yours dead? Is he too high and mighty to come?' So I have to go. How can I keep on good terms with them?"

"All right, no use complaining to me. I know you don't toe the line. But it's you I'm thinking of. A tall tree catches the wind, Wanju. You've done so well, other folk are bound to be jealous, may try to trip you up."

"You mean someone's informed against me?"

"Don't ask."

Li started wheeling his bike away, retorting:

"I've no intention of asking. So long!"

Qiu hastily called:

"Hey, come back!"

Li halted. Qiu approached and choosing his words with care said:

"You're quick in the uptake, Wanju, I don't have to hide this. Yes, someone has attacked you. But you needn't get het up...."

Li broke in:

"Het up? Why should I? I've been hoping you higher-ups would send someone down. You can hold a struggle meeting or a check-up. I'll ring the bell to summon everyone. If you want to check the accounts, I'll find the accountant for you. If you don't trust our accountant, I'll get the school teacher to help go through the books and we'll give him work points...."

"Come off it. This isn't a clean-up movement, Wanju. I just advise you to be more careful in future. Don't antagonize too many people."

"I'm no Buddha in a temple!" Li laughed, his beady eyes screwed up.

"A village cadre is bound to antagonize people. I have endless headaches. I'm looking forward to being chucked out so as to spend a couple of days in peace. To stop my wife nagging at me for being an official."

"All right, all right, enough of that. Let's get into the shade where it's cool, I've something to tell you."

Having parked his bike Qiu drew Li under a tree to sit down, then offered him a cigarette. Li produced a light and both men started smoking.

Wreathed by smoke, Qiu considered how best to word his question.

"Tell me frankly, Wanju, was the yield of grain you reported accurate?"

"What do you mean?"

"Did you exaggerate it?"

"I'm not such a fool! If I'd given a higher figure, where would I have got so much grain?"

"So the figure you gave was correct?"

"Yes!" With a glance at Qiu Li leant back against the willow, narrowing his eyes to stare into the distance.

"All right then. How did your village boost production?" Qiu was watching Li's expression.

"With the help of the county and the correct leadership of the commune!"

"That can't be the whole story." Qiu laughed. "Other villages have the same leadership, but their output hasn't risen."

"Ask them why not." Li chuckled. "How should I know?"

"Quit beating about the bush! Tell me, how did you boost production?"

"What's got into you, Chairman Qiu? I summarized our experience at that last meeting. There isn't anything else."

"Harking back to that speech of yours! The fact is that's why someone's gunned for you."

Li said nothing.

"Tell me, was what you said at the meeting true or not?"

Li widened his eyes and retorted indignantly, "In front of so many people, with the county heads sitting on the rostrum, how could I tell a pack of lies?"

"Well, some people aren't convinced. They ask why you have all the luck, raising production in every single movement, whether criticizing Confucius, Deng Xiaoping or the 'gang of four'. Other villages joined in those movements, so why didn't *their* output go up? Only yours."

"So they're saying I'm always red, under each new reign."

"You've pinned that label on yourself," Qiu chuckled.

"Very well, Chairman Qiu, you're welcome to come and inspect our village." Li stood up and added drily, "Whether I'm red or not isn't for me to say. And I wasn't the one who started those different movements. I'm a small village Party secretary with no special ability or power. I do as the higher-ups say, criticize whoever I'm told to. If I do it right, everybody's pleased and our brigade prospers too."

"Wanju!" Qiu also stood up. "You don't have to worry. I shall see you're all right."

Li snorted as he went over to his bike.

"That's good of you, Chairman Qiu. But I'm not one of the 'gang of four'. I've never gone in for beating, smashing and looting—what have I to worry about?"

"You—" Qiu shook his head. "The County Committee has never called you 'red under each new reign'...."

"I don't doubt that." Li smiled. "If not for the support and concern of the higher-ups I couldn't have got anywhere. Frankly, Chairman Qiu, I don't like being in the limelight. It's simply asking for trouble...."

"Will you let me finish?" Qiu cut him short.

Li clamped his lips together.

"Wanju, the fact is someone did inform against you. I've been into it and it's nothing to worry about. Still there's one thing I can't figure out. How did you boost production?"

"That's easy." Li's eyes crinkled in a smile. "You're in a hurry to get back now, right? Some day when you've time come back to my place. Bring a bottle of good grog and I'll cook a couple of dishes to go with it. While we're drinking I'll explain it to you in detail, how's that?"

Qiu smiled, thinking, This fellow's a regular monkey!

8. Fire in the Back Yard

There are no secrets in a village.

The least tittle-tattle flies somehow to every household. So of course everyone was talking about an important event like the visit of the county chairman. In vain Qiu had urged the people attending the meeting to keep the matter to themselves. As soon as he left the village the word went round, "Someone's informed against Wanju."

It was dark by the time Li got home and parked his bike under the eaves. Looking up he saw his hefty wife Lin Cuihuan in the doorway like a block of wood. She yelled at him:

"I told you to quit but you wouldn't. Wanted to cut a dash. Now you've done it! Got yourself accused to the county court! Serves you right."

Li feared nothing on earth but the rage of this "block of wood". He adopted his usual tactics now and said nothing, just slunk indoors. Having ladled out some cold water and had a quick wash, he stole a glance at her and asked sheepishly:

"Have you all eaten?"

"No! We're starving to death waiting for you."

He slipped inside to sit on the *kang*, then took out his tobacco pouch and slowly filled his pipe, pretending not to realize that his wife had followed him in.

"Did you stuff yourself at your meeting?" she snapped.

"I honestly haven't eaten. Anything left?" he asked with a conciliatory smile.

Scowling she growled at him:

"Plenty. Deep-fried dumplings, pork with vermicelli, scrambled eggs, plus two ounces of sorghum liquor."

"Ha, you're spoiling me!" He grinned.

"No one will take you food when you're in prison."

"Don't say that, they've two meals a day. With any luck I may get spending money too."

"Go on in then!"

With that she turned and went out. He heard the clatter of dishes and bowls. Presently she brought in a bowl of cornmeal porridge which smelt good, a plate of rolls made with scallion and a dish of pickles.

' Stuff yourself before they nab you."

' Don't worry, they won't. I haven't chopped down any

telegraph poles or filched brigade property. Haven't broken any law, so there's no place for me in prison." Li was so ravenous that he wolfed down the food without noticing what he was eating.

"If you were really a thief and they put you away for a few days, fair enough. But what's all this about? You've never feathered your own nest. Hard at it from dawn till dark you've worked yourself to the bone."

"Don't let that worry you."

"Damn!" He was so rascally she couldn't go on scowling. She went huffing to the cupboard and added a generous dollop of sesame oil to a bowl of crisp sliced turnip, then reached for a salted duck egg. Going back to the *kang* she dumped these on the table and through clenched teeth ordered, "Eat!"

Smiling at her he raised his chopsticks and took a big mouthful of turnip. Then he picked up the duck egg and looked at it.

"Keep this for the kids."

"Cut that out."

"All right, I'll eat it." He promptly peeled off the shell.

"I'm not kidding. Just think where you're heading. Rushing right and left, wearing yourself to a frazzle, you've put many people's backs up. You're so crazy to be an official, it'll be the death of you. Just you wait."

"Stow it! You're making a mountain out of a molehill." Li put down his bowl and told her, "Don't listen to that village gossip. On my way back I ran into Chairman Qiu. See, he gave me these good cigarettes. He says he's checked up and everything's all right."

"Really?" She sounded doubtful. Before she could ask more questions, they heard rapid footsteps and turned to see Mother Liu raise the door curtain and burst in.

"So you're back, Wanju!" There were beads of sweat on

Mother Liu's broad face and the tip of her nose. She picked up a fan and perched on the edge of the *kang*. "Today was terrible," she blurted out.

"Steady on, take your time." Li guzzled his hot porridge.

"How can I help being het up? Someone came from the county to bring to light everything that's gone on in our village."

"Why should we be afraid of everything coming to light?" he countered with a smile.

"We attacked Deng!" she whispered, fixing her big bright eyes on him.

"So what?" asked Li casually, screwing up his eyes as he extracted the duck yolk with his chopsticks.

"Oh, how can you be so stupid?" Mother Liu climbed on to the *kang* and sat there cross-legged, looking much spryer than a sixty-year-old. Frantically slapping one knee she demanded, "What times are these? Isn't attacking Deng just asking for trouble?"

When he smiled and said nothing she stuck her head over the table. Her white hair flashing in the lamplight she went on:

"The man from the county kept asking if we'd criticized Deng or not. I gritted my teeth and refused to let on. Just swore we never had. But I wasn't the only one there. That Grandad Ma and Second Sister Lu gave the show away. And finally Meifeng and Dequan admitted it too. It was written up in the minutes, and Chairman Qiu has taken them back to the county. So here's a pretty kettle of fish!"

"It doesn't matter, Mother Liu, don't worry," Li assured her.

"It was all Second Sister Lu's fault for blabbing. Many's the time I've told her to watch her tongue. But that's the way she is, she blurts everything out. And that business of fried dough-cakes, he didn't ask about that but she blurted it out. . . ."

"Fried dough-cakes?" Li was at a loss.

"Yes, during the wheat harvest didn't everyone get two big fried dough-cakes. Had you forgotten?" Mother Liu fixed him with her eyes.

Li chuckled and slapped the back of his head, replying:

"I've a memory like a sieve. But that doesn't amount to anything, Mother Liu."

"It doesn't? Wanju, didn't you announce: Harvesting makes everyone dead tired. So the brigade has decided to give everyone two fried dough-cakes a day. We'll see to the frying, you see to the eating. When you've finished and wiped your mouths you can forget it. If anyone asks, say you know nothing about it. Otherwise those busybodies may report us for going in for material incentives. Right? I remember perfectly."

"Well I never. What a good memory you have!" Li couldn't but believe her.

"Of course. It doesn't do to forget. If word leaked out who'd take the blame?"

"Well, nowadays eating dough-cakes is no crime."

"It isn't?" She sounded rather disappointed. "You must find time, Wanju, to explain in detail to everyone what's allowed nowadays and what isn't. Then we'll know where we are."

Li sighed to himself as this was a tall order. These days they were trying to bring order out of chaos. There was an old saying: No mirror is always bright, no balance always correct. Who knew the correct yardstick? What rules could he give their commune members?

All he could say was, "Anyway, we've nothing to be ashamed of, nothing to hide."

"Well, can you tell them about the grain?" Mother Liu, leaning over the table, had lowered her voice.

"That —" Li's chopsticks stopped in midair and he

looked grave. "We must tell everyone not to breathe a word about that."

Mother Liu was satisfied that she hadn't come in vain and had shown her shrewdness. She got off the *kang*, smoothed her tousled hair and prepared to carry out his instructions. As she walked out she assured him:

"Don't worry, I'll see to it. First I'll find those blabbermouths, starting with Second Sister Lu."

"Don't go raising a rumpus everywhere," he warned her uneasily.

"Oh, you can trust me!" She hurried out.

When she had gone Cuihuan came in to clear the table and gesturing towards the window said:

"So you're still deploying troops. What do you think she knows?"

Li took out a cigarette and lit up, then answered slowly: "Nowadays who knows anything? I'm all confused myself."

9. Report of the Investigation

Three days later Qiu Bingzhang wrote the following report for the County Committee:

Secretary Feng, Deputy-Secretary Qi and Members of the County Committee:

We recently received an anonymous letter denouncing Comrade Li Wanju, the Party secretary of Crown Prince Village. Secretary Feng and Deputy-Secretary Qi sent me to that village to investigate. Here is my report.

In line with our principle of mobilizing the masses to seek truth from facts, I lost no time in calling a meeting of representatives of cadres, commune members, members of the Party and Youth League and demobilized soldiers. This was in Li Wanju's absence, to encourage them to speak freely. The three chief questions raised were those brought up in the letter.

1. Li Wanju's working style. All approved of this. He has close, democratic relations with the villagers and shows concern for their welfare. For instance, when the poor peasant Second Sister Lu fell ill he took her to hospital. Mother Liu of the pig farm reported that he consults the masses, acts on their suggestions and is on good terms with them. No instances were given of coercion on his part.

2. The question of "attacking Deng". The letter exposed this, and the villagers did put up a reactionary cartoon criticizing the saying, "Black cats, white cats, whichever catches rats is a good cat." But according to the villagers they didn't hold a mass meeting, just made the usual show of joining in the movement. The accountant Yang Dequan who drew that cartoon made a clean breast of it and the others endorsed what he said. It had nothing to do with Li Wanju.

3. The question of Li Wanju always coming out on top. This is rather more complex. Ever since 1964 they've had good crops, due to Li Wanju's hard work. This is why he was singled out for praise by successive county committees. Thus it is unfair to distort the facts and accuse him of being "red in each new reign".

My preliminary investigation of these three questions leads me to believe that Comrade Li Wanju is a good or relatively good cadre.

I submit this for your consideration.

Qiu Bingzhang
August 24, 1978.

10. The Second Anonymous Letter

Respected Leading Comrades of the County Committee,

First, I am extremely grateful that you took my letter seriously. Busy as you are you sent someone to check up whether Li Wanju, secretary of Crown Prince Village, has been deceiving the Party and the masses. This shows that Secretary Feng is concerned for us common people, is a leader we can trust. So we can be optimistic about our future.

This being the case I'll write frankly. The investigation made by the County Committee was an utter failure. Not a single problem was brought to light, let alone solved. Of course people like myself have no means of knowing exactly what took place and no right to ask. But as the saying goes, Walls have ears. Though I'm an outsider I have an idea what happened. So here are my views for your consideration.

Chairman Qiu only went through the motions of checking up. He didn't stay in the village, simply called a few people in to hold a meeting in the morning and afternoon. And during the afternoon meeting he fell asleep. Then he just up and left. These years we've seen plenty of work teams, and no one dares speak to them frankly. Such investigations are bogus; how can they get at the truth. Chairman Qiu owed a duty to the people of the whole county, a duty he shouldn't have shirked.

Worse still, Chairman Qiu ignored organizational principles by telling Li Wanju that someone had informed against him and asking him if he'd offended anyone. It's a good thing I was careful last time not to give my name, or else I'd be in trouble. I'd never have any peace.

With Chairman Qiu backing him, Li Wanju has grown more cocksure. He boasts to everyone, "Don't worry, I'm all right." Doesn't that show a guilty conscience? If you're all right, why should other people worry? Why waste breath urging them not to? The more you try to conceal, the more you reveal.

Secretary Feng, this is the way I am. If I butt in, I have to go through with it. To help your respected committee I'll give you another clue. Li Wanju has no clear class line. He can talk all right but won't practise what he preaches. He eats and drinks with landlords and rich peasants, acts as matchmaker for those reactionaries' sons, attends their wedding feasts, and allotting work often gives them cushy jobs. This is the truth I'm telling you, please look into it yourself. How can such a man with no class stand grasp revolution and promote production? How can he boost the output of Crown Prince Village?

Chairman Mao teaches us to pay attention to great affairs of state. I see from the paper which I read every day that now our Party policy is to bring order out of chaos, and we ordinary people are all for that. After ten years of chaos we must set our house in order. And so should Crown Prince Village. I beg the County Committee to expose the true state of affairs there, so that everyone can judge it for themselves.

As I said in my last letter, I'm a coward. Now I've braced myself to write again, but still don't dare sign my name. Please excuse me. I hope your committee will soon send investigators to clear this up.

Respectfully wishing all your committee members good health,

> A commune member
> September 2, 1978.

11. A Sign of Trust or a Test?

Feng Zhenmin took this letter to Qi's office.

"Here's another letter, Old Qi, attacking Crown Prince Village." Feng sat down sideways in a chair opposite Qi and handed him the letter.

Qi took it with a glance at him. Recently Feng had lost weight. His orderly said he ate less than two steamed buns at a meal. It obviously was no joke heading a county. In his ten years out of office he'd imagined that once reinstated he could make sweeping reforms, but it wasn't that easy. These last few months had exhausted him.

Qi on the other hand had put on weight. For months the County Committee had been checking cases large and small, and Feng had shown himself able to deal with them all correctly, in accordance with the Party policy. He had arrested men with criminal records, let off those who had owned up to minor offences or to saying something wrong. Some cases involved Qi, who had made several self-criticisms which Feng had not followed up. So Qi's impression of him had improved. He found him principled, and felt secure working as his second-in-command. But the checking up hadn't yet ended. Was Feng holding his fire till the last stage of the movement, to launch a sudden assault? Hard to say. If the higher-ups changed their policy, Feng would have to follow suit. So Qi didn't like to take too much responsibility. He did the jobs assigned him and didn't interfere in anything else. Getting by like this for several months he had put on weight.

Qi opened the letter, read it carefully, and felt chilled. That anonymous "commune member" again! Who could he be? How come he knew so much? It sounded as if he had gone to the village with Qiu, or followed him there to make a counter-investigation. What did this mean?

"What action do you think we should take on this, Old Qi?" Feng leaned against the desk, his face turned to him.

Instead of answering, Qi said:

"Comrade Qiu isn't all that thorough. When he came back from Crown Prince Village I told him he ought to have stayed there for a few days...."

"We needn't be in a hurry to criticize him," Feng cut in. "Do you think this worth looking into further?"

Was it worth it? The County Committee received so many visitors and letters every day, they obviously couldn't send to check up on everything. But this letter denounced Crown Prince Village, held up for years as a model brigade. Nowadays sham models were being exposed by the papers every day as fabrications of the "gang of four". He'd looked into the work in Crown Prince Village in the past, so if he opposed a check-up it would look as if he had a guilty conscience. Besides, since Secretary Feng had sent someone to investigate last time, he clearly took the matter seriously. Now that the anonymous writer had even denounced Chairman Qiu they'd have to look into it.

"Of course we must check up thoroughly," Qi declared.

Feng took out his cigarettes and tapped one on the packet while he thought, then said slowly:

"At first I didn't think we need follow this up. We should be concentrating now on righting wrongs. Think how many cadres and people inside and outside the Party were persecuted in the ten years of chaos. We should first rehabilitate them and take this weight off their minds."

Qi nodded. That made sense. It was a question of policy and of priorities.

"Take this letter-writer." Feng glanced at the letter on the desk. "He doesn't accuse Li Wanju of persecuting or attacking him. He isn't someone who was unjustly treated. He accuses him of deceiving the higher-ups and those below, of a wrong working style. Of course those questions ought to be looked into. But right now we're so short-handed we can let them wait."

Qi nodded again. It seemed he'd been swayed by personal feelings. Feng's analysis was correct. This letter could wait.

"But since you propose going into it, I agree. Make another investigation."

Feng lit his cigarette and puffed out a cloud of smoke.

This time Qi didn't nod. He thought, Feng is really tricky. If he wanted to check up I wouldn't have stopped him. Why beat about the bush like that to bamboozle me? That's no way for Party members to discuss questions. He said:

"If this letter had denounced any other village, we wouldn't have to check up; but in the case of Crown Prince Village we must." He enlarged on this, "Crown Prince Village has been held up as a model by us for years. Although Li is attacked he's clearly not the main target. As you said, Li never persecuted this letter-writer, so why inform against him? I'm the one he's gunning for!"

Qi was quite worked up now, his pale face had flushed. Feng was at a loss for words.

"I agree that we need priorities in our work," Qi fumed. "We must concentrate on righting wrongs. But exposing, denouncing and investigating has top priority. And that's where this letter comes in. So I'm all in favour of finding out the truth."

When presently Qi had calmed down a little Feng said:

"Old Qi, I see no connection between you and Crown Prince Village. This letter isn't gunning for you. If it were he'd have named you and listed your crimes. An anonymous letter, why should he be afraid? Why write in this roundabout way?"

Qi lowered his head to think. Yes. It would be easy to inform against me without being so devious about it.

"We never worked together before so don't know each other too well," Feng went on. "But I'll tell you what I think.

In the ten years of chaos some comrades made mistakes, others didn't; I don't believe this proves that they had different levels of understanding. In my case I was pounced on as soon as the 'cultural revolution' started; and being locked up for ten whole years I'd no chance to make mistakes. You were liberated early on and appointed to the leading group. Holding a leading position in that time of chaos you couldn't but make some mistakes."

On hearing this Qi began to look more relaxed.

"So let's send someone to Crown Prince Village again, to find out what's been going on there." Feng stood up to leave.

"We'll have to send someone from the Standing Committee," said Qi. Since Qiu Bingzhang hadn't got anywhere they'd have to send someone senior.

Feng turned round at the door to suggest:

"I think, Old Qi, you'd better go yourself."

"Me?" Qi was taken aback. Did Feng think he was the power behind Li Wanju? Afraid that if he stayed in the county town he might be obstructive. Did he think no one else could handle this tricky business? Or that he was so useless that he might as well stay in the village? Was this equivalent to being "sent down to the countryside"?

"Well, Old Qi, how about it?" Feng asked.

"Am I the right man to go?" Qi blurted out.

"Of course you are. You were the one, Old Qi, who made Crown Prince Village a model. If there's something wrong with Li Wanju's style of work and feeling against him runs high, you can put someone better in his place. If you find no big problems there you can go on helping them to summarize their experience and do still better. It's not easy to groom a model brigade; it would be a pity to drop it for no good reason."

"In that case I'll go," Qi had to acquiesce.

12. Qi Yuezhai's Diary

September 9. Fine.

I came to Crown Prince Village this afternoon with Young Wang from our office.

I had thought of asking the commune to send a vice-secretary to join in this investigation, but Secretary Feng advised against it on the grounds that if there were too many of us the villagers might take fright and it would be harder to get at the truth. Qiu Bingzhang was against it too for different reasons. According to him Li Wanju is not on good terms with the commune. So if the commune joined in that would most likely complicate matters. There is some truth in that. But everything has its pros and cons. If someone came from the commune and picked a few faults we might get a better overall picture. Still, as this was Feng's decision I didn't insist.

It's years since I last stayed in a village, so I was very glad to come this time. On the banks of Crown Prince River the sorghum is ripening, the maize is in the milk, and it looks like being another bumper harvest. The credit for this can't go to our County Committee. It was Old Man Heaven who helped by sending good weather. Not to recognize this would be a big mistake.

The brigade has put us up with Mother Liu. There's only the old couple at home as their son is a worker in town, so the place is very quiet besides being clean. Mother Liu is most hospitable. She insists on giving us a new mattress and says we mustn't catch cold, as old people easily get rheumatism in autumn. Chinese peasants are really warm-hearted!

This evening we met the brigade cadres but didn't discuss any important questions. I didn't say why we'd come and

Wanju didn't ask, as if he took my coming very lightly. But I suspect he's worried. He's bound to wonder why the County Committee should send people here twice in less than one month.

September 10. Fine.

This morning I made a gaffe.

I went out while it was barely light to have a stroll in the fields and breathe the fresh air. When I reached the west end of the village I saw an old woman with two buckets of water. She was short and stooping under her carrying-pole. Thinking she must be a widow all on her own I offered to help. At first she refused but finally I persuaded her to let me take her pole.

It's years since I helped a villager carry water, but I found I could still manage. She behaved very strangely, not saying a word and keeping some way behind, as if afraid to walk beside me. When I reached her gate she rushed forward to block the way. "Don't go in," she whispered. "We're landlords."

That startled me. I looked round. Luckily there was no one about apart from two bare-bottomed kids squatting down to play. If anyone had seen a County Secretary carrying water for a landlord goodness knows what rumours would have been spread.

I hesitated on the threshold. Not to go in would seem unduly cautious and make me appear a coward; but going in might lead to trouble and be hard to justify later. Still I decided to go in for a look. In several dozen years of working in the countryside I'd actually never been through the gate of a landlord or rich peasant, and had no idea how they lived. So I said nothing, giving her tit for tat. When she opened the gate I carried the water in.

There seemed nothing special about the small well-swept yard. There was a bed of sunflowers, and by the wall a pigsty and a hen coop. A fat pig was lying sound asleep in the sty. Some hens had already come out in search of food. Ridiculous as it sounds, this peaceful rustic scene made me feel that landlords weren't too badly off — they hadn't the headaches of a County Secretary. That was really a dangerous notion.

I carried the buckets into the hall and, before I could empty them into the vat, an old man scurried out from the inner room. Of medium height and scrawny, he had a hooked nose and kept blinking his bloodshot eyes. He really looked like an old landlord. Unlike his wife he was talkative. He invited me into his room.

I didn't go in. If I had, I'd have had to sit on the *kang*, unable to get away. He'd have offered me tea and cigarettes so that there was no clear class line between us. Worse still he might have complained to me of injustice. On the other hand how could I beat a retreat? So I stood talking to him in the hall. Asked his name, he said it was Li Qiangfu, and as he was his family's fifth son the neighbours called him Fifth Uncle. These villagers are quite hopeless. After all these years of class education they're still in the grip of clan relationships, and you don't know whether to laugh or cry at the way they address each other. Old customs die so hard. Not even the storm of the "cultural revolution" could sweep them away.

"Fifth Uncle" announced with a smile that Li Wanju, his nephew, called him "Fifth Uncle" too. No wonder that letter accused him of having no clear class line. So I asked him his opinion of Wanju. He just said, smiling, that he had nothing against him. I asked if Wanju was a good cadre. The old fox answered, "That's not for me to say."

This slip-up brought home to me the need for a firm class

stand. Next time I come down to some village I must do as
I used to and first call together the cadres to find out the
number and whereabouts of the landlords and rich peasants
there, to avoid making a fool of myself by going through the
wrong gate.

In the morning I harvested beans.

It's some years since I did any field work. It made me
rather tired, made my back ache and the calves of my legs
swell. But I'd told Young Wang before we came that we must
join in the farm work for half a day every day.

Wanju was working in the fields too. He didn't try to
sound me out, just chatted and smiled as he had yesterday.
That made me suspicious because it wasn't logical or natural.
When the higher-ups send a work team to your village
shouldn't you ask what they want? Why keep so quiet?

But what can Wanju's problem be? Although I'm not all
that close to him I've known him for some time. Each year
when the local cadres came to the county for meetings I went
to hear the speeches made in his group. When later those of
us on the county's Standing Committee were assigned to visit
different brigades each year, I met him at many meetings
large and small. I know the general situation in Crown Prince
Village, and Wanju has done fine!

Of course we must investigate before coming to
conclusions. The "cultural revolution" was so disruptive
that many fantastic things happened, and nobody can vouch
for anyone else.

We're basically clear about Bingzhang's investigation here
last month. As the letter said, he simply called a fact-finding
meeting then left. And he did fall asleep during the afternoon
meeting. That fat fellow is always sleepy.

Still, according to the villagers, the people attending the
meeting talked very freely. The business of painting cats to

criticize Deng was pretty well cleared up too. It was nothing very unusual. And all agreed that Wanju was a good or relatively good cadre. So Bingzhang's report was based on facts.

It appears that only one person at the meeting seemed tongue-tied and rather depressed — that was Zhang Guilian of the sidelines group. Was she afraid to speak out? I've told Young Wang to talk to her tomorrow.

What puzzles me is who wrote those two anonymous letters? He knew too much for an outsider, so must belong to this village.

September 11. Fine.

This morning I dug up sweet potatoes.

To clear up any suspicions the cadres and commune members might have, I called a meeting before work and talked to them for half an hour. Mainly about the excellent situation in the country and our county. I also explained that we'd come down this time to fill in gaps in my knowledge — although I was supposed to keep an eye on Crown Prince Village, I'd actually seldom come here and never stayed long. This time I meant to stay longer and hear what they had to say. They relaxed and livened up after hearing this, further convincing me that there's much to be said for short meetings and short talks. They are in the masses' interest, as long meetings hold up their work. When cadres come down in future they should hold meetings in the fields like this.

This afternoon I called on various households. As I'd spoken to all the commune members that morning, everyone knew me. (In fact, as soon as I arrived, grown-ups and children alike knew I was here.) I received a hearty welcome wherever I went. I sounded them out about their living conditions. They seem to be doing rather well here and aren't short of grain or money. That's no mean achievement. But asked about their grain ration they gave different answers. Some said 400 catties of grain per year, others 420, and some just hummed and hawed. Mother Liu says the rule is 386.

When I asked their opinion of the cadres, especially Wanju, they all said he was fine, "Whole-heartedly for the collective". When I asked what faults he had, they said he had none. This is a bit dubious. How can any cadre be perfect? I asked casually if he had any enemies in the village. Again they said none. Strange. If he has no enemies, who wrote those anonymous letters?

After calling on some villagers I went to see the brigade's beancurd mill. It's quite a size. The beancurd, made of soya beans, is snow-white and soft. They sell beancurd milk too every morning. No wonder Mother Liu gives us a bowl of beancurd milk for breakfast every day. It's much better than that in our county canteen which is made of beancurd powder. They make vermicelli too in a big courtyard, with vermicelli hanging there like sheets hung up to dry. Quite a few people from other villages had come to buy some. They were doing a brisk business.

A man in his thirties called Li Chengde is in charge of the beancurd mill. With his big flashing eyes and an apron tied round his slim waist he looked most efficient as he bustled about. Since he was so busy I didn't like to interrupt him.

Crown Prince Village's affluence seems to owe a lot to its successful sidelines. Some villages can't make a go of sidelines. Depending solely on grain crops they grow poorer and poorer and have no means of raising the peasants' income. The villagers complain about the cost of chemical fertilizer, insecticides, machinery, water and electricity, and the state loses money. I've always doubted the need to use so much chemical fertilizer, which isn't as good as organic manure. And the use of insecticides needs to be more carefully controlled. One team sprayed so much on that their vegetables turned out too toxic to eat. This isn't an obvious problem yet, but it's bound to become one.

Mother Liu is really warm-hearted. She takes such good care of Young Wang and me, she cooks us different dishes every day. This evening we had pancakes and a bowl of beancurd with shallots. It was so tasty that I really tucked in.

This old lady takes an interest too in affairs of state, and asks all sorts of questions. She sticks up for Crown Prince Village, not letting anyone say a word against it. She's obviously loyal to Li Wanju and the other brigade cadres and seems to have guessed that someone has informed against Wanju so that we're making a private investigation. That's made her rather worried and put out. I'd like to assure her: Li Wanju is a good comrade; I haven't come to gun for him. But it's too early for that.

Today Young Wang had a talk with Zhang Guilian. Sure enough she had reservations at that meeting. Yang Dequan, who is her busband, owned up to painting those cats and claimed it had nothing to do with Wanju. She said that wasn't true, and her husband shouldn't have shouldered all the blame. He'd got Li's approval beforehand. So he wasn't the only one responsible.

It looks as if Li Wanju was involved; we must go into this. But supposing he was involved, does it really matter?

What's more exasperating is that Young Wang heard in the village that Li Qiangfu is telling everyone how well Secretary Qi treated him by going to see him as soon as he arrived and helping them fetch water. This old landlord's despicable nature hasn't changed!

13. "Grasp Class Struggle!"

"Wanju, hurry up and decide what to do. Qi...."

Mother Liu had burst anxiously into Li Wanju's room. Seeing the old brigade leader, Youth League secretary and other cadres seated on his *kang* she swallowed back what had been on the tip of her tongue.

"What is it, Mother Liu? Speak out!" said Li cheerfully.

"Ach, it's nothing." She forced a smile. "Go on with your meeting."

"We've finished. If you've some problem let's hear it." He shifted to make room for her on the *kang*.

Whenever cadres from outside came to the village they put up with Mother Liu. So she thought it her duty to make a "report" every day or so to Li. Under the "gang of four" the commune had sent someone to see whether they had reported their output in full or had set some aside for themselves. He had stayed with Mother Liu too. And she had promptly passed on to Li what she had learned from him, so that the whole village agreed on what to say and kept their fraud secret. Otherwise they would have been made to sell more grain to the state. That boosted Mother Liu's prestige. She prided herself on her usefulness, so keen to improve her fine record that there was no holding her back.

She bucked up now, seeing all the cadres waiting to hear her "report". Sitting cross-legged on the *kang*, her eyes dilated, she started:

"My word, this Secretary Qi is a terror! He's all smiles and sweet talk like a scholar, but he knows what he's doing! Is just too tight-lipped to let on. I try to get him to talk at mealtimes. But he simply hums and haws, shadow-boxing with me. Yesterday evening, though, I saw this with my own eyes!"

Mother Liu was as long-winded as a padded-out report in a newspaper. The cadres knowing this all too well didn't take her seriously. But her mysterious look as she announced this made even Meifeng who had no patience with her prick up her ears.

"Last night when I came back from the pig farm they'd stopped talking, but the lamp was still on in Secretary Qi's room. I peeped through a crack in the door. Young Wang was tucked up in his quilt while Secretary Qi was writing in a big notebook."

Wu Yougui, hearing this, threw back his head and laughed.

"Don't all cadres bring notebooks to make notes? That's nothing to worry about, Mother Liu."

Meifeng snorted, "Why be so sneaky, peeping through a crack in the door?"

"Just what I thought." Not in the least put out, Mother Liu went on, "I told myself, why look in from outside, why not go in? Calling out, 'Not asleep yet, Old Qi?' I marched in. And as soon as he saw me he hid that notebook of his under the pillow."

"You're too suspicious, Mother Liu," laughed Li. "Why should he hide it from you when you can't read?"

"Yes, that's what I thought. If he'd left it under the lamp I couldn't have made head or tail of it. Well, I've had plenty to do with cadres, I'm not afraid of them. Though he's a big secretary from the county, I don't mince words with him. I sat myself down on the *kang* and we had a long talk. Old Qi was very friendly, he poured me a glass of water and praised my cooking. We had a really good chat. And in the end, when he was off guard, I got him to answer my question."

"What was it?" asked Meifeng quickly. "Go on."

Having looked round to make sure that no outsiders were present, Mother Liu whispered:

"Hiding—output."

When no one spoke she enlarged on this.

"Secretary Qi's come to check on whether we've been faking production figures."

This information dismayed everyone. Only Mother Liu, feeling a weight lifted from her mind, rubbed her chest and let out a deep breath.

After thinking it over Li said:

"What did you ask, Mother Liu, and what did he answer?"

Though thinking this question superfluous she said, "We chatted for over half an hour, asking each other questions, till I got the truth out of him."

"Yes, just what did you say?" Li seemed to think this most important.

"Why, it was easy. I said, 'You've come all this way, Secretary Qi, when you're no longer young. Why not stay in your office, why come down here and work in the fields too? You mustn't tire yourself out.'" She blinked thoughtfully. "He said he was filling up, filling up gaps in his knowledge."

"That's stale news," complained Meifeng. "That's what he told us at that meeting this morning."

"I asked what gaps he was filling up. He said all of them. I asked what he meant. He said staying all the time in the county they got out of touch with reality, didn't know the situation. So he'd come to the village to get a clearer picture. Once his tongue was loosed he asked all sorts of questions: had we painted cats to criticize Deng, were the landlords toeing the line. I could see he knew the answers and didn't have to ask. But last of all after beating about the bush he asked about grain. How much land has your village, how big a crop do you raise, what's your grain ration, how much flour do you eat—he wanted to know in detail."

"What did you tell him?" Wu Yougui put in.

"Don't worry, brigade leader, he didn't get anything out

of me." She glowered as if she would rather die than disclose secrets.

"What harm would it do to say?" cried Meifeng. "What if we did divide up the grain. After all, to each according to his work. We handed in our grain tax, sold what ought to be sold and kept what ought to be kept. If we ate a bit extra what was wrong with that? We didn't rob anyone, we worked for it!"

"What's got into you, Meifeng? This is no time to throw a tantrum," the old brigade leader scolded. "It says in the old books 'Food is the first necessity for the people'. We need that grain to live on! If you get a kick out of defying the higher-ups and let the cat out of the bag, we'd be ordered to hand in the extra grain we took. Even if we are not asked to do that but are just given a warning never to do it again, the whole village, old and young, would be out for your blood!"

"That's right!" Mother Liu nodded, delighted by his approval.

Li tweaked his moustache and blinked his small eyes, then said:

"I've heard it's no great crime to conceal your output and divide it up. When Chairman Mao was alive he said this was storing grain among the people. If grain is stored in the bins in our homes, we don't have to worry where our next meal's to come from and the provincial granaries can stop complaining that they've no storage space. It saves building extra granaries too."

"I don't agree!" burst out Meifeng. "It's not a question of nowhere to store the grain. What's wrong is this hard-and-fast rule that everyone in the county gets 386 catties no matter how they've done. If your brigade has slacked you should go hungry. But our brigade has slaved away, it's not fair for us to get 386 too. This injustice is what makes me angry!"

"Bah, what are you shouting about! Listen to Wanju." The old brigade leader snubbed the furious Youth League secretary.

"There's reason in what I say, in what Meifeng says too," said Li. "We can't do anything unreasonable. But nowadays what stands to reason may be illegal, right? Which has priority, reason or law? Who knows? These last few years it's the fast donkey that gets whipped. The more grain you reap the more the state requisitions, so as to level things out. If our people can't get more to eat they won't be keen to produce more, and I've no way to make them. We were forced to hide our output and divided up that extra grain. What other way out was there? Now the county's sent Secretary Qi to make a check-up. What do you all think we should do?"

As no one had any ideas he went on:

"As I said, this doesn't count as a crime. If it was wrong, the man in charge will be blamed and at most I'll be dismissed from my post. So much the better, my family keeps urging me to quit."

"Dismiss you, no!" protested the old brigade leader.

The others agreed, that would never do.

What way out was there then? Mother Liu proposed:

"Let's not make things hard for Wanju. Let's tell the truth. Old Qi is a good sort, we can beg him not to report us but help to cover this up."

"A fine idea!" scoffed Meifeng. "A cadre who eats commodity grain doesn't understand the peasants' difficulties. How could he cover it up?"

Faced by this dilemma the old brigade leader said calmly:

"Steady on. Our brigade has weathered plenty of storms. Last time they checked up we made out all right, didn't we? Why? Because there's strength in unity. If we watch our tongues there won't be any big trouble. Besides, Secretary Qi hasn't questioned us yet officially. We don't have to worry till he does."

The others agreed. They'd just have to wait and see.

As Mother Liu got up to go Li urged her:

"Look after the men from the county well, Mother Liu. You needn't try to ferret out anything else."

"I'm not nosy. You don't have to warn me," she retorted. "I know what questions to ask and when to keep quiet."

She turned back at the threshold to add:

"Oh, there's something I nearly forgot."

"What is it?" Li looked blank.

"Yesterday evening I met Second Sister Lu and she said that old scoundrel Li Qiangfu has been spreading rumours again."

"What rumours?" asked Li.

"The old wretch tells everyone how good Secretary Qi is," she fumed. "His first day here he called on him to show his concern and helped his wife fetch water. What do you say to that?"

"He's a hopeless case," Li sighed.

The brigade leader suggested:

"Suppose we call a meeting of bad elements tomorrow? We can pin this on him."

Li frowned. "Go ahead! We must grasp class struggle."

14. Qi Yuezhai's Diary (2)

September 12. Fine.

This morning Secretary Feng sent Bingzhang here with some documents for me to read. Feng is very conscientious. Actually since coming here I've shelved all county business. He can deal with it all himself without consulting me. He probably thinks I may resent being left out and is showing his goodwill.

I'm getting sick of Bingzhang's fussiness and his wild guesses when analyzing problems. I ticked him off sharply today. People were already saying that the County Committee had hidden reefs although to all appearances we had cliques like solid mountains. He kept telling me tales in such a sneaky way that anyone seeing us might really think we were plotting. When I flared up he seemed very hurt. Well this Fatty is an intelligent idiot. Sometimes most shrewd, sometimes most stupid.

I saw him off to the end of the village and tried to reassure him. Coming back I met a fellow of about fifty with a toper's nose. He accosted me to ask where I was from, yet as if he already knew me. I couldn't remember seeing him here before, so I asked him his village. He chuckled, "I'm from Lai Family Grave. Stroll over when you have time."

That surprised me. Coming down here I gave the commune a miss, and I've stayed in Crown Prince Village all the time. How do villagers from outside know I'm here? On second thoughts it's not strange. Though I'm a low-ranking official they consider me one of the county heads, so of course I attract attention.

At noon Wanju came to tell me an old landlord had been spreading rumours about me, and they were calling a meeting of bad elements to teach them a lesson. I wanted him to call it off. I told him it wasn't a rumour, I had gone to Li Qiangfu's place. But he said they made it a rule to hold such a meeting once a month and now it was time for it. So I didn't insist.

I didn't want to attend, but being involved myself felt that it wouldn't be right to stay away. I went to the meeting this evening. I'd been rather worried, because how could they blame Li Qiangfu for telling the truth? I hadn't realized Wanju's gift of the gab! He stood there and, for all he's so short, dominated the whole meeting. Told Li Qiangfu, Secretary Qi called at your house and helped carry two buckets of water — was that anything to broadcast far and wide? Do you know why he went to your place? Why he helped carry water? Secretary Qi wanted to see for himself how our Party branch is carrying out the policy of forcing bad characters to reform. He went on: Chairman Mao said, unless you go into the tiger's den you can't catch a tigercub; unless you eat a pear you can't tell how it tastes. His visit to your place was like going into a tiger's den or tasting a pear. You're not remoulding yourself properly but flaunting the banner of Secretary Qi to gild your ugly face. What does this show?

Li Qiangfu was left speechless.

Li Wanju's such a clever devil he can turn black into white, white into black, or justify something quite unreasonable. Of course this isn't strange: most brigade cadres have the gift of the gab.

It seems to me that Li has a strong sense of class struggle. The accusation that he has no clear stand is obviously not true.

I want to know though if it's true that he finds wives for landlords' sons and goes to feast in their homes.

September 13.   Wet.

Today I cleared up the question of Li Wanju matchmaking for landlords' sons and going to their wedding feasts.

Mother Liu insists that Wanju has a firm class stand and never blurs class distinctions. This old lady is a "staunch royalist". "Wanju has the best class stand in our village," she claims. "He steers clear of landlords and rich peasants." She goes on and on about this to hammer it into you.

I approached the question then from a different angle by asking how many sons their landlords and rich peasants had and how many had married. I discovered that the nineteen sons of marriageable age are *all* married. Fantastic!

Next I asked who introduced their brides. First she said nowadays young people choose for themselves, they don't need matchmakers, and as Crown Prince Village is well off girls from outside like to come here. She wouldn't let on who the matchmakers had been.

She may have been telling the truth. Village marriages aren't based on love but on output, income and whether or not the man has a brick house with a tiled roof. Some people think it's vulgar to look for a husband with a house; but this is a practical question. If he'd no house she'd have nowhere to live and couldn't be high-minded even if she tried. If they make do with two adobe rooms and then have children, they'll never be able to save up to build a house. So most village girls find themselves a man with a house. That's why the peasants say: You must plant a Chinese parasol tree if you want a phoenix to fly over. Those trees are big tiled houses. This village has plenty of houses like that, so phoenixes flock here regardless of whether they belong to landlords or rich peasants.

I learned from Mother Liu that Li Chengde whom I met in the beancurd mill had a bad class origin yet invited eight tables of guests to his wedding feast. I asked if Wanju had attended it. Mother Liu can't see things from the viewpoint of class. To her, marriage is the main event in life so everybody wants it to be lively. If they didn't invite lots of guests, how could they look their neighbours in the face? As Li Chengde was a dab at making beancurd and treated all his customers so politely, he had friends everywhere. So a lot of people, including her, sent gifts and went to his wedding feast.

When I asked Grandad Ma on the threshing-floor about this he told a different story.

He said Crown Prince Village has always thrived because of its good geomantic location. Its auspicious situation made some emperor have the Crown Prince buried here — his grave is still in the orchard. That's how the village and river came by their names. With the Crown Prince's imperial bones buried here the village has never been short of brides. And all of them have borne children.

Of course this is nonsense. But Grandad Ma believes it implicitly. The peasants are fettered by centuries of feudal ideology. How to educate them is a serious problem.

Not until I sought out Xiao Meifeng, the Youth League secretary, did I get at the truth.

This forceful girl with her prominent eyebrows and eyes rattles off like a machine-gun. She seems to have absolutely the same stand as Li Wanju. When I asked if he'd arranged marriages for landlords' and rich peasants' sons, she said emphatically: Sure, no need to investigate. Then gave me a detailed account of how Li Chengde had found a bride.

For a landlord's son to find a wife was not as simple as Mother Liu made out. Li Chengde had been through junior middle school. He was an able, intelligent young fellow, so clever with his hands that he could pick up any skill he wanted. He had long ago built himself a three-roomed tiled house and left his family to live on his own. He had plenty of money and grain, but because of his bad class origin several girls' families had turned him down. The girl he finally married had a good impression of him but wanted to know if the villagers discriminated against him. So her parents took her to his house for a meal. Since the matchmaker Second Sister Lu had told them that their Party secretary thought highly of Li Chengde, Wanju had to attend this betrothal.

Li Chengde had arranged this the day before, and Wanju had promised to go. Unfortunately the next morning he came back late from a meeting in the commune — maybe this had slipped his mind.

Second Sister Lu was waiting furiously at the end of the village for him. She trounced him for breaking his word and making the match fall through. For when the girl's family saw that the Party secretary hadn't come, they decided that Li Chengde had no face and if she were to marry him the other villagers would look down on her. So though he was able and had a house they left. This made Wanju frantic. Hearing that the three of them had only just gone, he turned his bike around to chase after them. He persuaded them to go back for a meal and kept them company. Seeing that the secretary of Crown Prince Village did think highly of Li Chengde, they agreed to the match. It took place in '74, and now Li had a son of three.

After telling me this Meifeng eyed me intently and asked, "Do you think this a good thing or a bad thing?" I didn't answer. I really have mixed feelings on the subject. It's common in these days in the villages for the sons of landlords and rich peasants to fail to marry. There isn't the same problem for men from bad families who work in government offices or factories. In the "cultural revolution" especially, the emphasis on "family extraction" exerted a most pernicious influence. So the way Li Wanju handled this should count as correct.

I would have let the matter rest there but was unable to. News of the questions I had asked got out, so that after supper people came one by one to whitewash Li Wanju.

One was Second Sister Lu. She told me she was the one who'd arranged Li Chengde's marriage: it had nothing to do with Wanju. Asked why she had done Li Chengde this favour, she said he was an honest young fellow, hard-working and able, so she wanted to find him a wife. The first few times she hadn't succeeded because of his bad class origin. Finally she hit on the idea of assuring the girl's family: He may be a landlord's son but he's as well regarded in the village as a poor or lower-middle peasant. When they heard that, they agreed to have a meal with Li Chengde, since she said the Party secretary would be there too. That was why Li Wanju had gone to that meal.

Snivelling as she spoke, she said the County Committee could beat or fine her but mustn't drag Wanju into this — he had done nothing wrong. I don't know how to cope with old ladies like this. I could only tell her not to worry and send her off.

Li Chengde came too. I was surprised to see how glum and crestfallen he looked, quite unlike his usual self. According to him this had nothing to do with Wanju or with Second Sister Lu. It was because he hadn't remoulded his thinking that he'd roped in the Party secretary to give him face. He volunteered to analyze his mistake and expunge the brand of his class, ready to accept any punishment or criticism. He also handed in a self-criticism entitled "My Serious Mistake Four Years Ago in Inviting the Party Secretary to a Meal". It was both pitiful and laughable. I thought: I can't follow this up, there's no need to.

To wind up this case I went to see Wanju that night.

He was very frank and readily admitted that he had asked Second Sister Lu to act as Li Chengde's matchmaker, telling her just what to say. If the girl's family objected to Li's class origin she was to tell them that he was well thought of in the village, and if they went to his house Li Wanju would certainly go to drink with them.

But Wanju saw nothing wrong in this and proceeded to justify it. He said a few years ago they'd always chosen poor and lower-middle peasants for jobs, to join the army, as barefoot doctors, school teachers, or even as performers in their propaganda team. As the proportion of poor and lower-middle peasants among the young people actually farming had dropped, the sons of landlords and rich peasants had become their "main force". So you had to give them responsible positions, didn't you? And that being so you had to show concern for them. If these young men couldn't find wives, slept on a cold *kang* and came home to an empty house, how could they go all out? As Party secretary he had to see to such things.

One has to admit that what Wanju said made sense.

September 14.   Fine.

After breakfast Wu Yougui took me round the orchard and to have a look at the Crown Prince's Tomb. This brigade puts a lot of work into its orchard and gets a good income from it. Wu says most of the cash paid to the commune members and the money for the brigade's chemical fertilizer comes from these fruit trees. The old brigade leader beamed and smacked his lips as he said this. Of course there's nothing wrong with growing fruit, but I'm afraid all the effort put into it may affect the policy of taking grain as the key link. This problem of orientation deserves attention.

Passing under rows of fruit trees we finally saw a brick grave the height of two men, with in front of it a white marble tablet inscribed Crown Prince's Tomb.

I asked Old Wu when the crown prince had lived. He couldn't say. According to him the story had come down that he was a crown prince of the Tang Dynasty who had been buried here, and the Emperor had conferred the imperial surname Li on the man looking after the tomb. That accounted for the number of Lis in the village — they were all descended from this custodian.

I don't know much Tang history, but I'm sure this legend is groundless. Since the Tang capital was Changan, how could a crown prince be buried here? Besides, if this were really a crown prince's tomb, instead of carving that big inscription they'd have got some famous calligrapher to write on the tablet. But this had only Crown Prince's Tomb on it without any signature or epigraph, showing that it was bogus. Wu was most upset to hear this. As if casting doubt on the authenticity of that tomb was suspecting him of having a shady past. Ridiculous!

This orchard covering thirty *mu* was started in '62. As Wu showed me over it he detailed how this had happened.

Originally dozens of *mu* around the Crown Prince's Tomb had always been out of bounds as "sacred land". Not even old shepherds went there, for fear of disturbing the imperial bones which had been sleeping for centuries underground, thinking that if they offended the prince he might destroy the whole village. In '58 during the nationwide smelting of steel, the commune wanted to "send up a sputnik" and organized a "tree-felling company" which came to Crown Prince Village. The villagers begged them to spare these trees, saying that if they felled them they would be struck by lightning. In the end, to appease them four big trees in front of and behind the tomb were left, while all the rest were cut down.

That Great Leap Forward should have taught us a lesson. We've done too many crazy things like this in the last few decades.

Old Wu said: In '60 at the start of the hard years, some villagers said the Crown Prince had caused this famine to pay them back. Not till Li Wanju was elected Party secretary did he propose using these thirty *mu* for an orchard. The Party branch agreed, but many commune members opposed the idea. They said: Haven't we been punished enough for '58? If we disturb the soil over the Crown Prince's head again, he may wipe out the whole village. The Party members reasoned with them, but still some villagers were adamant. Finally Wanju called a mass meeting to accuse a landlord of sabotage. In fact, the landlord had simply said that if they planted an orchard the Crown Prince would take offence. Wanju had meant to "kill a chicken to frighten the monkey", debunking the landlord to stop the others from making trouble. But it didn't work. Some villagers were unconvinced. It looked as if the meeting would have to break up, till Wanju had a bright idea. He stepped forward and announced: "Growing an orchard wasn't *my* idea. The Crown Prince gave it to me in a dream." He embroidered on this, describing how the Crown Prince had appeared to him three nights in a row, dressed in imperial yellow, and had reiterated: Trees are clothes, grass is bedding. You've felled the trees and uprooted the grass so that I have no clothes to wear and am wretchedly cold. Hurry up and plant trees and I'll let bygones by bygones. Wanju made this sound so convincing, he fooled and frightened everyone into agreeing to it. The next day they raced each other digging pits and planting trees. Now the orchard brings them in ready money each year. The youngsters all grasp the advantages of a diversified economy, but some people still attribute this to the Crown Prince's protection.

Ah, Wanju sometimes plays monkey-tricks, but he really knows how to cope.

At noon Secretary Feng phoned asking me to go straight back to prepare to go to the provincial capital for a week for a meeting about cotton.

Looks as if this investigation will have to stop here.

Young Wang and I have pooled our information and

exchanged views. We agree that Li Wanju did arrange marriages for the sons of landlords and rich peasants, but can't be said to have lost his class stand. After all, the sons are different from their fathers. Our Party policy is to consider class status but not to judge solely by it, paying more attention to a man's political record. Li Wanju has a comparatively good grasp of this policy. And judging by the monthly meetings to make bad characters toe the line he has a relatively strong sense of class struggle.

Young Wang pointed out that certain things haven't yet been cleared up. For instance, was it Wanju who proposed finding Li Chengde a wife, or did Second Sister Lu take the initiative? And was it the accountant who decided to draw those two cats for their criticism column, or did he discuss it first with Wanju?

If we had time we could of course probe further. But I don't see much point in that. If Wanju put Second Sister Lu up to matchmaking, and got Yang Dequan to draw those cats, what does that prove? All the energy and money spent these last few years on detailed investigations into fabricated charges could probably have built ten big new steel works.

This afternoon I called the cadres to a meeting to affirm the good record of their Party branch, raise certain criticisms, and encourage them to go further in exposing the "gang of four" and to make a good job of their harvesting and sowing, so as to reap a bumper harvest this year and strive for an even better one next year. Naturally I said nothing about investigating Li Wanju. As usual he tweaked his moustache and screwed up his eyes in a smile. It's hard to make him out. If he had no idea he was under investigation he'd have to be very stupid, and how could a dolt run the village so well? If he knew all about the investigation he must be over-confident, and eight out of ten over-confident Party secretaries make serious mistakes, yet so far he's come no bad croppers.

Wu Yougui wanted to call a mass meeting so that I could say a few words to the villagers before leaving. He said it's so seldom a county secretary comes here, if I left without saying a few words the commune members would blame the cadres for not showing us proper respect. This fellow Wu looks very honest but he's deep. This high-sounding talk was to get me to assure the villagers that there was nothing wrong with their leading group. I had to agree to this. Since there's nothing wrong with Li Wanju and we've been chasing around here for a week, if we up and left without a word it would certainly make things harder for them in future. So in the mass meeting after work I once more endorsed the village's leading group. I could see from the faces of the commune members that they all side with Wanju and were delighted to hear him cracked up. That's how peasants are, simple and lovable. Of course, to avoid one-sidedness I urged Li Wanju to guard against pride and complacency.

This evening Mother Liu made us dumplings stuffed with scallion and egg for our farewell meal. The old lady is really warm-hearted, she treated us like rice tubs and kept filling my bowl with dumplings. I'd never eaten so many at one time. After supper, while we waited for our jeep, Second Sister Lu, Xiao Meifeng and Yang Dequan, as well as Li Wanju and Wu Yougui all came to see us off. They sat on the *kang* and chattered away on topics ranging from the authenticity of the Crown Prince's Tomb to this year's harvest, from the fall of the "gang of four" to the improvement in the peasants' life. I really love Crown Prince Village and these honest peasants.

Unfortunately I can't spend longer here.

15. The Third Anonymous Letter

Respected Leading Comrades of the County Committee:

How hard you work! A democratic atmosphere is really prevailing now, with our leaders' hearts linked to those of the masses. I feel very bad about adding to your trouble. I never expected our new leadership to be so conscientious or take two letters from a nonentity so seriously. First you sent Chairman Qiu out to make an investigation, then sent Secretary Qi to stay in the village. Secretary Qi didn't spare himself but got down from his high horse to live, eat and work with the villagers. We ought to learn from his fine spirit. I'm determined to work whole-heartedly at my post and make a good job of reaping and sowing this autumn, to show my gratitude to our leadership.

Secretary Qi is our old county secretary, I've nothing against him. His coming down in person to the countryside should first of all be approved. But I have to point out that this trip of his was a failure. Not only did he fail to clear matters up, he concealed the true situation. Li Wanju's matchmaking for landlords' sons was exposed by me and confirmed by Secretary Qi — there's no denying it. The crucial question is Secretary Qi's attitude: he stated explicitly that this wasn't wrong. Of course I know that the sons of landlords and rich peasants are human beings who need to work and eat and also to marry. This is beyond any doubt. What I can't understand is why it doesn't count as wrong for a village Party secretary to shelve important affairs and find the time to act as go-between for bad elements. And to go and drink at their wedding feasts — what does that count as? Does it show that Li has a firm class stand?

What is really the limit is that Secretary Qi actually

commended Li Wanju in public for his firm grasp of class struggle and of the proletarian revolutionary line, saying that each month he gave the landlords and rich peasants a dressing-down, and each time a new trend in the class struggle appeared he kept a close grip on it. The truth is, Secretary Qi was completely taken in! As I pointed out in my first letter, Li Wanju is so crafty that very few people can get the better of him. He calls a landlord "Fifth Uncle", did Secretary Qi know that? This form of address isn't something superficial; its substantive. This is such an important matter, I hope Secretary Feng will look into it again.

Recently they have been saying in Crown Prince Village that anyone who tries to topple Li Wanju is an idiot, dreaming. Since he is supported by the higher-ups and solidly backed by the masses, no one can harm a single hair of his head. So it seems this visit of Secretary Qi's not only achieved very little but, because of his indiscreet talk, has become an "umbrella" for Li. I foresaw that it wouldn't be easy to check up on Li Wanju but would require deep probing and repeated investigations; otherwise it would be like trying to draw water in a bamboo basket or to dredge the moon from the bottom of the sea. It would only waste time and disappoint the people.

I humbly suggest that the County Committee sends to make another investigation and learns from the revolutionary spirit of Song Jiang's* three attacks on Zhu Manor. The first time he attacked, he nearly lost his life there. The second time he fled ignominiously, chased by Third Mistress Hu. Why were both these attempts failures? It was Chairman Mao who analyzed this correctly: Song Jiang lost because he didn't know the situation and used the wrong methods. Later, after careful investigation, he learned the way out of the maze and broke up the alliance between

---

*Hero of the *Outlaws of the Marsh*.

the Li, Hu and Zhu manors. Then only did he change defeat into victory.

History repeats itself. In my humble view the way to solve the problem of Crown Prince Village is by learning Song Jiang's spirit when he attacked Zhu Manor for the third time. I hope the County Committee will resolve to overcome all difficulties and win victory!

This is the third letter I have ventured to send. I feel most guilty about disturbing you so often, as you are all busy leading cadres. I wait respectfully to learn your reaction.

With respectful greetings, I wish all our leaders good health! May we soon achieve modernization!

A commune member
October 16, 1978.

16. Placed on File

This anonymous letter arrived by registered post, and the office handling correspondence and callers passed it on without any delay.

At a meeting of the County Committee's Standing Committee, after the main business had been discussed the committee members picked up their thermos flasks and notebooks and some of them stood up, just waiting for the chairman to close the meeting. But Feng in the chair suddenly produced this letter.

"Wait a bit," he said. "You've all read this. Let's hear, briefly, what you think of it."

The committee members had to sit down again.

Feng put on his presbyopic glasses, which at once made his swarthy lantern-jawed face look rather intellectual. Riffling through the letter he said:

"This is the third letter from this man, again denouncing Li Wanju the Party secretary of Crown Prince Village. The last two times he wrote, first Bingzhang went and then Old Qi himself. Still he's not satisfied and thinks Li Wanju deceived them. See, he wants us to 'learn the revolutionary spirit of Song Jiang in attacking the Zhu Manor', to make a third investigation. Well! He's obviously well-versed in the *Outlaws of the Marsh*. How about it? Shall we explore the 'maze' of Crown Prince Village?"

Feng took off his glasses and looked at his colleagues.

Since this letter accused a village Party secretary and involved two leading members of the County Committee, nobody wanted to express any opinion.

One man said tentatively:

"This doesn't strike me as the usual type of informer's letter. He accuses Li Wanju without listing his mistakes or citing facts. It's so cryptic, he seems to be playing hide-and-seek with us."

"Right." Feng nodded. "It's rather like a game of hide-and-seek."

Now that someone had set the ball rolling, others joined in. Some said Crown Prince Village had always been advanced and Li Wanju was a very able Party secretary; others commented that it was odd not to write explicitly; yet others proposed ignoring this senseless letter, as they were so busy winding up old cases and needed to concentrate on storing the autumn harvest.

"What do you say, Yuezhai?" Feng looked at Qi.

Since his return from the provincial capital Qi had felt much surer of himself and shown more initiative. Called on to speak he said:

"I stayed in Crown Prince Village for some time, mainly investigating the charges in the second letter. We checked fairly thoroughly but couldn't find any irregularities. On my return I talked it over with Secretary Feng. The letter-writer must have had something to go on, but we didn't uncover any substantial evidence."

"That's right." Qiu Bingzhang put in. "I went to investigate after the first letter, which was also very cryptic, but I didn't discover anything."

Qi shot him a glance. Recently Qiu had made two self-examinations in the Standing Committee of his bourgeois factionalism, and his behaviour had improved, but Qi didn't like the way he still echoed him in meetings. When Qiu scratched his bald head and said no more, Qi went on:

"I'm not saying we didn't discover certain facts. We did. But the criticism of Deng and Li Wanju's matchmaking for landlords' sons were definitely not as reprehensible as the letter alleged. So now that I've read this third letter, I think the writer is holding something back. If he overcame his scruples and spoke out frankly, the business would be easy. Otherwise, just going by this letter, sending to make another investigation wouldn't get us out of this 'maze'."

Qiu burst out:

"I agree completely. First track down the letter-writer. That's what I've thought all along. . . ."

Qi glared at him and cut him short:

"I didn't propose tracking down the letter-writer. When the rank and file write to reflect the situation, especially to inform against our cadres, no matter whether they sign their names or not they should be protected. We mustn't track them down, much less take reprisals. What I meant was seeking out this letter-writer and persuading him to give his frank opinion of Li Wanju."

"That's right, that's right." Qiu promptly changed his tune. "Not track down but seek out."

Feng was twiddling a pencil. When everyone had spoken he looked up at them again.

"I've read all three of these letters. As I told Old Qi, he's gunning for Li Wanju but says not a word about Li persecuting him, so obviously there's no personal feud between them. Why, then, should he keep picking on him? Did Li Wanju start off as a rebel? No. Was he a smash-and-grabber? No. So this is rather strange. I've felt all along that these letters leave something unsaid and just make insinuations. If we could really find the man who wrote them and ask what he means, that would save trouble. It's too bad he's kept back his name, so we can't find him. I don't think we should go to the village to check up again. We're up to our ears in work now, and haven't the time to play hide-and-seek with him or let him lead us by the nose. There's no need to seek him out. Since he refuses to give his name, even if we found him he mightn't be willing to speak out. If all of you agree, I propose we give this letter to the correspondence office to file."

All nodded their agreement. At once Feng raised the pencil in his hand and wrote on the letter, "File this."

17. Secretary Feng Goes Down to the Country

At the end of the year the Party Central Committee held the Eleventh Session of its Third Plenary Conference. The papers published its communiqué: The nationwide mass movement to expose Lin Biao and the "gang of four" has on the whole ended in triumph. Now the emphasis in the Party's work has switched to socialist modernization.

The County Committee spent a whole week studying this communiqué. All the Standing Committee members realized that a new turning point had been reached, and felt their thinking lagged far behind the times. The documents issued said: "Now not a few comrades are afraid to raise and solve problems in a practical and realistic way." Feng spoke for three hours on this, urging his colleagues to liberate their minds and get down to work.

By the Spring Festival great headway had been made in all the work of Qingming County, and the leading members of the County Committee were more united. Before long the Central Committee took the decision to remove the labels of landlords and rich peasants. As soon as this was published in the papers it was discussed in every village and household. Some said it was high time for this, as the landlords and rich peasants had been remoulding themselves through labour for years. Others said: If they have their labels removed, who are we to exercise dictatorship over? The families of the landlords and rich peasants were even more agitated. Some saluted each other, declaring that they had never dreamed this day would come; others suspected that this was a scheme to allow them more latitude so as to pounce on them.

The Provincial Committee issued instructions that the Central Committee's directive must be carried out in each county before the spring ploughing, and each village and brigade must post up a list of those whose labels had been removed, to bring everyone's enthusiasm into play and make a better job of 1979's spring ploughing and field work. Qingming County's Standing Committee divided up the work between its members, and they travelled their districts day and night to implement this important policy.

Feng, responsible for the southeast of the county, went one afternoon to Crown Prince River Commune to hear its report. The commune secretary Zhou Yongmao described the situation in Crown Prince Village.

"There's an old landlord there called Li Qiangfu who spread counter-revolutionary talk in every movement, but the brigade wants to take off his label too. We don't consider he belongs to the category of landlords and rich peasants described by the Central Committee as having 'abided by the law for many years, worked honestly and not done anything wrong'. He's one of 'the small minority who have stuck to their reactionary stand and not yet reformed'. So he can't have his label removed."

"Ah, Crown Prince Village!" Feng at once thought of Li Wanju and asked, "What does Li Wanju think?"

"Li Wanju is the one who wants to remove his label," said Zhou. "This Li Wanju is unreliable and does whatever he pleases. He used to be so keen on grasping class struggle that when we asked him for material he listed many examples of sabotage by landlords, and described how effectively their Party branch had clamped down on them. This time as soon as the directive came down, he removed the labels of all the landlords and rich peasants to keep in step with the times, doing nothing by halves but making a clean sweep. Regardless of whether they'd reformed or not, he treated them all alike and took off their labels! How can we allow that, eh?"

Feng had kept on the go these last few days hurrying from village to village. He was sunburned but more vigorous than ever. Perhaps because the work was going smoothly, he felt fairly relaxed and his eyes sparkled under his shaggy eyebrows. When a commune disagreed with a brigade, he had always tended to pay more attention to the brigade's opinion.

"I suggest you have another good talk with Li Wanju to hear his views," he said. "He's in the village in daily touch with those landlords and rich peasants, so he has more right to speak than we do!"

To his surprise Zhou turned red in the face and bellowed:

"The material we have was handed in by Li Wanju!"

With that he pulled some material out of a drawer and pointed out

"See, this dates from '67. It says Li Qiangfu claimed that Liu Shaoqi had been unjustly treated. This is the report of how they set up a beancurd mill in '74, when Li Qiangfu said: Our village is dreaming to think it can set up a beancurd mill and go in for sidelines, like a toad lusting after a swan's flesh! This. . . ."

He would have gone on fulminating, but Feng raised a hand to stop him.

"All right," he said. "No need to read any more. Let's both go to Crown Prince Village to have a look."

In less than half an hour Feng and Zhou reached Crown Prince Village. Having parked their bikes they called the brigade cadres together to discuss whether Li Qiangfu should have his label removed.

"I think he should," said Wu Yougui. "He's nearly seventy, not long for this world, and we can't let him go labelled into his coffin."

"That's no reason." Zhou had a red face and booming voice, and being worked up now he bellowed, "Since he's behaved badly, he shouldn't be cleared but take that label with him into his coffin."

Before Wu could answer, Xiao Meifeng cut in:

"That's beside the point, old brigade leader. It's because of Li Qiangfu's record that we want to remove his label. In the thirty years since Liberation he's submitted to remoulding, worked honestly and not done any sabotage. So why not take off his label?"

Zhou pulled a long face. He asked:

"All that reactionary talk of his — wasn't that sabotage?"

Li Wanju, holding a tobacco pouch in one hand, with the other tweaked his moustache as he said slowly:

"Everyone has some fault, landlords too. Li Qiangfu's is that he can't keep his mouth shut. When anything new crops up, other landlords dare not comment on it in public, but he's not afraid to blether. That's his weakness, ferreting out the news and then airing his views. It's true he's often been criticized for this, but it's easier to change hills and streams than a man's nature — his tongue runs away with him. That year Liu Shaoqi was accused of opposing the Party and Chairman Mao and of representing the landlords and all the bad elements, no other landlords got involved, not caring whom he represented. Li Qiangfu was the only one to sound off about it. Working in the fields he bawled, 'When did Liu Shaoqi ever represent us? What nonsense!' At the time that sounded most reactionary, but today it doesn't seem wrong."

"Let me remind you," Zhou said coldly, "The Third Plenary Session didn't clear Liu Shaoqi; he's still wearing that label."

Not giving ground Li screwed up his small eyes to say:

"I think it's just a question of time. What did he do wrong?"

"You're going too far!" Zhou flared up.

Feng hastily made clear his stand:

"This is an inner-Party meeting where we can all say what we think. Even saying something wrong doesn't matter."

"All right, we'll drop that for the time being," Zhou said sullenly. "When your brigade set up that beancurd mill what did Li Qiangfu say?"

Li was at a loss. Deflated, he answered vaguely:

"Even if he said something wrong we can't hold it against him for ever. Think of all the wrong things we cadres say every year. Isn't a landlord bound to slip up sometimes?"

"I've something to say about the beancurd mill," Meifeng put in.

Li hastily stopped her by saying:

"Why bring up isolated instances? Don't we judge cadres by their overall records? We should do the same with landlords. Li Qiangfu...."

Zhou cut him short:

"Don't try to talk your way out of this, Wanju. You can't turn black into white or white into black. Are they valid or not, the reports your brigade handed in each year?"

"You've stumped me!" Li's eyebrows twitched and his lips parted in what looked like a smile. Then he retorted, "Whether they're valid or not depends. Some of them are. Some the commune badgered us to write. When the higher-ups press for reports, those lower down concoct them: Don't be angry, Secretary Zhou, that's the truth."

"In other words all that material was bogus, squeezed out of you by the commune!" Feeling he'd been put on the spot in front of the county secretary, Zhou's hands were trembling with fury.

"You can't say it was all bogus."

"If it was true, why should you take off his label?" Zhou thought he had Li cornered.

Before Li could justify himself, Feng said:

"All right, all right, let's drop this subject for now. I've another question to ask you. Did all the poor and lower-middle peasants in your brigade agree to remove Li Qiangfu's label? Did all the cadres agree?"

Li kept silent. Wu Yougui answered:

"Our cadres held a lot of meetings to discuss his case, and the poor and lower-middle peasants held several too. Careful study of the policy deepened our understanding, and then everyone agreed."

"Was that how it was?" Feng asked the accountant beside him, clapping him on the shoulder.

Yang Dequan didn't know what to say. He turned his round face to look first at Li and Wu, then at Zhou. Finally he mumbled:

"Yes, that's how it was."

Annoyed by his density Meifeng blurted out:

"Can't you talk sense, Yang Dequan? We've done nothing wrong, so why try to cover things up? The truth is some people were against removing Li Qiangfu's label. They still are. We've several hundred villagers, not all out of the same mould. How can everyone see eye to eye!"

This burst of "machine-gun" fire made the atmosphere tense.

Feng watched her intently, forgetting to light the cigarette he had put to his lips. Zhou looked rather astonished. He clearly hadn't expected to find an ally here.

"Who were against it then?" asked Feng.

Meifeng answered readily:

"Gu Qiushi for one."

Wu stretched out his long arm and hastily interposed:

"Don't drag Qiushi in, Meifeng, he's an honest lad."

"Did I say he isn't? That doesn't follow." She glared at Wu and demanded, "Didn't you know he opposed removing Fifth Li's label?"

Feng naturally had no idea what Gu Qiushi did. He asked Li:

"Who's Gu Qiushi?"

Li had lowered his head to smoke and was looking listless. He answered briefly:

"A demobbed soldier, in charge of the field crops."

Feng decided to let Zhou go back to the commune while he spent a night in the village.

Once again Mother Liu's cottage served as a hostel. But as this was the first time the cadre staying there was the top man in the county she went all out to entertain him well.

First she bought two packets of good tea from the co-op, made tea and settled her visitor on the big *kang* in the main room. Then from her clamp she picked out her finest cabbage, cracked and beat up a dozen eggs and deftly made a large batch of dumplings with thin wrappings but bulging with stuffing, to treat Secretary Feng.

Feng, his padded jacket unbuttoned, sat propped up at one end of the well-heated *kang*, finding this more comfortable than having electro-therapy for his back in the provincial hospital. Unable to refuse Mother Liu's hospitality, he ate her fried peanuts and sipped a small cup of liquor till his swarthy face was flushed. After bringing in the dumplings, Mother Liu sat sideways on the edge of the *kang* to keep him company. And as they ate they chatted.

"Does your village have a landlord called Li Qiangfu?"

"Yes, we do."

"What's he like? Does he toe the line?"

"Oh yes. Does whatever he's told and goes wherever he's sent."

"So now he should have his label taken off."

"That's right. He's sixty-seven. We can't let him wear that label into his coffin!"

She put some more hot dumplings into Feng's bowl. After eating a couple he asked:

"How much land did they have before Land Reform? Was he the head of the household?"

"I can't say how much land they had. But Li the Fifth wasn't the head of the household, his old man was. That old devil treated us poor folk viciously. He didn't die till the year after Land Reform."

"And Li Qiangfu?"

"He was no good. Couldn't carry a shoulder pole or lift a load. When the family had land he lived it up, keeping pigeons and other birds, a good-for-nothing glutton. His old devil of a father, seeing how useless he was, sent him to town to study. They had money! But how could he study? He didn't become a scholar but learned all sorts of bad habits. He made up to actors and started smoking opium. When his old man knew he fetched him home and found a wife for him. Not from a wealthy family but pretty. Then guess what, his mother gunned for her! That old lady was a tigress, everyone knew. She kept beating or cursing her daughter-in-law, not letting her live a single day in peace. So after less than three years she hung herself. Left not even a son behind. Later, just think, who'd be willing to marry into his family? Fifth Li's present wife didn't marry him till after his mother died. Her looks were only middling, not a patch on his first wife, and she had no children either. Old Li had four elder sisters but he was the only son; so he's no one to carry on the family and it'll be the first to die out in Crown Prince Village. Isn't that retribution, Secretary Feng? Who told their family to do so many wicked things? People can't charge ahead without considering the consequences, isn't that right?"

Feng smiled and asked:

"So you'd say this Li Qiangfu toes the line?"

"That's right."

"Then why did I hear he's often been struggled against?"

"Well, to make him toe the line."

Smiling all over her face Mother Liu helped Feng to more dumplings.

Feng smiled too as he asked:

"Is it true that some people opposed removing his label?"

"At the meeting all agreed, no one opposed it."

"Someone did."

"Who?"

"Gu Qiushi."

"Oh, young Qiushi was away for so long he doesn't know what happened in the village. What he says doesn't count."

Feng had other questions to ask, but Mother Liu kept bustling in and out to fetch more dumplings, vinegar and soysauce, talking away all the time.

"Eat up, Secretary Feng, mind you make a good meal.

We've fine rice and flour in the village but can't cook well, you must excuse us. At any rate our new wheat was husked by an electric mill. You should find it a change. At least it's much finer than the flour you buy in town."

"Yes, it's first-rate, I've eaten a lot. About Gu Qiushi...."

Mother Liu went out to fetch a bowl of dumpling soup and said:

"Have a bowl of soup now to wind up."

18. "Zhou Yu Fights Huang Gai"*

It was dark. Mother Liu urged Feng to turn in early and went off to the pig farm. Feng felt he should find Gu Qiushi to sound him out, but he'd forgotten to ask the cadres to arrange this. He was wondering what to do when he heard steps, the door curtain was raised and in came a strapping young fellow. Standing straight as a ramrod by the door he introduced himself:

"I'm Gu Qiushi."

He was wearing a clean but faded old army uniform, had closely cropped hair, thick eyebrows and big eyes. The way he held himself erect like a soldier made a good impression on Feng, who urged him to sit on the *kang*. But the youngster turned to pick up a stool which he set squarely in the middle of the room.

"Secretary Feng, I'm against removing Li Qiangfu's label." Gu didn't beat about the bush.

"Why are you against it?"

"I don't trust him." Gu went on with a frown, "I've only been demobbed two years so I don't know too much about

---

*This is an episode from the classical novel *The Romance of the Three Kingdoms*.

the brigade's affairs. Once, though, when I went to buy beancurd I bumped into Li Qiangfu who was buying some too. I noticed him strolling around, prying and looking quite smug. And he said with a grin to someone that he deserved a share of the credit for setting up the beancurd mill. I thought it very strange for a landlord to have the nerve to talk like that. The beancurd mill was set up under the leadership of the Party branch, how could it reflect credit on him? Then he boasted that it was due to his reactionary talk. He'd said, 'Crown Prince Village wants to set up a beancurd mill, like a toad lusting after the flesh of a swan.' They'd pounced on that as a new trend in the class struggle, and so were able to start this money-making mill. Hearing that I was furious and said he was spreading rumours. He told me if I asked around I'd find it was true. What's more, he said Wanju had put him up to it. The two of them had put on an act — 'Zhou Yu Fights Huang Gai' — one willing to be beaten by the other."

This sounded so amazing that Feng was staggered. How could a Party secretary work in cahoots with a landlord to stage such a scene of "class struggle"?

Gu went on gravely:

"I was so mad I hauled him straight off to see Comrade Wanju, who ticked him off very sharply, warning him that if he talked such rubbish again they'd hold a meeting to struggle against him. Later Uncle Wanju told me to pay no attention to Fifth Li's filthy lies. All this happened so long ago I'd nearly forgotten it. But this time when we discussed removing the labels of landlords and rich peasants, Comrade Wanju insisted on taking off Li Qiangfu's label. Then I remembered this business and felt something was wrong."

"What do you think was wrong?" asked Feng.

Gu lowered his head to think hard, then replied:

"Three things, as I see it. First, Li Qiangfu's reckless

behaviour shows that he's kept his reactionary stand and his attitude is very bad. Secondly, since his attitude is so bad yet Comrade Wanju insists on removing his label, that means Comrade Wanju hasn't drawn a clear class demarcation line. Thirdly, if grasping class struggle to set up the beancurd mill was really as Fifth Li said and they were in cahoots, then the brigade's grasp of class struggle was a fraud, and that's a more serious matter."

Feng, smoking, nodded as if he saw reason in Gu's analysis, but presently shook his head as if in disagreement.

However, the words "their grasp of class struggle was a fraud" haunted his mind. He suddenly remembered that the anonymous letters had hinted at this. Could Gu Qiushi be the writer of those letters?

"It won't do! I must clear this up!" Li Qiangfu, his hands behind him, his back bent, was pacing the room like an ant on a hot pan.

His wife sitting sewing on one corner of the *kang* said not a word.

"Secretary Feng's come to our village over the business of removing labels, and it's my case he's checking on. If I don't speak out now I'll have no other chance. That would be the death of me! The unfairness of it!"

Turning round he halted abruptly to fix his beady bloodshot eyes on his wife, as if about to strike her. Too scared to hold her needle steady, she faltered:

"Don't, don't...."

"Don't what?" he bellowed.

"Don't go to complain...."

"Don't go to complain!" Grinding his teeth he stared at her head, bald except for a few brownish hairs. "If I don't speak up now," he fumed, "everyone else will have their labels removed, leaving only me wearing one. What a fool I'd look!"

His wife, afraid to say any more, sobbed without shedding tears.

As Mother Liu had said, her looks were only middling. She had always been timid, afraid of thunder and lightning, afraid of men and rats. And because it's hard for a landlord to change his nature, Li Qiangfu might nod and bow outside but at home reared up to bully his wretched wife. A few sharp words and a glare always made her knuckle under. Their positions as master and slave were firmly established.

Now he was having a fierce mental struggle and couldn't decide what to do. He badly needed to consult someone he trusted so as to boost his courage. But here was only this zombie who couldn't speak. Still it was better for her to keep her mouth shut, if she opened it he felt even more at sea. What could he do? If he missed this chance it was no use begging heaven for another.

"To hell with it! I'll find Secretary Feng!" He set off on his spindly legs.

"Don't, don't go!" His wife in desperation plucked up her courage to grab hold of him, and finally came out with a whole sentence, "Haven't you had enough of being criticized?"

Taken by surprise the landlord unconsciously stopped scowling.

"This time I won't be criticized," he said. "This time they're taking off labels. If my label's taken off I can sit on the same bench at meetings as the poor and lower-middle peasants. I'll be a commune member. Understand? Bah, it's no use explaining to you."

To his astonishment his "zombie wife" showed unusual perception and came out with quite a speech:

"If they won't take it off for you, and you rush around trying to do something about it, at best you'll not have submitted to surveillance or, worse, you'll be wanting to reverse the verdict. Just think, won't you be criticized again?"

Li Qiangfu let out a cold breath. Yes, that made sense, carried weight. He looked again at his "zombie wife", unable to believe that such weighty words had fallen from her lips. Going up to her he spoke more affably than he ever had before:

"Don't worry, I know what I'm doing. Wanju hasn't treated me badly. Each time they held a struggle meeting against me, he let me know half a day ahead — didn't that show consideration? You've forgotten how once on the threshing-floor at noon, in the middle of summer, I was standing in the sun, sweat pouring off me. And what did Wanju say? He said, are you dead that you can't take two steps to stand in the shade? Are you doing this on purpose? If you pass out we're not going to carry you back! Wasn't it clear what he meant? He was on my side."

His wife nodded, remembering the incident.

Li Qiangfu screwed up his eyes, looking unusually smug, and reached out for his hat. But she caught his hand and whispered urgently:

"Think again! So many struggle meetings against you all these years, how can they reckon that you've behaved yourself?"

Her scepticism provoked him. Pulling a long face he grabbed his hat and dashed out to argue his case.

But he hadn't the nerve to go to Secretary Feng. The biggest cadre he'd seen since Liberation was the head of the commune's security office, who bawled him out much more forcefully than Li Wanju. On the rare occasions when the commune secretary came to their village he kept well out of his way. And Feng was the county secretary. Better go and find Wanju. At least they were fellow villagers.

It was already dark, but knowing the way he hurried straight to their house.

Wanju was sitting blankly alone on the *kang*.

He'd had a lot on his mind these last few days, removing the landlords' and rich peasants' labels. His anxious face and glum silence annoyed, worried and upset his wife Cuihuan. At supper he ate only a couple of mouthfuls and when she urged him to lie down and rest he simply shook his head. She felt his forehead. It was very cold, so she knew he had no fever. She couldn't help sighing and scolding:

"I told you not to stick your neck out and ask for trouble, but you wouldn't listen. You had to show off! What good came of setting up that beancurd mill?"

"It's brought our commune members some cash," he retorted.

He had gone to a great deal of trouble setting up that little mill. That was in '74 when they had to criticize Lin Biao and Confucius and do away with private plots, those remnants of capitalism. Propaganda teams and work teams kept coming to the village so that everybody was afraid to move. Every single household was desperately hard up. The orchard, which was all they had to rely on, couldn't cover the cost of chemical fertilizer or insecticide. They wanted to start some sidelines but these were forbidden. Then they hit on the idea of a beancurd mill. They had soybeans and labour power, they could clear out a room, set up a pan and make money. The beancurd could be sold, the dregs fed to the pigs, giving them more pigs, more manure and more grain. Their small investment would make a ten thousand-fold profit. The idea was a splendid one, but carrying it out had been hard. The higher-ups complained that this wasn't their proper job, that they were hankering after capitalism; the villagers were afraid of losing money, of coming a cropper without catching a fox; even the old brigade leader was against it. If he hadn't thought up a clever dodge, that mill might still be nowhere. Today it wouldn't count against them, but in those days he was taking a big risk.

If he hadn't pounced on a "new trend in the class struggle", they couldn't have set up the mill, but neither would he have landed in trouble now. In those days it was believed that anything opposed by class enemies was the right thing to do. When they seized on that remark of Li Qiangfu's he had a brainwave. If they found something the enemy opposed, it was all right to support it.

"How you love to shine! You're called smart but you're the biggest fool of the lot! Everyone knows what a scoundrel Fifth Li is, so why did you seek him out? See, now that's a handle against you."

"I wear my heart on my sleeve to let the world see if it's red or white," he countered.

Had he sought Fifth Li out? He'd known without asking that the old man must have sounded off. As a landlord, a class enemy, if he opposed the mill the others should be for it, and they could bring this off. They'd held a struggle meeting and reported it to the higher-ups, thereby silencing their objections, and so the mill got started. The villagers shared the proceeds, getting paid more for each workday, and that benefited them all. But who knew how hard it had been!

Cuihuan, seeing him in a brown study, speechless and motionless, was worried about him and urged:

"Never mind, why be so upset if the commune won't take off his label? Is Fifth Li any good?"

True. Fifth Li was really no good. He'd been criticized for reactionary talk and owned up to it, the beancurd mill had got started, and if he'd behaved himself the affair would have blown over; but he had to brag about it. And Gu Qiushi, what did he understand? Why raise such a rumpus over that talk about Zhou Yu and Huang Gai? Why wrangle with a senseless old devil like him? The whole village knew what gibberish he talked.

Now, dammit, even Secretary Feng had been alerted. This was a muddled up case, true mixed with false, how could it be cleared up? Ah, these days a village cadre didn't mind hardships or occasional curses, but injustice was hard to take. Still, take it he must. Let them do whatever they pleased.

He was thinking this over when someone shouted from the yard:

"Are you in, secretary?"

This was Li Qiangfu's rule when he called. He wasn't allowed to visit the poor and lower-middle peasants, for fear that he might corrupt them; and he didn't call on other landlords or rich peasants, for fear they'd be accused of ganging up. Li Wanju's house was the only one he could visit. Wanju as Party secretary was in charge of the brigade. It was all right for a landlord to call on him to report his ideological or other problems; but he dared not go indoors. There were often cadres in there discussing the work. If he burst in they might accuse him of eavesdropping. So he always stood in the yard and called out. If they were having a meeting Wanju would go out to see what he wanted and then send him off. If there was no one there he would ask him in.

Hearing his shout, without letting her husband speak Cuihuan called furiously through the window:

"Are you calling up the dead? He's just breathed his last!"

Knowing what a terror she was, Li Qiangfu kept quiet. And now Wanju went out. He didn't invite the old man in but stood on the steps, his padded jacket draped over his shoulders.

"Why have you come?" he demanded.

"To ask about having my label removed."

"It's not for you to ask. It'll be removed or not as we see fit."

"Put in a good word for me, secretary!"

"Don't ask *me*! You're still blethering right and left. Did you or didn't you blab about Zhou Yu's Fight with Huang Gai?"

"I...." Li Qiangfu stepped back in dismay and stammered, "I was joking."

"Have you learned nothing all these years? What sort of joke was that!" Growing more worked up, Wanju lashed out at him, "Do you know what you're guilty of? Zhou Yu and Huang Gai were generals in the same camp. Who are you? And who am I? Can you lump us together? What were you trying to do? Think for yourself!"

Li Qiangfu panicked. Wasn't that collusion between a class enemy and a Communist? What could be done? He couldn't retract what he'd said, it was spilt water. He turned pale and trembled.

Before Wanju could say more Cuihuan behind him called out:

"Don't waste your breath on such a swine. Ignore him!"

Wanju waved the landlord away and he started to stagger off. Seeing how terrified he was, Wanju took pity on him.

"Go home and have a good sleep," he yelled. "Others will see to the removing of labels."

19. Li Qiangfu's Label Is Removed

Feng hadn't slept so soundly for days. When, opening his eyes, he heard hens clucking and birds chirping in the yard, he wondered where he was. Lying on the *kang* he stretched his arms a few times, then sat up. Two women were talking just outside the window.

"Will Fifth Li's label be removed this time?" one of them asked.

"It will. I've told Secretary Feng all about it," said Mother Liu.

"Take it off and be done with it then. You've no idea, the old fellow hasn't worked properly for days. He's kept on at me about that label of his until my ears feel callused. The last couple of days just the two of us have worked in the orchard and my heart bleeds for him, he looks so wretched."

If that old lady worked with Fifth Li, she should be able to clear some matters up. Feng promptly dressed and stepped outside with a mug to clean his teeth.

"Oh, did we wake you!" Second Sister Lu beamed at him.

"Secretary Feng, this is Second Sister Lu from next door," said Mother Liu.

Starting that morning Feng made mental notes of what many people told him.

This was Second Sister Lu's account:
Secretary Feng, you've really been working hard. Yesterday evening when I heard you'd come I wanted to come over, but my old man stopped me. He said Secretary Feng has come to look into a case and his time is precious, so don't you go butting in! I argued: Now that the "gang of four" has fallen, aren't we taking the mass line in everything? Whatever my faults I'm one of the masses, are't I? That shut him up. Was I right, Secretary Feng?

You want to know about Fifth Li? Why yes, I work with him in the orchard. Does he do a good job? Well, what can you expect of a scrawny old man! They just record work points for him to let him get by. Reactionary talk? Oh yes, but he wasn't the only one. There was nothing special about the way he talked.

What did he say about setting up the beancurd mill? You've asked the right person. I know all about it. I remember we were sorting out turnip seeds, just the two of us. As we chatted, the business of the mill came up. I said, "Wanju's biting off more than he can chew. We're not even allowed to raise poultry, they'll never let us eat beancurd. He must be dreaming." He said, "It's like a toad wanting to eat the flesh of a swan — no way!" Later, talking about Wanju, he said, "Wanju's a good sort, he sometimes calls me Fifth Uncle." I said, "Well, you're the generation above him."

A few days later, at noon, I was sewing a shoe-sole by the field when I saw Wanju come and take Li Qiangfu aside to whisper something to him. When he'd gone the old fellow came over and sat down without a word, just smoking pipe after pipe. I asked, "What did Wanju say to you?" He grinned at me and said, "Second Sister, you'll have half tomorrow off for a criticism meeting." I asked, "Who's to be criticized this time?" He said, "Me of course. Who else?" I asked, "What for?" He said, "For that remark of mine about a toad wanting to eat swan's flesh." I said, "Just for that? That's nothing. You weren't the only one saying that." He hung his head and sighed. Presently he stuck out his chest and said, "I don't give a damn. A meeting to criticize me will get the beancurd mill started, everyone will get more money, and I'll have done the village a good turn." Wasn't that a joke, Secretary Feng. As if he could do anyone a good turn!

This was what Li Qiangfu said:

Sit where you are, Secretary Feng, I prefer standing. The fact is I'm sixty-seven this year, and this is the first time I've seen a county official. I never saw one in the old society or in the new. Of course the two are quite different. If I say anything wrong, please don't hold it against me. The village cadres often criticize me, but I can't keep my mouth shut. Sending for me today shows you don't look down on me, it gives me face. Just to repay your kindness I can't tell you the least fib. As heaven is my witness, all I'm saying is true. I'll tell things the way they were. If you find there's anything I've made up you can sentence me to several years in prison.

I was brought up an exploiter. I don't have to tell you, I'm a criminal. Why am I grateful to the Communist Party? Because the Party has remoulded me so that now I can work and support my family. Though I'm getting on in years and only able to do odd jobs in the orchard, when the brigade issues flour I get my share — the cadres and other villagers make allowances for me. I understand that and I'm grateful.

Yes, yes, I'll tell you about the beancurd mill. When they discussed starting one, the commune members didn't see eye to eye. I've this stinking fault, I like to gab about anything that happens. Others might get away with the things I say, but in my case they lead to trouble. Every few days I would be criticized. After each meeting I told myself to keep my mouth shut in future. If you keep quiet you can't be sold as a mute. But my memory's like a sieve. Once a wound heals you forget how it hurt. In a couple of days I would trip up again.

That's how it was then, I heard everyone say they couldn't start this beancurd mill, the higher-ups wouldn't let them, sidelines were capitalistic. I chipped in. Exactly what I said I can't remember. Anyway I likened us to a toad which could never taste the flesh of a swan. I heard I wasn't the only one to say that. I'm not accusing anyone else, Secretary Feng. I admit my crime, I'm just telling you what happened.

Then Wanju, I mean our Party secretary, came to find me and ask if I'd really said that. I said, "Yes." He said, "That's reactionary talk, tomorrow we'll hold a meeting to struggle against you." I asked, "What rule did I break?" He said, "You tried to sabotage setting up a beancurd mill." I thought, so I've done it again. Go ahead and criticize me. After Wanju left I wondered why I had such lousy luck. Then I thought, never mind, it only means standing in front of everyone for half a day. When I've been bawled out they'll all be able to eat beancurd, that's worth it. I felt that showed public spirit! So when Second Sister Lu asked me about it I told her how I felt. See, I never watch my tongue.

When the beancurd mill started the brigade called a mass meeting. Wanju said it was the fruit of victory, due to our Party branch's grasp of class struggle. I didn't attend that meeting, Secretary Feng, I heard about it. I thought: Don't I have a share in this victory? It seemed to me like Zhou Yu's fight with Huang Gai in "The Meeting of Heroes". One was willing to fight, the other to be beaten. Wanju wanted to criticize me and I was willing to be criticized. I should never, never have talked like that outside.

Yesterday evening I went to see our Party secretary. When he brought this up I realized that I was guilty of a capital offence — collusion. Now I've made a clean breast of everything, Secretary Feng. You've examined me and I've come clean. That makes me feel easier in my mind. With your discernment you can see I meant no harm by that remark.

This is what Li Wanju said:
Don't ask me to explain, I've nothing to say. I wanted to start a sideline to bring in a bit more money for our brigade. In those days to get anything done you had to grasp class struggle. Without big criticism campaigns you couldn't get anywhere. How did we grasp class struggle in our village? Our target was Li Qiangfu. He was the only landlord who liked to gab. I admit that my grasp of class struggle was bogus, I was really out to set up a beancurd mill. That's how it was. But I wasn't in cahoots with Fifth Li to stage a fight between Zhou Yu and Huang Gai.

This was what Wu Yougui said:
Seems to me the seriousness of this depends on how you look at it. If you take it seriously, it was simply making a

show of class struggle to get a beancurd mill set up. If you don't take it seriously, it was Fifth Li's senseless talk that confused the issue. Now that we've got to the bottom of the business it should be easy to handle. We must draw the right conclusions. Fifth Li's label should still be removed. Wanju should go on giving us all a lead.

This is what Xiao Meifeng said:

I don't think Wanju was wrong. He was driven by circumstances. What could be done without raising the banner of class struggle? If he hadn't, the higher-ups would have accused him of Right deviationism! But now he's said to have put on an act. A rat in a bellows can't get out at either end. How are cadres to manage, I ask you!

That evening Feng went back to the county town.

Three days later the County Revolutionary Committee issued the list of the landlords and rich peasants in Crown Prince Village whose labels had been removed. The brigade promptly posted it up. The names of Li Qiangfu and his wife were on it. No one in the village remembered the name of Fifth Li's wife. And she herself when questioned didn't know. Luckily Yang Dequan found a list of names dating from Land Reform where she was written down as Mrs Li, née Pan.

The day the list was put up, Mrs Li, née Pan washed and combed her hair, changed into new clothes and put on a black velvet cap to go and look at it. Actually she couldn't read a single character or see where her name was. But she came very solemnly and stood in the crowd for hours. Mother Liu seeing her told Second Sister Lu:

"Look, buddhas depend on gilt, people on clothes, that's a true saying. In that new tunic and shoes, Fifth Li's wife looks halfway human."

Those standing near by started joking. One said, "What

sort of name is Mrs Li, née Pan? Better give her another."
The names Apricot Blossom and Moon Cassia were
suggested. Covering their mouths to hide smiles others said
that giving an old lady such names was an insult to flower
names. One youngster proposed calling her New Life, but no
one seconded this.

This was the first time in her life that Mrs Li, nee Pan had
attracted so much attention. A smile appeared on her
wrinkled face. And for the first time in her life she spoke in
public:

"No other name is as good as Commune Member. I'll
trouble you, accountant, to change my name to Pan
Commune Member. All right?"

20. "Three Don'ts"

Very soon all the labels of the landlords and rich peasants
in the county had been removed. The County Committee
met to summarize the work, what they had learned and their
present understanding. It was a lively meeting.

Feng spoke of the importance of class struggle, then of the
magnification of class struggle, citing principles as well as
specific examples. He described the beancurd mill in Crown
Prince Village to illustrate the saying "Grasping class
struggle is always efficacious". He said:

"Comrade Li Wanju's case is most interesting. I went to
Crown Prince Village to settle the question of removing Li
Qiangfu's label, but I brought back with me many other
ideas. In the past, apparently, we often adopted a high moral
tone that forced comrades lower down to fake their reports.
This gave rise to a set of cadres like Li Wanju. They used both
truth and lies to cope with us. And we often believed their
lies There's an important lesson to be learned here."

After the meeting Qiu went glumly to Qi's office and sat down scratching his head. Qi ignored him till finally he burst out:

"Secretary Qi, I've something to say, but I'm afraid you'll accuse me of factionalism."

Qi asked coldly:

"In that case why say it?"

"I can't stand it! You're too good, Secretary Qi, that's your weakness. Can't you see what Secretary Feng is doing? That was an artful dodge, his going to Crown Prince Village in person. He's stolen your trump card."

"What trump card?"

"Crown Prince Village." Qiu moved his big head closer and lowered his voice. "I even suspect he may have had something to do with those three anonymous letters."

"Impossible!" Qi nearly shouted.

"It's not impossible." Qiu clicked his tongue. "Crown Prince Village was under your supervision; you made Li Wanju a model. As soon as Feng came he wanted to blacken Li, so as to pounce on the man backing him. That was clear from the first letter. Now he's absolved Wanju, putting all the blame on us. He just said we often adopted a high moral tone that forced comrades lower down to fake their reports. Who did he mean by 'we'? He wasn't here then."

Qi considered Qiu's analysis carefully, saw some sense in it and felt resentful. Did *I* want to adopt a high moral tone? he thought. It was set up above, so I'd no other choice. If Feng had been in charge then he'd have had to do the same. He sighed and looked up to say:

"Mind you don't say that to anyone else, Bingzhang. It's disruptive talk and would make a bad impression."

"I won't, I won't." Qiu nodded. "But I advise you not to be too good-hearted and soft. Now the check-up's finished. The facts prove that we had no connection with the 'gang of four'. And you were invited to that meeting in the provincial capital, showing that the Provincial Committee trusts you. From now on, I think, you should say what ought to be said and dispute what ought to be disputed. You can't let Feng grab Crown Prince Village. Wanju's not bad, you ought to keep hold of him."

"Forget it, I'm not fighting for them." Qi smiled rather bitterly

Qiu was getting up to go when Feng hurried in exuberantly.

"Wanju's here."

"Oh! Why has he come?" Qiu looked taken aback.

"He has business with the Farm Machinery Bureau. I asked him to have supper with us. The two of you must join us presently."

That evening Feng got the kitchen to cook four dishes and bought a bottle of hard liquor to entertain Li Wanju. Qi and Qiu came as requested to keep them company.

"Wanju, I've asked you here so that we can have a good chat." Smiling, Feng filled a cup with liquor. "The last few years, work in the countryside hasn't been easy, especially at the grass-roots level. You seem to know how to manage. Please tell us your methods."

"What methods have I? You've got it wrong,' Li demurred.

Qiu refilled Li's cup and encouraged him:

"Secretary Feng wants you to tell us, so go ahead. You've been Party secretary for over ten years, and Secretary Qi has always held your village up as a model. So you must have plenty of experience."

Li had hesitated at first, but three cups of liquor loosened his tongue.

"What experience have I? I've just fooled people. The last few years in the villages you couldn't get anything done unless you learned how to fool people. But you can't fool your belly. If cattle don't get enough fodder they won't move. If you don't get enough to eat, just boasting that you're bursting, what use is that? Bellies can't speak but they can rumble. They won't put up with bad treatment. The fewer muffins they get, the less strength they'll give you, so that when you see a pit ahead they won't let you cross it."

"Food is the first necessity for the people," laughed Feng.

Li took another swig of liquor and went on:

"In the three hard years our old Party secretary was still alive. He often said: Bellies are most impartial, you can't fool them. Because of the shortage of grain, the higher-ups called for 'double steaming', claiming that if a catty of rice was steamed twice it would increase by two ounces. Our old Party secretary said: Don't listen to them. You can steam it eight times and it's still only one catty. How can you conjure up two extra ounces? Later there were many new tricks. One day they said gruel was good, your stomach could absorb more, and less nourishment was lost; another day they said dry food was better and we should swallow uncooked grains of corn, as that would last longer instead of disappearing after two pisses."

Li had been joking, but Feng took this to heart. Yes, during the three hard years when he was secretary of the County Committee, he had passed on directives like this. What a thing to have done!

"These years our brigade has reaped a bit more grain, and today I'll come clean to you county cadres. I issued a bit more to our commune members than the ration you fixed. You can call it hiding output or secretly dividing it up, and I'll accept any punishment you see fit. Anyway, in my opinion, if we harvest more it's because our brigade has worked hard. So when we've handed in grain to the state and completed our state purchase quotas, I can let our brigade members have a little extra."

"No wonder," laughed Qi, "when I asked around in your village they couldn't give me an exact figure."

"I knew you were asking what their grain ration was." Li tweaked his wispy moustache. "We figured you'd come to see if we'd concealed our output or divided some up secretly. You had us really worried for a while!"

"No need to worry now." Feng refilled Li's cup. "The Provincial Committee has sent down a directive ending the hard-and-fast fixing of grain rations. In future those who harvest more can have more."

"Fine, fine, that's fine." In high spirits Li rolled up his sleeves, stretched out his lean swarthy arms and drained his cup.

Feng eyed him with interest, refilling his cup as he asked:

"Is there anything else that can't be fooled?"

"Yes, the crops. If you try to fool them they won't grow, so what good would that do you? These years I've dreaded your hard-and-fast rules. The higher-ups send down new orders every day. Now they order us to grow more sweet potatoes, and we can't sow half a *mu* less than the acreage fixed. Now they decide to root out sorghum, not letting us keep a single plant; each seedling must be pulled up. I could give you many examples. Today they order you to dibble beans, tomorrow the broadcast tells you to start harvesting. I ask you, doesn't each plot of land have its own peculiarities? And how can you sow and harvest at the same time? All this rumpus means that farmers don't know how to farm. That's why our commune members say these years the people farthest from the land know best how to grow crops!"

"What do you do when you get such senseless orders?" Feng asked with a smile.

"Me? I go all out to fool the higher-ups; but there's no fooling the crops." Li took another drink. Red in the face he went on, "Drinking so much I've gone a bit too far; I hope you won't hold it against me. It's mostly the commune I've been talking about. On the other hand where did the commune get those orders?"

"Of course the county's responsible," said Feng.

Qiu stole a glance at Qi, who pretended not to notice. Raising his cup he said:

"Yes, most such orders come down from above, and the County Committee can't block them. Don't worry, just speak your mind."

"All right then. The truth is, when we get senseless orders I make a show of complying but secretly oppose them. I've written off those few *mu* of land beside the highway and put up signs 'Experimental Plot' to mess about with. I call that 'growing flowers by the road'. When the higher-ups come to check up, they hurry along the road, just wanting to have a look. In the fields, though, we have to make an honest job of sowing and harvesting without fooling around. Our motto is: Reap a good harvest and sack the grain."

"Right." Feng nodded. "The bulletin of the Third Plenary Session says the autonomy of the brigades must be protected."

Topping up Li's drink Qiu chuckled:

"You know plenty of artful dodges! Go on. Any more?"

"Yes, commune members can't be fooled." Li thought before explaining, "We've several hundred people in the village. Each able to size things up, each alive and kicking—how can you fool them? You can't. If you're unreasonable they won't do as you say; if you're unfair they'll curse you behind your back. If they don't trust you, you're finished. Our old Party secretary told me, the main thing for a village cadre is to work honestly for the good of the commune members. It's no good trying to fool them. If you do they'll fool you. At least they'll slack and there'll be nothing you can do about it."

"Very true!" Feng had drunk only one cup, yet his swarthy face was as red as a picture of the God of War. Patting Li's bony shoulder he said, "First, you can't fool bellies; secondly, you can't fool crops; thirdly, you can't fool commune members.... Ha, 'Three Don't Fools', that's a good, profound summary. Seems to me that's the way to work in the countryside."

Li had drunk so much that he was rather tipsy. Feng looked drunk too as he patted Li's shoulder again.

"Good experience! But why didn't you talk about these 'Three Don't Fools' at the cadres' meeting last year? Why only talk about 'Three Contacts and Three Contrasts'? Were you fooling me, eh?"

Smiling broadly, Li looked at him sideways.

"How can you say that, Secretary Feng? We can only talk like this behind closed doors; how could I shout it through a big loudspeaker!"

"Because you weren't honest, after that cadres' meeting someone informed against you," said Qi with a laugh.

"I know."

He informed against you three times. You know that too?"

Li shook his head as if sobering up.

Feng asked Qiu to fetch the letters and read them to him. As Li listened he clicked his tongue:

"Good heavens! Knows all about our Crown Prince Village!"

When Qiu had finished reading the letters he asked:

"Wanju, who d'you think wrote these?"

Li looked up thoughtfully, then said positively:

"Someone from one of the brigades next to our village. I think I know who it was."

"Who?"

"I'm not telling. If I'm wrong I'd be making an enemy. If I'm right there's no point, as he didn't sign his name, did he?"

21. A Visit from the Anonymous Letter-Writer

Four days later, a farmer in his fifties came through the gate of the Qingming County Committee.

The gateman stopped him to ask:

"Who are you looking for, comrade?"

"Secretary Feng," he said boldly.

"Secretary Feng's at a meeting."

"Secretary Qi then."

"He's at a meeting too."

"Then Chairman Qiu."

Hearing him reel off the names of these leading members of the County Committee, the gateman felt this man must have powerful backing. He hastily asked:

"What's your business?"

"I wrote three letters to the County Committee."

The gateman pointed out to him the office handling letters. The caller went in and said brashly:

"Last year I wrote three letters denouncing Li Wanju the Party secretary of Crown Prince Village."

"Oh, so you. . . ." The men in charge saw that this was the writer of those three anonymous letters. They offered him a seat and lost no time in notifying Chairman Qiu, who hurried to consult Secretary Qi.

Qi at once invited the caller to his office.

When he came in Qi looked up and saw a man with the red nose of a drinker. He exclaimed:

"So it's you!"

"That's right, Secretary Qi. You've a good memory. We met once in Crown Prince Village."

"Aren't you from Lai Family Grave?"

"That's right," the other answered respectfully.

Qi invited him to sit down and, staring at him, asked:

"Are you the Party secretary of Lai Family Grave? What's your name?"   "No, no, my level's too low." The visitor half rose from his seat. "I'm Lai Jiafa. The villagers think well enough of me to have put me in charge of the sidelines in our brigade."

Qi poured him a cup of water which he stood up to accept in both hands, saying:

"You mustn't go to such trouble!"

"Was it you who wrote those three letters?" Qi sat down, eyeing Lai Jiafa and thinking he didn't look the sort of man who could have any connection with Feng. How ridiculous Qiu's analysis had been.

"That's right, that's right," replied Lai. "Before Liberation I studied for two years in a private school and liked to read the paper. But I hadn't time to learn to write, so I'm no good at writing. You must have found my letters laughable."

"Why did you denounce Li Wanju?"

"I've a daughter Biyu who married into Old Chao's family in the east end of Crown Prince Village. Our two villages are alongside, so I know Crown Prince Village's output and income are high. But how exactly they managed that I don't know. At the cadres' meeting last year when Li Wanju talked about 'Three Contacts and Three Contrasts', everyone thought that fishy. They said Li was too tricky. He didn't let on what his canon was, just fobbed us off with something bogus. Some said they didn't blame him, they blamed the County Committee for not being able to tell true from false. After hearing that I racked my brains till midnight. I decided the only way to get hold of the true canon of Crown Prince Village was by alerting the heads of the County Committee. That's why I wrote those three letters."

"Ah!" Qi let out a deep breath, thinking: What a headache they were, those senseless letters of yours.

"Please excuse me if I wrote something wrong," said Lai with a faint smile. "I've come today mainly to thank our County Committee heads for taking my letters seriously. I heard that as a result of those three visits to Crown Prince Village by you, Secretary Qi, Chairman Qiu and Secretary Feng, Li Wanju finally came clean. My daughter told me the village was in a hubbub because the County Committee decided they'd done nothing wrong."

Qi brushed this aside:

"You needn't thank us for that."

Lai leaned forward to say:

"I've a suggestion, Secretary Qi. Can you call a mass meeting and get Li to introduce his real canon? We poor brigades and villages could pick up some useful tips from it."

"I'll have to discuss that with Secretary Feng."

"Of course, of course." Lai nodded repeatedly.

Qi asked casually:

"Have you met Secretary Feng before?"

"Never."

"You don't know him?"

"Why, how could I know Secretary Feng!" Lai laughed at the idea.

Qi stood up, asking:

"Would you like me to take you to see him now?"

"No need, no need. You've done me an honour, letting me take up so much of your time. And I hear Secretary Feng is at a meeting. I don't want to disturb him. You've been too good!"

When Lai had left, Qi relaxed and smiled. This fellow was an honest-to-goodness peasant, nothing to do with Feng; yet Qiu had linked them, thinking himself very smart.

22. The "True Canon" Rally

After the spring ploughing and sowing the Qingming County Committee convened another meeting of cadres from the county, communes and brigades to discuss the bulletin of the Third Plenary Session and two documents concerning agriculture. Everyone was called on to bring order out of chaos and restore their practical, realistic tradition.

Li Wanju, asked to speak about his true canon, his "Three Don'ts", refused until Feng talked him round. This time he spoke freely and frankly so that everyone enjoyed his talk and said this was a "true canon" meeting.

In his summary Feng rated Li's "Three Don'ts" very highly. According to him, if they were carried out in the countryside that would strengthen the ties between the Party and the people, enabling those above and those below to work with one heart and one mind for modernization.

At once Li Wanju found himself in the news. Reporters and photographers from different papers, news agencies, radio and television stations came to his hostel to interview him and record what he said. They crowded round him firing requests at him:

"Comrade Wanju, that was a splendid talk you gave. We want to write it up. Please make time to repeat it for us."

"Comrade Wanju, our radio station wants to record an interview with you. We hope you'll talk for just ten minutes."

"Comrade Wanju, that 'true canon' of yours is completely in line with the Third Plenary Session's emphasis on a realistic style of work. We want to publish it in full in our paper."

"We called our office long distance yesterday, and our editorial board consider your experience most important. They're going to write an editorial about it."

"Comrade Wanju. . . ."

Li sat on a stool in the hostel without a word, his lowered head clasped in his hands. Small and lean, he looked blighted by frost, with none of the poise or spirit of a model worker. Not until all the requests had been made did he lower his hands and look up, tweaking his moustache. He pleaded:

"Have a heart!"

The experienced, knowing newsmen were taken aback.

"I'm no model character and I've no 'true canon'," Li muttered. "I'm a farmer, the Party secretary of our village, and it isn't easy leading our villagers. I was forced to do what I did, it's not worth talking about. If you boost me up today, tomorrow I'm bound to come a fearful cropper."

Seeing that he had no idea of the importance of the mass media and of writing up models, the newsmen went to urge Secretary Qi to persuade him.

"I can't do that," said Qi civilly. "You'd better apply to Secretary Feng."

After hearing what they wanted, Feng said:

"I don't think Li Wanju's 'true canon' can be reported."

The newsmen were both startled and indignant. Didn't this secretary of the County Committee grasp the importance of propaganda either?

Feng stood up, a cigarette in one hand, and took a few steps as he explained to them all:

"The gist of Comrade Wanju's 'true canon' of 'Three Don'ts' is seeking truth from facts. I spoke about this at the meeting, and you've raised the point again. But let me pose a problem which may not have occurred to you. Each time Li Wanju did something practical and realistic he had to play a trick. Why was that?"

Not one of the newsmen could answer.

Feng frowned and puffed hard at his cigarette. Pacing round the room he said:

"On the one hand practical work, on the other fraud. Or we could say on the one hand 'Three Don't Fools', on the other 'Fool Everybody'. These two completely different types of behaviour are harmoniously united in one man. Who can explain the nature of this problem?"

He halted and looked searchingly at the newsmen sitting there. When they eyed each other without a word he went on:

"As I said, this unity of a contradiction has reached the harmonious stage. You see, to do anything practical and realistic, Li Wanju had to resort to fraud. This is evident from everything he did. I hope you'll clear up the philosophic implications of this before discussing whether or not to report it."

The disgruntled newsmen had to prepare to leave.

As if to console these comrades on whom he had poured cold water, Feng said:

"Seeking truth from facts is going to become the practice, and it won't be necessary to play tricks at the same time. When that day comes you can report this. And of course I'll welcome your eagerness to write about our county."

A correspondent from the provincial paper countered:

"By then Li Wanju's true canon will have no point, so what will there be to report?"

Feng answered with a smile:

"So much the better!"

May, 1982

Translated by Gladys Yang

Ten Years Deducted

WORD wafted like a spring breeze through the whole office building. "They say a directive will be coming down, deducting ten years from everybody's age!"

"Wishful thinking," said a sceptic.

"Believe it or not," was the indignant retort. "The Chinese Age Research Association after two years' investigation and three months' discussion has drafted a proposal for the higher-ups. It's going to be ratified and issued any day now."

The sceptic remained dubious.

"Really? If so, that's the best news I ever heard!"

His informant explained:

"The age researchers agreed that the ten years of the 'cultural revolution' wasted ten years of everyone's precious time. This ten years debit should be cancelled out...."

That made sense. The sceptic was convinced.

"Deduct ten years and instead of sixty-one I'll be fifty-one — splendid!"

"And I'll be forty-eight, not fifty-eight — fine!"

"This is wonderful news!"

"Brilliant, great!"

The gentle spring breeze swelled up into a whirlwind engulfing everyone.

"Have you heard? Ten years deducted!"

"Ten years off, no doubt about it."

"Minus ten years!"

All dashed around to spread the news.

An hour before it was time to leave the whole building was deserted.

Ji Wenyao, now sixty-four, as soon as he got home, yelled towards the kitchen:

"Minghua, come here quick!"

"What's up?" At her husband's call Fang Minghua hurried out holding some spinach she was cleaning.

Ji was standing in the middle of the room, arms akimbo, his face lit up. Hearing his wife come in he turned his head, his eyes flashing, and said incisively:

"This room needs smartening up. Tomorrow go and order a set of Romanian furniture."

She stepped forward in surprise and asked quietly:

"Are you crazy, Old Ji? We've only those few thousand in the bank. If you squander them...."

"Bah, you don't understand." Face flushed, neck dilated, he cried, "Now we must start a new life!"

Their son and daughter as if by tacit consent hurried in from their different rooms not knowing what to make of their father's announcement. Was the old man off his rocker?

"Get out, this is none of your business." Old Ji shooed away the inquisitive young people.

He then closed the door and, quite out of character, leapt forward to throw his arms round his wife's plump shoulders. This display of affection, the first in dozens of years, alarmed her even more than his order to buy Romanian furniture. She wondered: What's wrong with him? He's been so down in the dumps about reaching retirement age, he's never demonstrative like this in the daytime, and even in bed he just sighs to himself as if I weren't there beside him. What's got into him today? A man in his sixties carrying on like those romantic characters in TV plays — she blushed for him. But Old Ji didn't notice, his eyes were blazing. Half hugging, half carrying her, he lugged his impassive wife to the wicker chair and sat her down, then whispered jubilantly into her ear:

"I'll tell you some top-secret news. A directive's coming down, we're all to have ten years deducted from our age."

"Ten — years — deducted?" Minghua let fall the spinach, her big eyes nearly popping out of her head. "Well I never! Is it true?"

"It's true. The directive will be arriving any minute."

"Oh my! Well I never!" She sprang to her feet to throw her arms round her husband's scrawny shoulders and peck at his high forehead. Then, shocked by her own behaviour, she felt as if carried back thirty years in time. Old Ji looked blank for a moment then took her hands and the two of them turned three circles in the middle of the room.

"Oh my, I'm dizzy." Not till Minghua pulled free and patted her stout chest did they stop whirling merrily round.

"Well, dear? Don't you think we ought to buy a set of Romanian furniture?" Ji looked confidently at his rejuvenated wife.

"We ought." Her big eyes were shining.

"Oughtn't we to make a fresh start?"

"We ought, we ought." Her voice was unsteady and there were tears in her eyes.

Old Ji plumped down on the armchair and closed his eyes while rosy dreams of the future flooded his mind. Abruptly opening his eyes he said resolutely:

"Of course our private lives are a minor matter, the main thing is we now have ten more years to work. This time I'm determined to make a go of it. Our bureau is so slack I must take a firm grip on things. On the back-up work too; the head of our general office is not a suitable choice at all. The airs our drivers give themselves, they need to be straightened out too. . . ."

He flourished his arms, his slit eyes agleam with excitement.

"The question of the leading group will have to be reconsidered. I was forced to appoint the best of a bad lot. That Zhang Mingming is a bookworm with no experience of leadership. Ten years, give me ten years and I'll get together a good leading group, a young one with really new blood, chosen from today's college students. Graduates of twenty-three or twenty-four, I'll groom them myself for ten years and then...."

Minghua took little interest in the overhauling of the leading group, looking forward to the wonderful life ahead.

"I think I'll get another armchair too."

"Get a suite instead, more modern."

"And our bed, we'll get a soft one in its place." She reddened.

"Quite right. After sleeping hard all our lives we shoud get a soft bed to move with the times."

"The money...."

"What does money matter." Ji Wenyao took a long-term view, filled with pride and enthusiasm. "The main thing is getting another ten years, ah, that's something no money could buy."

As they were talking excitedly, hitting it off so well, their daughter opened the door a crack to ask:

"Mum, what shall we have for supper?"

"Oh, cook whatever you want." Minghua had forgotten completely about the meal.

"No!" Old Ji raised one hand and announced, "We'll go out and eat roast duck, I'm standing treat. You and your brother go first to get a table, your mother and I will follow."

"Oh!" His daughter gaped at seeing her parents in such high spirits. Without asking the reason she went to call her brother.

Brother and sister hurrid off to the roast duck restaurant, speculating on the way there. He said perhaps an exception had been made in the old man's case and he was being kept on. She thought that maybe he had been promoted or got a bonus. Of course neither of them could guess that the deduction of ten years was worth infinitely more than any promotion.

At home the old couple were still deep in conversation.

"Minghua, you should smarten yourself up too. Ten years off makes you just forty-eight."

"Me? Forty-eight?" she murmured as if dreaming. The vitality of her long-lost youth was animating her plump flabby figure, to her bewilderment.

"Tomorrow buy yourself a cream-coloured coat for spring and autumn." Old Ji looked critically at her tight grey uniform and said decisively, almost protestingly, "Why shouldn't we be in fashion? Just wait. After supper I'll buy myself an Italian-style jacket like Zhang Mingming's. He's forty-nine this years; if he can wear one, why shouldn't I?"

"Right!" Minghua smoothed her scruffy, lustreless grey hair. "I'll dye my hair too and treat myself to a visit to a first-rate beauty-parlour. Ha, the young folk call me a stick-in-the-mud, but put back the clock ten years and I'll show them how to live. . . ."

Old Ji sprang to his feet and chimed in:

"That's it, we must know how to live. We'll travel. Go to Lushan, Huangshan, Jiuzhaigou. Even if we can't swim we'll go to have a look at the ocean. The fifties, that's the prime of life. Really, in the past we had no idea how to live!"

Not pausing to comment Minghua went on thinking aloud:

"If ten years are deducted and I'm just forty-nine, I can work another six years. I must go back and do a good job too."

"You. . . ." Old Ji sounded dubious.

"Six years, six years, I can work for another six years," she exulted.

"You'd better not," Ji said. "Your health isn't up to it."

"My health's fine." In her eagerness to get back to work she really felt quite fit.

"If you take up your old job who'll do all the housework?"

"We'll get a maid."

"But that lot of women from Anhui* are too irresponsible. You can't trust one of them to take over here."

Minghua began to waver.

"Besides, since you've already retired you don't want to make more trouble for the leadership, right? If all the old retired cadres asked to go back, well, that would mess things up." Ji shuddered at the thought.

"No, I've still six years in which I can work," she insisted. "If you won't take me back in the bureau, I can transfer somewhere else. As Party secretary or deputy secretary in some firm — how about that?"

"Well . . . those firms are a very mixed lot."

"All the more reason to strengthen their leadership. We old people are the ones to do ideological and political work."

"All right."

Ji nodded, pleasing her as much as if the head of the Organization Department had agreed. She chortled:

"That's fine then! Those researchers are really understanding. Ten years off, a fresh start — that's beyond my wildest dreams."

"Well, I dreamed of it." Quite carried away Ji cried out vehemently, "The 'cultural revolution' robbed me of ten of my best years. Ten years, think what I could have done in that time. Ten wasted years, leaving me white-haired and decrepit. Who's to make good that loss? Why did I have to take such bitter medicine? Give me back my youth! Give me ten years back! Now this research association is giving me back that decade of my youth. Good for them, this should have been done long ago."

---

*In recent years many young women from Anhui have come to work as housemaids in big cities like Beijing.

Not wanting her husband to recall painful memories, Minghua smiled and changed the subject.

"All right, let's go and eat roast duck."

Zhang Mingming, forty-nine that year, couldn't analyze his reaction. It seemed a mixture of pleasure and distress, of sweetness and bitterness.

Ten years off certainly pleased him. Working on scientific research he knew the value of time. Especially for him, a middle-aged intellectual approaching fifty, the recovery of ten years was a heaven-sent opportunity. Look at researchers overseas. A scientist in his twenties could win an international reputation by presenting a thesis at an international conference, then go on to head his field while in his thirties, his name known throughout the world — there were many such cases. Then look at him: a brilliant, most promising student in college with just as good a grounding as anyone else. But unluckily he had been born at the wrong time, and sent to do physical labour in the countryside. When he got down again to his interrupted studies the technical material was strange to him, his brain didn't function well and his hands trembled. Now with this extra ten years he could make a fresh start. If he went all out and research conditions improved, with less time wasted bickering over trifles, why, he could put twenty years' work into ten years and distinguish himself by scaling the heights of science.

He was pleased, just as pleased as everyone else, if not more so.

But a colleague slapped his back and asked:

"Old Zhang, what are you so bucked about?"

"What do you mean?" Why shouldn't he be bucked?

"Deducting ten years makes Ji Wenyao fifty-four. So he won't retire, you won't take over the bureau."

Quite true. That being the case Ji won't retire. He doesn't want to. He'll stick on as bureau head. And what about me? Of course I won't be promoted. I'll remain an engineer doing scientific research in the lab and library.... Yet two days ago the ministry sent for me to tell me that Old Ji would be retiring and they'd decided to put me in charge.... Does that still hold good?

He really didn't want an official post. The highest he had ever held was that of group head, and convening a group meeting was the height of his political experience. He had never expected an official title, least of all the imposing one of bureau head. He had always been a "bookworm". In the "cultural revolution" he had come under fire as "a reactionary revisionist set on becoming an expert". Since the overthrow of the "gang of four" he had spent all his time in his lab, not talking to a soul.

But somehow or other when it came to choosing a third-echelon leading group he had been chosen. In each public opinion poll his name headed the list, just as he had always come top in examinations. When he was summoned to the ministry it sounded as if the whole business had been settled. In that case he couldn't understand where or how he had shown any leading ability, to be favoured by the authorities and trusted by the rank and file. Thinking it over he felt most ashamed. He had never had any administrative ability, let alone any leadership qualities.

His wife Xue Minru, moderately good-looking and intelligent, was an admirable wife and mother. She took a keen interest in her husband's affairs and knew the disputes in his bureau very well. Her comment had been:

"It's because you're not leadership material that you've been chosen for a leading post."

Zhang Mingming was puzzled by this statement. What does that mean, he wondered. Then he thought: maybe there's some truth in it. Because I've no ability to lead or definite views of my own, and I've not jockeyed for position, no one need worry about me. Perhaps that's why I've been given this opening.

Of course there was also an "opposition party". It was said that at one Party meeting in the bureau his problem had been disputed all afternoon. What the dispute was about he wasn't clear. Nor what his problem was either. After that, though, he felt that he had become a "controversial figure". And this "controversy" wouldn't be resolved nor would his "problem" be cleared up till the day he became bureau head.

Gradually as these public opinion polls and arguments went on, Zhang Mingming became accustomed to his role as someone due to be promoted and a "controversial figure". Sometimes he even imagined that he might really make a good bureau head, though he had never held such a position.

"Better take the job," said Minru. "It's not as if you'd grabbed at it. When you're bureau chief at least you won't have to squeeze on to the bus to go to work."

But now he wouldn't get the job. Was he sorry? A little, not altogether. What it boiled down to was: his feelings were mixed.

He went home at a loss.

"Back? Good, the meal's just ready." Minru went into the kitchen to fetch one meat dish, one vegetable dish and a bowl of egg and pickles soup. The meat dish wasn't greasy and the green vegetables looked very tempting.

His wife was an excellent housekeeper, considerate, clever and deft. During the three hard years when their neighbours contracted hepatitis or dropsy, she kept their family fit by cooking coarse grain so that it tasted good, boiling bones to make soup and using melon rind in place of vegetables. Now farm products were plentiful but fish and meat had risen so much in price that everybody claimed they couldn't afford them. However, Minru knew how to cook tasty inexpensive meals. When Zhang saw the supper she had served he lost no time in washing his hands, sitting down at the table and picking up his chopsticks.

"What succulent celery," he remarked. "Is it expensive? The papers say celery keeps your blood pressure down."

Minru simply smiled.

"These pickles are good too, they give the soup a fine flavour."

Still she just smiled and said nothing.

"Bamboo shoots with pork...." He went on praising this simple meal as if he were a gourmet.

She laughed and cut him short to ask:

"What's got into you today? Has anything happened?"

"No, nothing." He made a show of surprise. "I was just admiring your cooking."

"You never do normally, so why today?" She was still smiling.

Feeling driven into a corner he retorted:

"It's because I don't normally that I'm saying this now."

"No, you're hiding something from me." She could see through him.

With a sigh he put down his chopsticks.

"I'm not hiding anything, but I don't know what to make of it myself or how to tell you."

Minru smiled complacently. Her husband might be an expert researcher, a top man in his own field, but when it came to psychoanalysis he was no match for her.

"Never mind, just tell me." She sounded like a teacher patiently encouraging a child.

"Today word came that a directive's coming down to deduct ten years from everybody's age."

"Impossible."

"It's true."

"Really?"

"Really and truly."

She thought this over and looked at him with big limpid eyes, then chuckled.

"So you won't be bureau head."

"That's right."

"Does that upset you?"

"No. I can't explain it, but I feel put out."

He took up his chopsticks again to fiddle with the rice in his bowl as he went on:

"To start with I'm not leadership material and I didn't want this job. But they've made such a mess of things these last few years, it seems I ought to take over. Still, this sudden change makes me feel a bit...." He was at a loss for words.

Minru said incisively:

"If you don't get the job so much the better. You think it's a cushy post?"

Zhang looked up at his wife, surprised by her decisive tone of voice. A few days ago when he'd told her about his impending promotion, she had shown genuine elation. She'd said, "Look at you — you didn't grab at the job and now these laurels have been put on your head." Now the laurels were lost she wasn't upset or angry, as if there had never been any talk of promotion.

"As bureau head, head of the bureau, you'd have been expected to solve every problem big or small — could you have stood it?" she asked. "Allocation of housing, promotions, bonuses, private squabbles, financial affairs, finding jobs or kindergartens for people's children. How could you manage all that?"

True, no one could manage it all.

"Stick to your speciality. An extra ten years will make all the difference to what you can achieve...."

Yes, it would certainly make all the difference.

Zhang felt easier in his mind, with a sense of light-hearted well-being.

He went to bed expecting to sleep soundly. But he woke in the middle of the night with a feeling of faint regret and deprivation.

Thirty-nine-year-old Zheng Zhenhai shot out of the bureau and cycled swiftly home. There he took off his old grey jacket and tossed it on to a chair, conscious of inexhaustible energy. This deduction of ten years seemed to call for prompt action to solve many major problems.

"Hey!"

No one answered his call. His ten-year-old son was fooling about as usual in the alley, and where was his wife who usually responded? Out visiting? Hell! What sort of home was this?

His home-made armchair was so misproportioned that his spine didn't reach the back, while the low arms and high seat made sitting there positively tiring. All because she had to keep up with the neighbours and since they couldn't afford an armchair had insisted on his making a set himself. What a philistine! It was sickening the way every family had armchairs like this, as standard as a cadre's uniform. So philistine!

Whatever had made him choose her? Such a vulgar family with no interests in life except food, clothing, pay and perks. Family education was all-important. She was the spitting image of her mother: the same crude way of talking, and fat as a barrel since the birth of the boy, with no good looks, no figure, no character. Whatever had made him choose someone like her?

Hell! It came of being in too much of a hurry. A bachelor nearing thirty couldn't be choosy. Now with ten years off he was only twenty-nine! He must think over this problem seriously. Yesterday she'd squawked and flounced about because he'd bought a carton of good cigarettes, threatening to divorce him — they couldn't go on like this. Divorce? Go ahead! Twenty-nine was just the right age to find a wife, a slender college graduate of twenty-two or twenty-three with a refined, modern outlook. College students should marry other college students. She was half-baked, just from a technical school. He could kick himself for making such a mistake.

He must re-organize his life, not muddle along like this. Where the hell had she gone?

In fact, after office she'd bolted out of the bureau to head for a shop selling women's clothes.

The thought of ten years off had thrown Yuejuan into raptures and fired her imagination. A woman one year short of forty, she was suddenly restored to a girl of twenty-nine. For her this heaven-sent stroke of luck was a boon not all the money in the world could buy.

Twenty-nine — to be so young was glorious! She glanced down at her faded, drab, unprepossessing uniform with a stab of pained resentment. Hurrying into the shop she pounded up to the section displaying the latest fashions, her eyes scanning the dazzling costumes hanging there till a scarlet dress with a white gauze border struck her. She asked to try it on. The salesgirl looked her up and down, her impassive face cold and stony, her cold look implying contempt.

"Well? Aren't I fit to wear this?" Yuejuan fumed inwardly, as she often had in recent years when shopping for clothes, because whenever something took her fancy Zhenhai always ticked her off: "That makes you look like mutton dressed like lamb." What was wrong with that? Did she have to dress like an old woman? Generally she went home in a rage without buying anything, to squabble with him all night.

How unlucky she was, landed for life with such a stick-in-the-mud.

Why stop to argue with the salesgirl? I'll pay for what I buy, you hand it over and mind your own bloody business! What did the silly fool know? Had she heard about the directive? This is just the dress for someone of twenty-nine. The Chinese are too conservative. In other countries, the older ladies are the more they prink themselves up. Eighty-year-olds wear green and red. What does it matter to you what I choose to wear? However you glare at me, I'm taking this.

Having paid up, Yuejuan went into the fitting room. In the long mirror the scarlet dress which hugged her plump figure so tightly seemed a rather outsize mass of fiery red, but really hot stuff, really smart. Well, she'd have to start slimming. Ten years could be deducted from her age by a directive from the higher-ups, but to deduct ten pounds from her weight she'd have to sweat blood. She'd long since stopped eating animal fat and ate only the minimum of starchy food, even cutting down on fruit. However was she to slim?

She huffed and puffed her way home, threw open the door and burst in like a ball of fire. Zheng leapt up in horror from his armchair to ask:

"What's come over you?"

"What do you mean?"

"Where on earth did you get that dress?"

"I bought it. So what?" She raised the hem of the dress and circled round like a model with a coquettish smile.

He at once poured cold water on her.

"Don't imagine that gaudy colours are beautiful — it depends on who's wearing them."

"Why shouldn't I wear them?"

"A dress like that is out of place on you; you're past the age for it. Just think of your age."

"I have thought; that's why I bought it. Twenty-nine! Just the right age to dress up."

"Twenty-nine?" Zheng was taken aback.

"That's right, twenty-nine. Minus ten years makes me twenty-nine, less one month. I insist on wearing reds and greens — so there!" She was gesticulating like an affectedly coy pop singer careering about the stage.

Confound the woman, at her age, so broad in the beam, what a sight she was carrying on like this because of ten years off! Zheng shut his eyes, then opened them abruptly to glare at her.

"The higher-ups are issuing this directive so as to give full play to cadres' youthful vitality and speed up modernization, not so that you'll dress up!"

"How does dressing up affect modernization?" She sprang to her feet. "Does the directive forbid us to dress up? Eh?"

"I mean you can't dress up without taking into account your appearance and figure...."

"What's wrong with my figure?" Touched on a sore spot she struck back. "I'll tell you a home truth. You think me fat; I think you scrawny, scrawny as a pullet, with deep lines like tramways on your forehead, and you can't walk three steps without wheezing. Bah! I wanted an intellectual for a husband. But with you, what better treatment have we had? You're nothing but an intellectual in name. No decent clothes, no decent place to live in. Well? Now I'm twenty-nine, still young, I can find a pedlar anywhere in the street who's better off than you, whether he sells peanuts or sugar-coated haws."

"Go ahead then and find one."

"It's easy. We'll divorce today, and tomorrow I'll register my new marriage."

"Let's divorce then."

With that the fat was in the fire. Normally Yuejuan kept

talking of "divorce" while to Zheng the term was taboo. Now that devil was using it too. Of all the gall! This wouldn't do.

It was all the fault of those damn researchers. She butted her husband with her head and raged:

"Deducting ten years has sent you round the bend. Who are *you* to want a divorce? No way!"

"You think by deducting ten years you can have your way in everything — you're crazy!"

"Little Lin, there's a dance tomorrow at the Workers' Cultural Paıace. Here's a ticket for you." Big Sister Li of the trade union beckoned to Lin Sufen.

Ignoring her, Sufen quickened her step and hurried out of the bureau.

Take off ten years and she was only nineteen. No one could call her an old maid any more. The trade union needn't worry about a slip of a girl. She didn't need help from the matchmakers' office either. Didn't need attend dances organized to bring young people together. All that was done with!

Unmarried at tweny-nine she found it hard to bear the pitying, derisive, vigilant or suspicious glances that everyone cast at her. She was pitied for being single, all alone; scoffed at for missing the bus by being too choosy; guarded against as hyper-sensitive and easily hurt; suspected of being hysterical and warped. One noon when she went to the boiler room to poach herself two eggs in a bowl of instant noodles, she heard someone behind her comment:

"Knows how to cosset herself."

"Neurotic."

She swallowed back tears. If a girl of twenty-nine poached herself two eggs instead of having lunch in the canteen, did that make her neurotic? What theory of psychology was that?

Even her best friends kept urging her to find a man to share her life. As if to be single at twenty-nine were a crime, making her a target of public criticism, a natural object of gossip. The endless idle talk had destroyed her peace of mind. Was there nothing more important in the world, no more urgent business than finding yourself a husband? How wretched, hateful, maddening and ridiculous!

Now she had been liberated. I'm a girl of nineteen, so all of you shut up! She looked up at the clear blue sky flecked with small white clouds like handkerchiefs to gag those officious gossips. Wonderful! Throwing out her chest, glancing neither to right nor left, she hurried with a light step to the bicycle shed, found her "Pigeon" bicycle and flew off like a pigeon herself through the main gate.

It was the rush hour. The crowded streets were lined with state stores, collectively run or private shops. Pop music sounded on all sides. "I love you...." "You don't love me...." "I can't live without you...." "You've no place in your heart for me...." To hell with that rubbish!

Love was no longer old stock to be sold off fast. At nineteen she had plenty of time, plenty of chances. She must give top priority now to studying and improving herself. Real knowledge and ability could benefit society and create happiness for the people, thereby earning her respect, enriching her life and making it more significant. Then love would naturally seek her out and of course she wouldn't refuse it. But it should be a quiet, deep, half-hidden love.

She must get into college. Nineteen was just the age to go to college. There was no time to be wasted. If she did well in a television college or night school she could get a diploma. Still those weren't regular universities, not up to Beijing or Qinghua. Her life had been ruined by the interruption to her education. Strictly speaking she had reached only primary school standard, because in her fourth

year in primary school the "cultural revolution" had started;
but after skipping about in the alley for several years she
counted as having finished her primary education. In middle
school she felt as dizzy as if in a plane, unable to grasp nine-
tenths of what they were taught, yet somehow or other she
managed to graduate. Sent down to the country to steel
herself by labour, she had forgotten the little she'd learned.
When the "revolution" ended she went back to the city to
wait for a job, but none materialized. She contrived to get
into the service team under the bureau, though that was a
collective, not state-run. Reckoning up like this, it seemed
there was only one way for her to spend the rest of her
life — find a husband, start a family, wash nappies, buy oil,
salt, soya sauce, vinegar and grain, change the gas cylinder
and squabble.

Was that all there was to life? It wasn't enough for Sufen.
One should achieve something, leave something behind. But
with her primary school level, unable to grow rice or to mine
coal, she was neither worker nor peasant, an "intellectual"
with no education, a wretched ghost cut off from
humankind.

She'd started from ABC. Spent practically all her spare
time attending classes, and most of her pay on school fees
and textbooks. Chinese, maths, English, drawing — she
studied them all. But this method of catching up was too
slow, too much of a strain. She wanted a crash course. Her
age was against her. If she couldn't get quicker results, even
if she ended up fully proficient it would be too late for her
to win recognition.

She concentrated on English, hoping to make a
breakthrough. Studied different textbooks, radio materials,
TV classes and crash courses all at the same time. After a
month she discovered that this breach was already besieged
by countless others. All elderly bachelors or unmarried girls

like her, trying to find a short cut to success. And this wasn't a short cut either. Because even if you gained a good grasp of English what use would it be in China which is still backward as far as culture is concerned? Translate English into Chinese? Chinese into English? There were plenty of good translators among the graduates from foreign languages colleges. Who was going to look for new talents among young people waiting for employment?

She transferred to the "Correspondence College for Writers". Why not write stories or poems to disclose all the frustrations, uncertainties and aspirations of our generation? Let the reading public and youth of the twenty-first century know that for one brief phase in China the younger generation was unfairly treated and stupefied by history. Through no fault of their own they had lost all that should have been theirs by right and burdened with a heavy load they hadn't deserved. They would have to live out their lives weighed down by this crushing burden.

To talk of writing was easy. But how many works written by her age group made any appeal? When you picked up your pen you didn't know where to start. She'd torn off so many sheets from her pad that her family were desperately afraid that she was possessed. Apparently not everyone could be a writer.

Then what about studying accountancy? Accountants were in great demand....

She couldn't make up her mind. She vacillated, frustrated and unsure of herself, not knowing what she wanted or ought to do. Someone advised her, "Don't be senseless. At your age, just muddle along." Someone else said, "Once you're married you'll feel settled."

But that was the last thing she wanted.

Now this stupendous change: flowers were blooming, birds singing, the world had suddenly become infinitely beautiful. Subtract ten years and I'm just nineteen. To hell with all hesitation, frustration and wretchedness. Life hasn't abandoned me, the world belongs to me again. I must treasure every single moment and waste no time. Must set my life goals, not turn off the right track again. I mean to study, go to college and get myself a real education. This is my first objective.

Yes, starting today, as of now, I'll press towards this goal.

Cycling along and smiling all over her face, she headed for the textbook department of the Xinhua Bookstore.

The next morning the whole bureau seethed with excitement. Upstairs and down, inside and out, all was bustle, talk and laughter. Cardiac cases climbed up to the fifth floor without wheezing, changing colour or heart palpitations, as if nothing were wrong with them. Men of over sixty who normally talked slowly and indistinctly now raised their voices and spoke so incisively that they could be heard from one end of the corridor to the other. The doors of all the offices stood wide open and people wandered about as if at a fair to share their excitement, elation, dreams and illimitable plans.

Suddenly someone suggested:

"Let's parade through the town to celebrate this new liberation!"

At once everyone went into action. Some wrote slogans on banners, some made little green and red flags. The head of the recreation committee fetched out from the storeroom a drum the size of a round table and the red silk used for folk dances. In no time they all assembled in front of the bureau. Written in yellow characters on the red banners was the slogan, "Celebrate the return of youth". The small flags voiced their inmost feelings: "Support the brilliant decision of the Age Research Association", "Our new youth is devoted to modernization", "Long live youth!"

The big drum beat a rousing tattoo. Ji Wenyao felt his blood was boiling. Standing at the top of the steps he meant to say a few inspiring words before leading this grand parade, when suddenly he saw dozens of retired cadres rush in. Charging up to him they demanded:

"Why weren't we notified of this deduction of ten years?"

"You . . . you've already retired," he said.

"No! That won't do!" the old men chorused.

Ji raised both hands and called from the top of the steps: "Quiet, comrades. Please. . . ."

They paid no attention, the roar of their voices rising to the sky.

"Ten years deducted applies to everyone. It's not fair to leave us out."

"We must carry out the directive, not just do as we please." Ji's voice had risen an octave.

"Where's the directive? Why hasn't it been relayed?"

"Show us the directive!"

"Why don't you let us see it?"

Ji turned to the head of the general office.

"Where's the directive?"

The man answered bluntly:

"I don't know."

They were in this impasse when shouts went up from some newly recruited workers in their late teens:

"Ten years taken off — nothing doing!"

"Have we grown up for eighteen years and landed a job, just to be sent back to primary school — no way!"

The children of the bureau's kindergarten trooped up to Ji too like a flock of ducklings. Clinging to his legs and grabbing his hands they prattled:

"Ten years off, where can we go?"

"Mummy had to be cut open when I was born."

In desperation Ji called again to the head of the general office:

"The directive — hurry up and fetch the directive."

Seeing the man at a loss he thundered:

"Go and get it, quick, from the section for confidential documents."

The man rushed off to hunt through all the directives there, but failed to find it.

Well-meaning suggestions were made:

"Could it have been put in the archives?"

"Could it have been lent out?"

"Dammit! Suppose it's been thrown away!"

In all this confusion Ji kept a cool head. He ordered:

"Everybody's to make a search. Look carefully, all of you, in every corner."

"Shall we call off the parade?" asked the head of the general office.

"Why should we? First find that directive!"

Translated by Gladys Yang

To Save Them Trouble

IN the West, a person's age, particularly a woman's, is a secret, and to ask a woman her age is considered impolite.

But in present-day China age is a popular subject, so meticulously recorded on birth certificate, identity card and residence booklet that it is absolutely impossible to keep secret. Now that the importance of appointing younger people as leaders at all levels is being stressed, age is widely discussed at Party and organizational meetings, in polls and in idle sitting-room talk. A difference of one or two years, even six months or a hundred days decides the fate of an official, whether he soars to the clouds or is dismissed to civilian life, rises meteorically or goes home to rock his grandson.

It was only natural for me, therefore, amid such enthusiasm about age, to write "Ten Years Deducted".

To deduct anything from one's age is just as impossible as to retrieve time gone by. Zhu Ziqing has a famous paragraph on the passing of time in his essay "Haste": "Departed swallows always return. The withered willow puts out green leaves again, just as fallen peach blossoms will come again another year. But tell me, smarty, why does time never return?... It slips from the basin when we wash our hands, from our rice bowls when we eat, and from our staring eyes when we meditate." What an incentive to melancholy!

Sixty-eight years ago Mr Li Dazhao exhorted the world otherwise in his article "The Present": "The present is the most precious thing in the world for me, all the more so since it is the easiest to lose. The minute you talk about it, it passes like lightning into the past. A shame, is it not, to let it go so idiotically?'' Anyone who hears this can feel its weight.

I have exploited fiction, then, to deduct ten years from everybody's age, to save them sighs, to save them worries and to save them trouble.

June 16, 1986

Translated by Yu Fanqin

目　录

人到中年

谌 容

熊猫丛书

*

中国文学出版社出版

（中国北京百万庄路24号）

中国国际图书贸易总公司发行

（中国国际书店）

华利国际合营印刷有限公司印刷

1987年第 1 版

ISBN 7－5071－0005－7/Ⅰ·6

00640

10－E－2215 P